International College
Information Resource Center
2655 Northbrooke Drive
Naples, Florida USA 34119
www.internationalcollege.edu

LAWYERS,

LAWSUITS, AND

LEGAL RIGHTS

THE CALIFORNIA SERIES IN LAW, POLITICS, AND SOCIETY

Robert A. Kagan and Malcolm Feeley, General Editors

LAWYERS,

LAWSUITS, AND

LEGAL RIGHTS

The Battle over Litigation
in American Society

THOMAS F. BURKE

UNIVERSITY OF CALIFORNIA PRESS
Berkeley   Los Angeles   California

Portions of chapter 2 were originally published as Thomas F. Burke, "On the Rights Track: The Americans with Disabilities Act," in *Comparative Disadvantages? Social Regulations and the Global Economy*, ed. Pietro Nivola (Washington D.C.: The Brookings Institution, 1997), 247–272, and are reprinted in revised form with permission of the Brookings Institution.

University of California Press
Berkeley and Los Angeles, California

University of California Press, Ltd.
London, England

Library of Congress Cataloging-in-Publication Data

Burke, Thomas Frederick.
  Lawyers, lawsuits, and legal rights : the battle over litigation in American society / Thomas F. Burke.
    p.   cm. — (The California series in law, politics, and society ; 2)
  Includes bibliographical references and index.
  ISBN 0-520-22727-1 (alk. paper)
    1. Actions and defenses—United States.   2. Lawyers—United States.   3. Justice, Administration of—United States.
  I. Title.   II. Series.

KF380 .B87   2002
347.73—dc21   2002019162

Manufactured in the United States of America
10   09   08   07   06   05   04   03   02
10   9   8   7   6   5   4   3   2   1

The paper used in this publication meets the minimum requirements of ANSI/NISO Z39.48-1992(R 1997) (*Permanence of Paper*).

To my mom, Juanita Burke, whose love
of learning was the beginning of all this

CONTENTS

ACKNOWLEDGMENTS

This book is the end of a long and mostly enjoyable journey, eased by the support of several generous institutions and graced most of all by the friends I met along the way. The first interview I conducted for this book was in San Francisco, the last in Stockholm, Sweden. In between were stops at such varied locales as Charlottesville, Virginia, Simi Valley, California, Turton, South Dakota, and of course, Washington, D.C. I am indebted to the many people, famous and not so famous, who kindly agreed to be interviewed.

This book began as a dissertation at the University of California, Berkeley. I spent much of my time as a graduate student at Nelson Polsby's Institute for Government Studies, a marvelous place that provided generous financial support, camaraderie, intellectual stimulation, and room for my books. I learned much from my fellow graduate students at Berkeley, especially Sandra Bass, Jon Bernstein, Alyson Cole, Paul Edwards, Eric Patashnik, Ron Schmidt, Craig Thomas, Elaine Thomas, Christine Trost, and Kathy Uradnik. My friendships with Nate Teske and James Martel sustained me both at Berkeley and beyond. Among the faculty, I especially want to thank Sandy Muir, Judy Gruber, Bruce Cain, Laura Stoker, and Jack Citrin, as well as my extraordinary thesis committee: Martin Shapiro, Hanna Pitkin, and Nelson Polsby. Thanks above all to my chair, Robert Kagan, who has been an unending source of advice and support. In the unlikely event that an academic advisor Hall of Fame is created, I will make sure he is one of the first inductees.

I was fortunate enough to be a Brookings Research Fellow, which entitled me to spend 1993–94 in Washington, D.C., at the Brookings Institution, another source of both financial and intellectual support. Thanks to Robert Katzmann, Pietro Nivola, John Kingdon, Margaret

Weir, Constance Horner, and Tom Mann, as well as my "classmates," Doug Reed, Valerie Heitshusen, and Dan Tichenor.

My lucky streak continued after graduate school, when I became a professor at Wellesley College, just outside Boston, a great environment in which to write and teach. Among many friends at Wellesley I particularly want to thank Adrienne Asch, Brock Blomberg, Roxanne Euben, Jeff Gulati, Kyle Kauffman, Sally Merry, Craig Murphy, Kathy Moon, Rob Paarlberg, Ellie Perkins, and Alan Schechter. Susan Silbey is a friend and mentor who teaches me something every time I am fortunate enough to be in her company. Moreover, she provided her good judgment about my manuscript at a crucial point. My Boston-area friends kept me sharp and helped even out the peaks and valleys of academic life: Nancy Aykanian, Barb Connolly, Keith Bybee, John Gerring, Anna Greenberg, David Hart, Dan Kryder, Martin Levin, Paul Pierson, and Steve Teles. Gerring, Greenberg, Gulati, and Kevin Esterling all nursed me through the quantitative roll-call study that appears in chapter 5, but they are not to blame for any statistical sins I may have committed. I had wonderful research assistance at Wellesley from, among others, Ruth Zeable, Lydia Chan, Cortney Harding, Christine Ho, and Belinda DelaCruz. I thank Jane Choi, whose research assistance was supported by the National Science Foundation Awards for the Integration of Research and Education Program (award no. 9873771). Thanks for superb administrative assistance to Cyndy Northgraves and Sue Lindsey.

A fellowship with the Robert Wood Johnson (RWJ) Scholars in Health Policy Research Program brought me back to Berkeley and allowed me to put the finishing touches on this book in the California sun. I thank Nathan Jones and Claudia Martinez, the program's Berkeley site administrators, for their hard work, dedication, and flexibility in responding to the diverse needs of RWJ scholars, and I thank the Robert Wood Johnson Foundation for creating this generous program. I am grateful to Chuck Epp and Frank Baumgartner, my University of California Press reviewers, whose comments stimulated major improvements in the book. Thanks also to Steve Rotman, a lifelong friend who contributed his razor-sharp editing skills (to only two chapters, alas), John Skrentny, who provided a thorough and helpful critique of an early draft, and Lauren Leve, whose moral support was invaluable.

And thanks to my family, who have patiently stood by while this manuscript slowly, painfully at times, became a book.

INTRODUCTION

Although Alvin Laskin grew plants for a living, no one would ever accuse him of being an environmentalist. Yet Laskin's entrepreneurial efforts managed to create employment for many environmental scientists—and hundreds of lawyers.

In the early 1970s, when Laskin's Ohio nursery business slumped, he found a more lucrative trade: used oil. Laskin bought the oil from factories and sold it for a variety of uses, particularly dust control. Most of Laskin's old oil presumably ended up with his customers, but hundreds of thousands of gallons of the stuff were inadequately stored in corroded tanks and ponds. By the late 1970s, when Ohio officials first investigated the Laskin Poplar storage site, a chemical sludge containing lead, dioxin, and PCBs had leached into the soil and threatened the groundwater.[1] An extensive cleanup was required, eventually costing about $32 million.[2]

The Environmental Protection Agency, which administered the cleanup, would have been happy to bill Mr. Laskin, but he was "judgment proof"—too poor to make it worth going after him. So instead the EPA sued seven of Mr. Laskin's largest customers, big corporations who had either bought or sold the waste oil.

That was just the beginning. The seven corporations decided to sue Laskin's other customers, eventually more than six hundred, to help pay for the bills. The federal government became involved in these lawsuits as a third party. Then the big companies sued each other. Later some of the companies sued their insurers. At one point the disputants literally ran out of lawyers in the Cleveland area to handle all these suits and countersuits.[3]

It took five years for the first group of defendants to settle, and four more years for most of the rest.[4] In 2001, seventeen years after the first lawsuit, lawyers were still battling over who would pay for Alvin Laskin's environmental sins.[5]

LITIGIOUS PEOPLE/LITIGIOUS POLICIES

Stories like this, about litigation seemingly run amok, are common in American popular culture. Anyone who regularly reads a newspaper or watches television has heard, for example, the story of Stella Liebeck, the woman who sued McDonald's after she burned herself with its coffee.[6] Through the media we encounter despondent New Yorkers who jump in front of subways and sue for their injuries, students who sue their professors for bad teaching, parents who sue because their toddlers came to blows on a playground, golfers who sue after being hit by errant tee shots, nonprofit agencies that sue to collect from wavering donors, snackers who sue when their overcooked Pop-Tarts catch fire, prisoners who sue to get chunky peanut butter instead of the smooth kind, game show contestants who sue over a disputed question, and overweight people who sue movie theaters because their chairs aren't sufficiently spacious.[7] There are also "urban legends" that radiate out from the media with ever more outrageous (and almost entirely fanciful) claims, of handymen who sue after their ladders slip on cow manure, restaurant customers who collect thousands of dollars after eating "Kentucky Fried Rat," and psychics who assert that CAT scans withered their powers and receive hundreds of thousands for their troubles.[8]

These are not simply amusing vignettes. Although they appear in the media as unconnected anecdotes, a serious theme underlies these stories. They are parables about a fundamental breakdown in American society. The prerequisites for peaceful community life, the stories suggest, have evaporated. Greed, individualism, and contentiousness are winning out over, as one book puts it, "common sense."[9] This theme is so readily accepted that such stories resonate even when demonstrably false. Meanwhile, careful academic research that debunks the notion of a "litigation explosion" in the United States fails to make much of an impression.[10] Nearly everyone, a few lawyers and legal academics to the contrary, seems to believe that litigation is out of control.

Explanations for litigiousness are eagerly pronounced. Many blame greedy lawyers, always an easy target.[11] Others point to changes in American culture, with its growing emphasis on individual rights and neglect of the common good. Americans, it is said, have become whiny victims who sue at the first opportunity.[12] These explanations share a common feature: they focus on the individual's decision to sue. From this perspective the problem is that Americans have chosen to litigate rather than tolerate their discomforts or settle their disputes amicably. The communal spirit and stoic temper that once kept Americans out of court have withered. Americans, this perspective suggests, have become a litigious people.

It seems a persuasive view. Yet though the anecdotes that punctuate this narrative of cultural decline are vivid, the evidence to support it is surprisingly scarce. Research typically shows Americans rarely take their disputes to court. Of every one hundred Americans injured in an accident, only ten make a liability claim, and only two file a lawsuit.[13] Of every one hundred Americans who believe they have lost more than $1,000 because of someone else's illegal conduct, only five file a suit.[14] When medical malpractice results in serious injury, only one of eight victims makes a claim.[15] Far from a nation of litigators, the United States seems to be filled with "lumpers," people inclined to lump their grievances rather than press them. Further, claims of a "litigation explosion" are overblown; indeed some studies suggest that those supposedly stoic pioneers of frontier America were far more inclined to sue than their allegedly litigation-loving descendants.[16] Nor do Americans today seem much more litigious than citizens of other nations, though comparisons are difficult and the data skimpy. Some researchers even believe that Americans are no more innately lawsuit prone than the Japanese, the supposed saints of nonlitigiousness.[17]

If all this is true, one might ask, why is there so much complaining about litigation in American life? How can the image of sue-crazy Americans creating a litigation explosion be so far removed from the reality?

Part of the answer is that there is a dedicated corps of image-makers, business interests that have conjured a litigation "crisis" for their own political ends. As several researchers have shown, these interests have mounted a self-serving attack on one form of litigation, personal injury lawsuits, that has succeeded in convincing Americans of their society's descent into the wickedness of litigiousness.[18]

But this, I believe, is only part of the story. Complaints about the place of litigation in American life are not, in fact, merely the artifact of the conjurers' skills, the residue of a cultural con job. For while there is little evidence that Americans are more sue happy than citizens of other nations or that there has been an "explosion" in personal injury lawsuits, litigation clearly does have a distinctively important role in American life. As sensational and unrepresentative as the litigation horror stories are, they do reveal one important truth: the range of matters that can be litigated in the United States is broader than in other nations and growing each year. Forms of litigation that are unknown elsewhere have in the

United States become significant avenues for political controversy and even social change. Although the aforementioned prisoners who sued for chunky peanut butter rather than the smooth kind were undoubtedly laughed out of court, the important fact that remains is that it is *imaginable* in the United States for a prisoner to bring such a lawsuit. Indeed, prisoners with far more serious claims have been able, with the help of sympathetic federal judges, to reshape many aspects of the penal system in the United States.[19] Prisons, schools, playgrounds, game shows, even churches: there are few "litigation-free" zones in twenty-first-century American life, domains in which no lawsuit can be brought. And on this point it's clear that the United States *is* different. From coal mines to high schools, administrative decision making to workplace regulation, comparative research has shown that the United States relies more than any other nation on lawyers, rights, and courts to address social issues.[20] Although there are exceptions to this generalization, and though courts and litigation are a growing part of public policy in many nations, the American pattern still stands out.[21]

In castigating Americans for being too individualistic and sue crazy, commentators have themselves committed the sin of *methodological* individualism: focusing on individual behavior while downplaying the significance of social structures.[22] The evidence that individual Americans have a greater lust for litigation than their counterparts in Japan is murky at best. The evidence that the United States, as compared to Japan, has adopted policies that encourage litigation is overwhelming.[23] I take no position in the ongoing debate over the proclivities of individuals, whether in Japan or the United States, in the eighteenth century or the twenty-first. It is the comparison of institutional arrangements that arouses my interest. My focus, then, is on the litigiousness of American laws rather than on the purported litigiousness of the American people.

This book examines the causes of America's uniquely litigious public policy style. *Litigious policies** are laws that promote the use of litigation in resolving disputes and implementing public policies by (1) creating rights to sue, (2) lowering barriers to litigation, or (3) increasing the rewards of litigation.[24] These policies produce an environment in which lawyers and legal concepts structure everyday practices and where the *threat* of a lawsuit always looms—even when, as is usually the case, no lawsuit is filed.

---

*I am aware that *litigious* is normally used as an adjective applied (almost always as a criticism) to groups of people. It is a bit strange to call a policy "litigious," but I have not found another way to adequately describe the phenomenon in which I am interested.

Without litigious policies there could be no anecdotes about the purported litigiousness of the American people. The parties in the Laskin
Poplar oil-dumping case, for example, would have been powerless to sue
if not for the "Superfund" law, which was devised by Congress in 1980.
The Superfund law commits the federal government to fund a large share
of the cost of toxic dump cleanups through litigation against polluters. In
addition, Superfund allows the government to hold any individual or
business implicated in the waste site liable for the entire cost of cleanup,
whether or not the individual followed state and federal dumping laws
and no matter when the waste was dumped. The law also allows "partly
responsible parties" to sue each other so as to spread costs around. Thus
Superfund created the legal structure that allowed the explosion of litigation in the Laskin case.

This structure did not, of course, ensure litigation. The parties could
have worked out their differences without suing, as has been done in
many Superfund cleanups.[25] Yet the net effect of Superfund has been to
make Superfund disputes a matter for lawyers and legal doctrine as well
as engineers and engineering practices.

In toxic waste as in many policy realms, the American approach is distinctively litigious. Every industrialized nation has a problem with toxic
dumps, but no other nation uses such a court-oriented solution. Some
European nations hold polluters liable for cleanup only if their waste disposal methods were illegal when they did the dumping.[26] Others promote
the principle of "polluter pays" in all cases but grant the government
only a limited power to enforce the principle.[27] By contrast, the American
approach, which grants the federal government powerful litigation rights
and encourages "partly responsible parties" to sue each other, makes litigation a central aspect of disputes over toxic waste dumps.

But Superfund, like many litigious policies, is under attack. Researchers
have long criticized Superfund for its litigiousness, and in recent years a
plethora of groups have mobilized to reform or repeal it.[28] In 1994 the
Clinton administration created a Superfund reform plan aimed at reducing litigation in the program and assembled a grand coalition of manufacturers, insurers, and environmentalists in support of the plan. The
administration's bill was beaten, however, by Republicans and business
groups who wanted more radical change. Since then Congress and both
the Clinton and George W. Bush administrations have continued to
wrestle over how best to fix the Superfund liability scheme.[29]

The battle over the Superfund program is only one small part of what
has become a widespread debate over litigious policies in the United

States. In recent years business groups, journalists, academics, and politicians have attacked what they see as an excess of litigation in American life. George W. Bush in his 2000 campaign promised to be "a president who's tough enough to take on the trial bar" and, like Republican presidential candidates before him, including his father, criticized Democrats for cozying up to trial lawyers instead.[30] Books like *The Litigation Explosion* and *The Death of Common Sense: How Law Is Suffocating America* have in recent years found a popular audience.[31] Advertising by business groups suggests that excessive litigiousness is limiting access to doctors and closing down parks and playgrounds.[32] The media dramatize the negative effects of litigation with an array of lawsuit horror stories and overwrought pronouncements.[33] In television sitcoms such as *Seinfeld, The Simpsons,* and *Ally McBeal* overzealous lawyers and greedy litigants are portrayed pursuing outrageous claims. Meanwhile in academia, second thoughts about the use of litigation to promote social justice proliferate. Litigation is criticized as ineffective,[34] costly,[35] and divisive.[36] Even among jurists there is "failing faith" in adjudication and greater attention to encouraging settlement and alternative means of resolving disputes.[37]

Antilitigation sentiment has rolled through the nation's legislatures, resulting in a profusion of bills designed to limit lawsuits. The movement for "tort reform," heavily funded by business groups and debated in every legislature in America, is the most prominent example. But tort reform is just part of the struggle. In areas as diverse as the environment, civil rights, crime, welfare, and family policy, litigiousness has become part of the political debate, and one group or another has pledged to reduce or limit it.

Antilitigation reformers, however, confront powerful forces in American culture and politics. It would seem that no crusade would be more popular, but in fact antilitigation campaigns have often met with strong resistance, and their record is decidedly mixed. Despite the exertions of a cavalcade of researchers, journalists, public relations specialists, and lobbyists—and despite the millions of dollars spent in their quest—most litigious policies remain in place. Moreover, for every successful effort to limit litigation, several new species of lawsuits seem to pop up nearly every day, some brought into the world by the very politicians who campaign against litigiousness.

If lawyers, litigants, and lawsuits are so regularly vilified in American culture and politics, why are litigious policies difficult to dislodge? Commentators often point to the machinations of politically powerful lawyers and to the seemingly inbred inclination of Americans to see social issues in terms of rights. There is some truth to both these answers, and later chapters explore them in some detail. But both fall well short of a full explanation.

The roots of America's litigious public policy style, I contend, lie much deeper. Building on the work of Robert Kagan,[38] I locate these roots in fundamental features of the American constitutional tradition. This tradition, Kagan points out, combines a profound distrust of centralized governmental power with a set of structures—federalism, separation of powers, an independent judiciary—designed to tame that power. In this book I demonstrate how those structures induce litigious policy making and how they help resist antilitigation reforms. The constitutional tradition, I argue, creates powerful incentives for activists[†]—those who favor governmental action on social problems—to implement their schemes through courts. Thus it takes powerful forces to reform litigious policies.

Litigious policies appeal to activists for two basic reasons. First, courts offer activists a way to address social problems without seeming to augment the power of the state. Litigious policies nicely match the preferences of Americans, who want action on social issues yet are ambivalent about the typical tools of the state—bureaucratic regulation and welfare programs. Courts and individual rights provide a promising alternative.

Second, litigious policies offer a means of overcoming the barriers to activist government posed by the structures of the Constitution. The Constitution's dispersion of power, to states and localities on one hand and to the branches of national government on the other, makes it difficult for activists to control the implementation of their schemes and easy for enemies to derail them. Courts offer a way around these problems. Courts can, for example, enforce national mandates against recalcitrant localities, thus mitigating the impact of federalism. Within the national government, courts can protect policies from "capture," a danger that separation of powers exacerbates. Through litigious policies, activists seek to surmount the fragmented, decentralized structure of American government, which (as its creators intended and James Madison famously boasted) makes activist government difficult. Attempts to limit litigation,

---

[†]I use the term *activists* to refer generically to legislators, "policy entrepreneurs," "moral entrepreneurs," interest group leaders, government officials, and others involved in the policy-making process who favor governmental action on some issue. I do not attempt to analyze how different actors might, because of their distinctive positions in the policy-making process, differ in their incentives. Instead I focus on something they all share—the incentives created by the American constitutional tradition, which affects each of them.

then, run up against powerful motivations, rooted in the basic structure of the framers' handiwork. Thus those who despair at the prominence of litigation in American life would be well advised to stop blaming the Stella Liebecks of the world and focus instead on Mr. Madison and his compatriots. Their influence looms over the politics of litigation.

THE EXPANSION OF LITIGIOUS POLICIES

In *Democracy in America,* Alexis de Tocqueville, the great French observer of American society, famously declared after traveling through the United States in the early 1830s that "there is hardly a political question in the United States that does not sooner or later turn into a judicial one."[39] Tocqueville's statement contained an essential truth about American politics, particularly true in his day, when the absence of a strong national administration left courts as the primary regulators of the economy.[40] Yet Tocqueville's observation was made in an age when the scope of American government—and thus of "political questions"—was relatively limited.

That is no longer the case. In the twentieth century, American government took on more and more of society's problems and conflicts. The growth of the federal government, punctuated by the New Deal, World War II, and the Great Society, is a well-known story. Less attention has been paid to a parallel growth in the responsibilities of courts, an expansion that has made Tocqueville's proclamation even more accurate today than when he wrote it. Beginning after World War II and accelerating in the 1960s and 1970s, courts and legislatures created new avenues of litigation across many realms of law and politics.

One of the first arenas in which this trend developed was tort law, the law of personal injury. In the first half of the twentieth century, tort law severely limited the ability of potential plaintiffs to be compensated for their injuries. Beginning in the 1940s a new emphasis on compensation and loss spreading developed. In 1952 the California Supreme Court for the first time allowed plaintiffs to recover for "intentional infliction of emotional distress," and over the next two decades the Court abolished the doctrines of charitable, familial, and governmental immunity.[41]

Those were just the first steps in a series of major changes in tort law. California Supreme Court judge Roger Traynor had urged in a famous 1944 case that manufacturers of products be strictly liable for injuries arising from the use of defective products. Plaintiffs, he argued, should not have to show that the manufacturer was negligent to collect damages. That suggestion was finally adopted in the 1960s in California, and it soon spread throughout the nation. One result of this change surfaced in 1968, when a federal court ruled that auto manufacturers were liable for injuries sustained in cars that inadequately protected passengers in a crash. Design defect cases have since become an important area of product liability law.

In the 1970s, in perhaps the biggest change of all, the California Supreme Court eliminated the contributory negligence rule, which had barred any recovery for plaintiffs partly responsible for their injuries. Instead the court substituted the "comparative negligence rule," instructing juries to reduce awards by the percentage that plaintiffs contributed to their injuries through their own negligence. Legislatures and courts in other states followed California's example. Meanwhile courts made it much easier for plaintiffs to sue in medical malpractice cases, eliminating defenses, creating new causes of action, and extending the statute of limitations. Changes in procedural rules made it easier to bring "mass torts" and class action lawsuits for injuries either proven or alleged to be caused by asbestos, Agent Orange, breast implants, diet pills, genetically modified foods, HMOs, even the Holocaust—as well as such lesser evils as defects in the Pentium computer chip.[42] Enterprising plaintiff lawyers developed new theories of damages, and awards for "pain and suffering," loss of a family member, and punitive damages ballooned. As a result both the opportunities for and potential rewards of tort litigation have greatly increased.

A second source of litigation growth was the civil rights movement and the proliferation of antidiscrimination statutes that followed. Out of *Brown v. Board of Education,* the Supreme Court's 1954 ruling that segregation in public schools is unconstitutional, grew the notion that law could be used to transform society and achieve social justice. One of the crowning achievements of the civil rights movement, the Civil Rights Act of 1964, gave minorities the right to sue discriminating employers. That model—of giving victims of discrimination the right to bring lawsuits—has since been expanded to cover women, the aged, gays and lesbians, religious minorities, and people with disabilities, and has inspired a panoply of civil rights laws at the national, state, and local levels. Alongside these statutory antidiscrimination rights, the Supreme Court expanded the bases for claims under the Constitution's Equal Protection Clause to include discrimination on the basis of sex and other attributes. Both constitutional and statutory antidiscrimination law has grown to govern more and more domains, from education and employment to law enforcement and public accommodations. With the Supreme Court's 1964 *Baker v. Carr* decision, holding that unequally sized voting districts could be challenged under the Constitution, and with Congress's passage of the 1965 Voting Rights Act, many aspects of the U.S. electoral system have also become subject to litigation.

As the range of civil rights laws has grown, so have the damages available to plaintiffs. While the Civil Rights Act of 1964 allowed successful plaintiffs to claim only back pay, reinstatement in their jobs, and attorney's fees, courts and legislatures have in many instances also granted punitive and pain-and-suffering damages, enlarging the potential rewards of litigation. The 1991 Civil Rights Act, for example, gave plaintiffs in sex, race, and disability discrimination cases the right to collect up to $300,000 in punitive and pain-and-suffering awards. Thus the potential rewards of civil rights litigation have continued to grow.

Civil rights law was one of many areas of constitutional litigation enlivened by the jurisprudence of the Earl Warren–led Supreme Court in the years 1953 to 1969. The Warren Court's emphasis on protecting the rights of minorities vastly increased the reach of First Amendment protections of religion, speech, press, and assembly.[43] A new right of privacy was articulated by the Warren Court in 1965 and applied in 1973 by the Burger Court to abortion, one of the most controversial issues in American politics. Each of these expansions in constitutional law has created a new stream of litigation.

In terms of sheer volume, however, the Warren Court's criminal law cases have probably had the greatest impact. The *Gideon v. Wainwright* decision, for example, helped transform criminal law by giving every defendant, at least in theory, assistance to fully litigate his or her case. The Warren Court's expansion of *habeas corpus* rights similarly increased the ability of defendants to challenge the practices of police and of state courts through appeal to federal courts. Thus constitutional law became the means by which the abuses of local officials were regulated. The Court's rulings on the Fourth, Fifth and Sixth Amendments created new standards of criminal procedure—and new opportunities to challenge conduct that did not live up to these standards. Death penalty litigation, for example, has become lengthy and complex due largely to the Warren Court's rulings and later decisions on the Eighth Amendment's protection against "cruel and unusual punishment." Thus in criminal law the Supreme Court has produced a host of litigious policies.

Moving beyond the criminal justice system, courts became deeply involved in managing the conduct of a wide range of public officials.

Beginning in the 1960s, schools, prisons, and mental hospitals all fell under the supervision of courts when they were found to exhibit constitutional defects. The "due process revolution" commenced with the 1970 case of *Goldberg v. Kelly*,[44] which required hearings for those faced with the loss of welfare payments. In the wake of *Goldberg*, courts required hearings for loss of drivers' licenses, government employment, and tenancy in low-income housing projects and gave procedural protections to the mentally ill, students, parolees, and prisoners. Although these procedural rights did not always involve litigation, they created quasi-adjudicative forums in which lawyers and legal doctrine could influence governmental institutions. Moreover, defects in whatever process was employed could be challenged in court.

In the late 1960s, courts also increased their scrutiny of administrative agency decision making. They relaxed traditional limitations on lawsuits to allow various plaintiffs—frequently public interest groups—to challenge agency actions. Often the outcome of this litigation was an order to agencies to implement or enforce regulations or to explain why they had not done so.[45] Fearing that agencies were not consulting a sufficiently broad range of voices in their deliberations, courts required agencies to allow public interest groups to participate in decision making and to have their concerns addressed. Under the doctrine of the "hard look," courts scrutinized the actions of agencies to see whether they accorded with statutory guidelines, often in a way that slid over into second-guessing the substance of agency decisions.[46]

Litigants were not only allowed to challenge the decisions of agencies but also given the right to bypass those agencies by enforcing regulatory statutes themselves as "private attorneys general." The flurry of regulatory statutes passed in the early 1970s, like the civil rights statutes of the 1960s, often granted potential litigants one or both rights.[47] The ability of private litigants to enforce statutes by themselves was certainly nothing new: in the United States and elsewhere it has historically been a mode of criminal enforcement. But these regulatory statutes, governing clean air and water, consumer credit, and product safety, reinvigorated private law enforcement in realms that had been considered the province of the state.

How to pay for all this litigation? The Legal Services Corporation, created in 1965, became one source, though most of its resources were devoted to helping poor people in everyday disputes with landlords, businesses, and estranged spouses. In the 1960s, courts began awarding attorney's fees to be paid by defendants to prevailing plaintiffs in public interest cases. When the U.S. Supreme Court ruled in 1975 that it would not award fees without specific statutory authorization, Congress responded with a host of statutes doing just that. The most prominent of these statutes, the Civil Rights Attorney's Fees Award Act of 1976, created presumption in favor of awards from defendants to prevailing plaintiff attorneys *and* a presumption against awards from losing plaintiffs to prevailing defendants.[48] By 1983 a review by the Supreme Court found 150 such federal fee-shifting provisions.[49] The availability of these fees for plaintiffs stimulated heavy growth in public interest law firms and lowered the barriers to bringing lawsuits.[50]

Not content to sit by while private attorneys brought lawsuits on prominent social issues, public officials in the late 1990s got into the practice, as well. Thus grew yet another form of litigious policy making—lawsuits brought by government agencies themselves against producers of troublesome products. Lawsuits against the makers of cigarettes, guns, and lead paint were brought by states and the federal government, often in the absence of regulatory or legislative action. The threat of a federal lawsuit, for example, convinced Smith and Wesson to change the way it makes and sells handguns—changes Congress was unwilling to legislate. Government-led lawsuits are often brought by a partnership between public and private attorneys, with the possibility of enormous gains for both sides, an arrangement that has been heavily criticized.[51]

As if to spotlight the growth of litigious policies in the twentieth century, the two most dramatic moments in American politics at the turn of the century each took the form of litigation. First was Bill Clinton's impeachment trial, made possible by the development of sexual harassment law. Clinton's lies about Monica Lewinsky rose to the level of "high crimes and misdemeanors" in some (mostly Republican) eyes because they occurred during a legal proceeding, a deposition in a harassment lawsuit brought by Paula Jones. The impeachment struggle that ensued was largely a debate over the weight of the obligation to honor even those legal processes one considers illegitimate. The next great presidential political-legal battle was the fight between Al Gore and George W. Bush over the 2000 election. Bush commenced the barrage of lawsuits by arguing in federal court that a hand recount would violate the Fourteenth Amendment equal protection rights of voters—a novel argument that demonstrated once again that Republicans, like Democrats, are skilled at creating new species of legal claims when the need arises.[52] That didn't stop conservative commentators from excoriating

Gore's own legal strategy as excessively litigious or berating the Florida Supreme Court, Gore's greatest ally, as an "Imperial Judiciary."[53] In the end, Bush's equal protection argument won the day, and for the first time in American history, a Supreme Court decision concluded the presidential election.

The Clinton impeachment and the 2000 election struggle served only to underline a basic fact of American life that stretches far beyond presidential politics: across many areas of law and public policy, both the opportunities for and rewards of litigation have vastly increased. Throughout the second half of the twentieth century, Americans increasingly turned to litigation as a means of resolving troubling social issues. In other words, Tocqueville was, as usual, ahead of his time.

THE CONSTITUTIONAL THEORY

Why have Americans turned to litigation to solve social problems? Why, despite all the jeremiads against litigiousness that ring through the nation, has it been so hard to get them to turn away? The argument of this book is that the ultimate answer lies not with the usual suspects—rapacious lawyers and their rights-conscious clientele—but with fundamental features of the American constitutional tradition, which create incentives for activists to favor litigious policies.

Robert Kagan has highlighted the importance of the decentralization of American government in accounting for the distinctive role of litigation in American public policy.[54] He points to a fateful combination in contemporary American politics: a polity that demands governmental activism on social problems has been joined to an inherited governmental structure whose hallmark is division of authority. The framers of the Constitution, fearful of governmental tyranny, created a highly permeable, decentralized state structure. The object was to make it hard for the national government to do much of anything. In this object, the framer's design eventually failed: it did not forestall a massive expansion of the national government. Yet the design has had an effect on the forms that the expansion has taken. In particular, it has *channeled* many demands for action on social problems toward courts.

Kagan's research, with its linkage between the constitutional tradition and the shape of American public policy, is the basis for what I will call the *Constitutional Theory* of litigious policy making. The theory is constitutional in two senses. First, it focuses on the importance of three structures embedded in the U.S. Constitution—federalism, separation of powers, and judicial independence. These structures are a set of rules that shape the incentives of political actors. In particular, the rules lead those who seek action on social problems to favor litigious policies, since court-based implementation is a means of overcoming barriers to activist government created by the Constitution.

But the Constitution is not merely a set of rules that political actors strategically manipulate. It is, as its name implies, *constitutive*.[55] The Constitution shapes the way Americans view politics and government, even the way they see their own political interests. And this suggests the second sense in which the theory is constitutional: it emphasizes the significance of the distrust of centralized governmental power that is at the core of the American constitutional tradition. American activists support court-based schemes in part because of their ambivalent attitudes toward the welfare-regulatory state, attitudes that are strongly reinforced by the structures in the Constitution.

The constitutional tradition creates three specific incentives for activists to support litigious policies. Through litigious policies, activists can (1) insulate implementation of policy from political enemies (the insulation incentive); (2) do good things for constituents without spending governmental dollars (the cost-shifting incentive), and (3) gain power over the actions of states and localities (the control incentive). These three incentives—insulation, cost-shifting, and control—explain the prominence of litigious policies in American politics and the difficulty of dislodging those policies.

THE INSULATION INCENTIVE

American activists support litigious policies in part because they provide a means of implementing public policy that is relatively insulated from political enemies.[56] Implementation is, of course, a vital step in the policy process: for activists, a policy that is never implemented, or implemented in ways they abhor, can be worse than no law at all. But implementation is a particularly problematic enterprise in a system of separated powers, such as that of the United States. Federal bureaucracies assigned to implement policies in a separated system serve a thousand masters—the president, members of Congress, interest groups, and the public. Each of these masters can seek to derail implementation of a policy. The public policy literature is rife with tales of regulatory agencies "captured" by the regulated, resulting in lax enforcement of rules. Courts, because of their relative independence from the rest of the political system and because of their decentralized structure, can provide a seemingly safer route for implementation. Lodging enforcement of antidiscrimination rules solely in the Equal Employment Opportunity Commission puts the future of civil rights law in the hands of whoever gains control over the commission. Allowing individuals to sue for discrimination in court scatters control over civil rights to litigants, judges, and juries around the nation. In a nation with a constitutional tradition based on suspicion of centralized governmental authority, it's not surprising that activists often favor court-based enforcement.

THE CONTROL INCENTIVE

Activists are also attracted to litigious policies as a way to gain control over the actions of states and localities.[57] Federalism creates strong barriers to national controls over local policies. Within their own spheres, the Constitution says, the states are supreme and cannot be told what to do by the national government. Thus activists who wish to gain nationwide control over, say, school districts or police departments face severe constraints. In many nations the best way to control what's taught in schools is to become secretary of education. In the United States, by contrast, the secretary of education is relatively powerless: this official can only exhort school districts to change their curricula, or perhaps bribe the districts with federal aid. Litigious policies offer an attractive alternative to these routes. By enforcing court-protected rights against local agencies, activists can get federal courts to command the changes they wish. Civil rights laws, for example, gave civil rights activists a way to challenge the actions of local officials in the South. Fourth Amendment search and seizure lawsuits became a means to control the procedures of the police. Environmental laws have been used to control local development. These forms of litigation have the added virtue of appearing as "checks" on the abuses of local governmental officials, a frame that resonates strongly in a nation whose constitutional tradition is built around a fear of unchecked governmental power.

THE COST-SHIFTING INCENTIVE

The dream of all politicians is to do good things for their constituents without having to pay for them. Litigious policies make this fantasy a reality. Imagine, for example, that the public grows dissatisfied with the services rendered by health maintenance organizations (HMOs). Policy makers could address these concerns in numerous ways. For example, they could (a) create a publicly funded health care system to replace the despised HMOs, (b) establish a new regulatory bureaucracy to oversee HMO abuses, or (c) create a "patients' bill of rights" to allow individuals to sue HMOs for their sins. It isn't hard to understand the appeal of option (c), which unlike the others involves not a single penny of fiscal spending. By creating new rights—to be free of toxic waste dumps (as in the Superfund program), to sue when discriminated against, or to challenge HMO decision making—policy makers can claim credit for helping their constituents, but shift the costs on to others. Not only that, by lodging enforcement of rights in courts, politicians can transfer the cost of *enforcement* to private actors. In a constitutional tradition that stresses limited government and makes it particularly difficult to raise the revenue necessary to build the state,[58] litigious policies have the great virtue of addressing social problems without tapping the budget. Activists, recognizing this, support and defend litigious policies.

Taken together, the insulation, control, and cost-shifting incentives explain the staying power of litigious policies in American politics. That is not to say that these incentives are ever present and all-powerful. They vary in intensity both over time and across policy domains. The insulation incentive, for example, does not operate when activists are convinced that they can trust bureaucratic agencies to implement the law as they wish.[59] Similarly, the control incentive is relevant only to policy domains in which states and localities are significant actors. Control is not, for example, an incentive in a domain such as defense policy, where there is usually no need to wrest implementation from states and localities. Moreover, none of these incentives is relevant unless those who desire governmental action on a social problem gain the power to enact their desires into law—"activism" is a variable in itself. Thus to say that the insulation, control, and cost-shifting incentives have fostered litigious policies is not to claim that American public policy has been invariably litigious. It does suggest that these three incentives create a generalized tilt in American public policy toward courts as compared to the public policy of other nations. The three incentives explain why many areas of public policy that are bureaucratized in other nations are more judicialized in the United States.

More important for this study, the Constitutional Theory provides an explanation for why antilitigation efforts, despite their apparent popularity, face strong resistance. Courts provide an attractive way for American activists to meet their goals, and it takes an extraordinary effort to stop them or divert their energies to other channels.

The result of all this—greater judicialization of matters that in other nations are bureaucratized—takes on its full significance when we compare the organization of the American judicial system with that of the typical bureaucracy. Bureaucracies are centralized hierarchies: in the bureaucratic model, government policies are implemented by civil servants who are following fixed rules laid down by superiors. The American judicial system, by contrast, is based on what Kagan has called the model of "adversarial legalism." In an adversarial legal system, issues are organized as formal disputes between parties rather than as rules implemented by civil servants; the parties (individuals and organizations, mostly nongovernmental) have the burden of invoking and enforcing the rules. The decision makers in an adversarial legal model (judges and juries in the American court system) are not tightly bound to a centralized higher authority as in the bureaucratic model. The rules themselves are constantly in dispute and evolving: in the course of arguing how rules should be enforced, the parties also argue about what the rules should be. Public policy in an adversarial legal system, then, is decentralized, privatized, and fluid, often unpredictable.[60]

As the Constitutional Theory suggests, some of these features of adversarial legalism are what makes litigious policies so attractive to American activists. The decentralization inherent in adversarial legalism, for example, helps insulate the policy from control by enemies, while privatization means that implementation costs are not borne by the public fisc. But these features can also be sources of discontent. The fluidity and unpredictability of an adversarial legal system create troublesome uncertainties for the actors that system regulates. It is difficult, for example, to be certain about what kind of treatment a jury in a medical malpractice lawsuit might consider adequate, so doctors are tempted to practice "defensive medicine." Moreover, the privatization of public policy inherent in the adversarial legal model makes implementation dependent on the resources and choices of nongovernmental actors, thus creating further uncertainty, and great inequities as well. Finally, the process of implementing public policy through disputes among parties can be extraordinarily costly in both time and money, as the Laskin Poplar Superfund case demonstrates. Discontent with the costs, uncertainty, inequity, and inefficiency of adversarial legalism can provide a powerful stimulant to antilitigation reform, as the case studies in this book illustrate.

PATHS TO REFORM

This book describes a wide variety of antilitigation efforts, but at the outset it is helpful to contrast two basic forms, which I call *discouragement* and *replacement*. Discouragement policies aim to restrict or discourage litigation by making it harder or less rewarding to bring lawsuits. A typical discouragement policy, adopted by many states, is to cap the amount of money a plaintiff can win for pain-and-suffering damages in a personal injury lawsuit. Discouragement policies like this do not stop litigation altogether but can reduce the volume and intensity of claims. Replacement reforms, by contrast, eliminate whole categories of litigation and replace them with some alternative mechanism. One notable example of replacement reform is the New Zealand accident insurance system, in which accident victims apply to a government agency for compensation rather than suing their victimizers in court. Another, less exotic replacement reform is the American workers' compensation system, an employer-funded insurance system designed to replace litigation over workplace injuries. The most recent replacement reform is the September 11th Victim Compensation Fund, a federal program intended to replace litigation over the terrorist attack on the World Trade Center towers and Pentagon. Replacement reforms like these can eradicate whole species of lawsuits.

Discouragement campaigns, particularly the tort reform movement, have become the most prominent of all antilitigation efforts. This book, however, focuses on replacement reforms because they are the most revealing of the causes of America's litigious public policy style: replacement efforts, unlike discouragement campaigns, force policy makers to compare the costs and benefits of litigious policies to alternative mechanisms designed to achieve similar goals. The study of replacement politics, then, can spotlight what exactly makes the mechanism of litigation so enticing to American policy makers—and what makes alternatives, especially the bureaucratic approaches used in other nations, less alluring.

The study of discouragement politics is, by contrast, bound to be disappointing on this score, because discouragement campaigns aren't ultimately about the virtues and vices of litigious policies. Discouragement politics, instead, is a fight over distributional justice. Discouragement battles are waged on such matters as how much victims of accidents should receive for their injuries or how much companies should pay for manufacturing defective products, not whether litigation is a good way to decide these questions. Because the distributional consequences of such fights are usually clear-cut, the politics of discouragement is usually fairly simple: groups aligned with plaintiffs square off against groups aligned with defendants. So, for example, the debate over restrictions in personal injury law typically pits Democrats, liberal constituencies, and lawyers against Republicans and business and professional groups.

Replacement politics is much more complex. Reformers in this path focus on the negative effects of adversarial legalism, principally its high transaction costs and uncertainty, and argue that the social problems involved can best be solved by some alternative mechanism. They seek to bring together groups associated with both plaintiffs and defendants to agree on the alternative. This path can lead to the elimination of whole species of lawsuits, but it is fraught with difficulties, as the case studies in this book demonstrate.

The first and most important barrier to replacement reforms is suggested by the Constitutional Theory. Many of the alternatives to litigation involve bureaucratic regulation or welfare programs. These alternatives are common in other economically advanced nations, but in the United States the constitutional tradition creates strong incentives for groups to favor litigation over these other forms of governmental action. The incentives—insulation, control, and cost-shifting—have to be overcome if governmental antilitigation reforms are to be adopted.

Related to the Constitutional Theory is a second, more general barrier. Replacement reforms are usually controversial because they reverse one of the major features of adversarial legalism—the privatization of public policy—by socializing what seems to be a conflict between individuals. This movement from individualized dispute to socialized solution is often resisted in American politics. In litigation, problems appear as discrete disputes between individuals. When, for example, your car is hit by a careless driver, both the problem and the solution seem clear: the numbskull who hit your vehicle should be punished by a lawsuit. Replacement reforms reconceive individual conflicts as social problems. So, for example, "no-fault" auto insurance is premised on the view that accidents are a predictable social hazard produced by automobiles and that the problem is best solved not by punishing individual drivers but by pooling the risk of accidents through the most efficient insurance system possible. As later chapters illustrate, the no-fault idea is controversial in part because it seems to neglect the individual dimension of the problem: the bad driver appears to get away with his or her misdeeds. The problems in this book's case studies—auto accidents, bad reactions to vaccines, unemployment among people with disabilities—can be viewed either as social issues or as the product of individual transgressions. As the cases demonstrate, the weight of American political culture appears to favor the latter interpretation, and so proponents of reform policies face an uphill battle in creating a socialized alternative to litigation.

A third barrier to replacement reforms is the difficulty in bringing groups associated with plaintiffs and defendants together, even on the basis of common interests. The two sides usually have bitter rivalries, disparate cultures, and conflicting alliances. Each deeply distrusts the other. Coming to agreement on some alternative is hard enough; working together against opponents of reform is even harder. It takes an unusually gifted politician to create an effective plaintiff-defendant alliance, as we will see.

A fourth barrier is uncertainty about the alternative to litigation. Replacements for litigation are often complex and their effects hard to measure in advance. Replacements involve complicated trade-offs and mechanisms the likes of which only the most dedicated policy wonks are likely to understand. In an atmosphere of distrust, it is easy for opponents of the replacement reform to sow doubts about the alternative and hard for proponents to assuage those doubts.

Together these are formidable obstacles. Nonetheless, replacement proponents sometimes overcome them and enact sweeping reforms. The struggles over replacement proposals, though, reveal the deep political roots of America's litigious public policy style.

THE PLAN OF THE BOOK

Many studies have compared the social policies of the United States to those of other advanced industrialized nations and found American policy to be uniquely court oriented. This book probes the political origins of these differences, the mechanisms that have kept litigious policies in place, and the conditions under which they may be successfully attacked. Thus the bulk of this book offers selected scenes from the struggle over litigation in American politics. Chapter 1 is an overview of the politics of litigation in the United States. Chapters 2 through 4 tell the stories of three antilitigation campaigns: the (feeble) attempt to forestall the creation of the Americans with Disabilities Act, the effort to enact no-fault auto insurance in California, and the drive to establish the Vaccine Injury Compensation Program. Chapter 5 summarizes the findings of the cases and suggests how they might lead Americans to rethink the way they argue about "litigiousness."

This is a book about litigation, but as the reader will soon discover, there is very little in these pages that directly examines the legal process or how courts do their work. Instead this book focuses on activists, lobbyists, policy experts, and legislators as they wrestle over litigious policies.

Why travel to legislatures to understand litigation? So far, most academics who have written about the litigation debate have analyzed it at the level of popular culture. They have highlighted the ways in which those who campaign against personal injury lawsuits use cultural myths or beliefs about litigation to strengthen their position.[61] These studies are fascinating but necessarily limited in scope. First, they are limited to personal injury law and do not explore other arenas of antilitigation politics. Second, they focus on the production of litigation myths and so do not closely examine the policy-making process. In this book I closely scrutinize the role of ideas and interests in the making and unmaking of litigious policies.

There are several works that examine aspects of the politics of litigation, but no comprehensive study.[62] American political scientists are quite familiar with the long-standing struggles over regulation and deregulation in the United States and the unending battle over the welfare state. Hundreds of books have been written about the politics of welfare and regulation. In this book I describe a parallel universe, the world of litigation politics, a realm that is just beginning to be explored.

CHAPTER 1

THE BATTLE OVER LITIGATION

Litigation is under siege from many directions, but as I argued in the introduction, some attacks turn out to be more significant than others. While tort reform, for example, are aimed simply at reducing the volume and cost of litigation, other antilitigation efforts can eradicate whole species of lawsuits. It is these more sweeping campaigns, in which policy makers are led to ponder the merits of litigation versus other problem-solving devices, that teach the most about the roots of America's distinctively litigious public policy style. In focusing on two of the most visible components of the attack on litigation, tort reform and alternative dispute resolution, commentators have missed broader, more theoretically significant patterns. A review of the many struggles over litigious policies in American politics and the political forces involved in the litigation debate puts the individual battles in context.

THE ATTACK

It would be arbitrary to pinpoint a moment when the attack on litigation began. There have always been antilitigation impulses and even antilitigation reforms in the United States.[1] Yet as late as the 1960s, in the midst of an enormous expansion in litigious policies, there was little mention of litigiousness as a major problem in American life. Indeed, within the legal profession the major criticism of the legal system was that it was inaccessible and so unavailable to poor and middle-class people. *More* litigation, not less, was needed.[2] At some point in the 1970s, however, a shift began. Concerns about accessibility faded, and misgivings about litigation took center stage. A wide-ranging debate over the costs and benefits of litigation began.

Within the bar an indicator of the shift was the 1976 Roscoe Pound Conference on the Causes of Popular Dissatisfaction with the Administration of Justice. Number one among the causes cited by the participants—federal judges, elite lawyers, and law professors—was "overload," both in the sheer number of cases filed and in the expectations people had about the problem-solving capacities of courts. "The American public today perceives courts as jacks-of-all-trades, available to furnish the answer to whatever may trouble us," said Simon Rifkind, a corporate lawyer and former federal judge. As a result, courts were carrying a "backbreaking burden."[3] Others complained of the expanding length and complexity of litigation. With the growth of procedural rights for defendants, criminal cases "never seem to end," said Walter Schaefer, a judge.[4] Francis Kirkham, a corporate lawyer, claimed that in some kinds of civil litigation "discovery knows no bounds" and that class action lawsuits in the federal courts were "reaching flood stage."[5] Echoing the aquatic metaphor, U.S. Attorney General Edward Levi said that courts were "deluged with business."[6] The problem of overload was so serious, claimed Solicitor General Robert Bork, that "the integrity of the federal system is threatened."[7] Kirkham worried whether the nation was "retaining the capacity to achieve justice by rational means."[8]

The Pound Conference participants suggested a myriad of solutions to the problem of overloaded courts, proposals that would set much of the agenda for antilitigation reformers over the next two decades. Contrary to their image as lawsuit mongers, the elite lawyers at the conference took a very critical stance toward litigation.

Beginning in the 1970s, a new skepticism about the utility of litigation also arose among academics. Researchers in law and the social sciences argued that courts lacked the capacity to be good policy makers and that litigation wasn't a very effective way to make society more just.[9] Although these themes were hardly novel, they took on particular poignancy coming after two decades in which reformers had turned repeatedly to litigation as a tool of reform. Indeed, some of the criticisms of litigation came from those who had eagerly accepted the premises of the legal reform model. Gerald Rosenberg went to law school hoping to become a social reformer but discovered that social change through constitutional litigation was a *Hollow Hope*.[10] Radical lawyers in the critical legal studies movement, some of them veterans of civil rights struggles, analyzed the limits of liberal legal reform; critical race theorists, though more sympathetic to rights laws, joined in.[11] Meanwhile communitarian critics of liberalism articulated yet another set of complaints about the influence of litigation on American life. Mary Ann Glendon, for example, argued that American politics was overly legalistic, dominated by "rights talk" that polarized citizens and oversimplified issues.[12] Economists condemned litigation for its high costs and impact on American competitiveness.[13] Conservatives and a few liberals criticized the Warren Court's expansion of procedural rights in the criminal justice system.[14] Even many tort law professors, a group that had promoted the liberalization of liability in the 1950s and 1960s, were by the 1980s deeply troubled by the shortcomings of litigation as a means of compensating injury.[15] Echoing their criticisms was a flurry of research on civil litigation that began in the 1980s, much of it supportive of antilitigation reforms.[16]

By the 1990s antilitigation reform even became the stuff of national politics, thanks largely to the efforts of Vice President Dan Quayle. During the Bush administration Quayle developed litigation reform into a political issue, and mainly through his rhetorical attacks it occasionally popped into the national spotlight.

The apex of Quayle's antilitigation campaign was his 1991 speech to the American Bar Association (ABA). Applauding Walter Olson's *The Litigation Explosion* and estimating that tort litigation cost over $300 billion each year, Quayle called the civil justice system a "self-inflicted competitive disadvantage." In one of the more widely discussed sections of his speech, Quayle asked, "Does America really need 70 percent of the world's lawyers? Is it healthy for our economy to have 18 million new lawsuits coursing through the system annually?"[17] As a step toward remedying these conditions, Quayle proposed fifty antilitigation reforms recommended by the President's Council on Competitiveness, which he chaired.[18]

Rising to the challenge, John Curtin, president of the ABA, said his organization was willing to consider the proposals, but "Anyone who believes a better day dawns when lawyers are eliminated has the burden of explaining who will take their place. Who will protect the poor, the injured, the victims of negligence, the victims of racial discrimination, and the victims of racial violence? . . . Lawyers are the simple yet essential means by which people seek to vindicate their rights and we must not foreclose that means."[19] Quayle had not actually proposed the extermination of lawyers, so Curtin's response was a bit of a non sequitur. But the exchange was dramatic and drew media attention.[20] Sophisticated critics, besides noting Quayle's use of dubious statistics,[21] pointed out that Quayle, like Curtin, was shadowboxing: his reforms were far less sweeping than his rhetoric suggested.[22] Many were minor procedural measures that the ABA itself had supported; others sounded major but on inspection turned out to be narrow in scope.[23] Nonetheless, a splash was made.

None of Quayle's suggestions found its way into federal legislation, though President Bush did sign an executive order implementing some of the procedural ideas.[24] But in legal reform Quayle and Bush found an agreeable, albeit minor, political issue, one that has since become a staple of Republican politics. In the presidential election of 1992 President Bush's first television ad mentioned "legal reform," and his campaign criticized Bill Clinton and the Democratic Party for accepting massive contributions from plaintiff lawyers. Republicans even picketed Bill Clinton with signs reading "Stop the Trial Lawyers' Takeover of the White House."[25] Newt Gingrich made "Common Sense Legal Reform" the ninth plank in his Contract With America and pushed various tort reform bills through the House. In one of the highlights of his otherwise uninspired 1996 presidential campaign, Robert Dole joked after falling from a stage during a campaign event that trial lawyers had begun calling him on his cell phone even before he hit the ground.[26] And during his 2000 presidential campaign, George W. Bush, proud to be considered an enemy of plaintiff lawyers, pointed to tort reform as one of his major accomplishments as governor of Texas.[27] Dole and both Bushes have mentioned litigation reform in their televised debates, and the Republican platform since 1992 has contained antilitigation language.[28]

Although their antilitigation rhetoric sweeps broadly, these politicians are in fact mainly focused on one species of lawsuit, the personal injury claim. They tend to ignore other, more common forms of litigation— over contracts, property disputes, and family issues. Business-to-business contract disputing, for example, is at least as important a source of lawsuits as tort, but in the litigation debate this is obscured. In 2000, tort lawsuits constituted 7 percent of the civil case load of a sample of state courts; contract cases amounted to 23 percent.[29] Yet when politicians, pundits, and journalists criticize "litigiousness," they are speaking almost invariably about personal injury lawsuits.

Why does tort litigation receive such a disproportionate share of attention? The simplest explanation is that those on the receiving end of tort lawsuits—business groups, governments, and professional organizations—have the means and the incentive to publicize their discontents. These powerful interests have set the agenda both for politicians and the media. Other forms of litigation—for example, contractual disputes— have business interests on both the giving and receiving ends, creating a much more ambivalent attitude.[30] Moreover, many common types of litigation—family disputes, for example—don't involve business interests at all. It is only those forms of litigation in which powerful interests appear solely as defendants—tort, civil rights, and environmental lawsuits—that are most visibly attacked.

Even in this grouping, however, tort litigation seems to get the lion's share of the attention. Aside from the interests behind it, there seems to be a special resonance to complaints about personal injury law. David Engel has argued that tort litigation stories serve as symbols of community disintegration in a way that anecdotes about, for example, contract disputes cannot. Engel studied attitudes toward tort law in a rural county in the Midwest. In the view of Engel's subjects, plaintiffs in tort lawsuits deserved special scorn because they had used the coercive powers of the state to get money they did not earn from defendants who never agreed to assume responsibility for their injuries. Thus for Engel's subjects, as for many Americans, stories about tort litigation symbolize the decline of personal responsibility in society.[31] Moreover, tort stories are dramatic and easily understood, making them easily digestible fodder not just for everyday gossip but also for the news and entertainment media. The story of Stella Liebeck, who had the infamous encounter with McDonald's coffee, radiated through public discourse because it dramatically illustrated what "everyone knows"—that Americans routinely sue others for accidents they themselves are responsible for, that big corporations are excessively punished because they are "big pockets," and that tort plaintiffs are overcompensated by runaway juries. Indeed, aspects of the Stella Liebeck story that were inconvenient to this portrayal—such as the fact that Liebeck eventually settled for roughly one-fifth of the widely publicized $2.9 million jury verdict, that her burns were horrifyingly severe, or that McDonald's coffee had previously scalded hundreds— were widely ignored.[32]

The notoriety of tort litigation, combined with the powers of persuasion of corporate and professional interests, has put personal injury lawsuit reform at the top of the antilitigation agenda. Yet the range of antilitigation politics sweeps much more broadly than tort suits. Business-to-business disputing, though not the subject of television sitcoms or Republican platform planks, has been the target of several antilitigation efforts, especially alternative dispute resolution, discussed below. Indeed, some of the more obscure antilitigation reforms, though not the stuff of advertising campaigns or presidential speeches, are among the more significant.

FOUR TYPES OF ANTILITIGATION EFFORTS

There are a vast array of antilitigation efforts spanning varied policy areas and levels of government, but they can be usefully divided into four basic forms: (1) *discouragement,* attempts to discourage plaintiffs and so reduce litigation; (2) *management,* attempts to make the disputing process more efficient and harmonious; (3) *replacement,* attempts to replace litigation with some other problem-solving device; and (4) *resistance,* opposition to new forms of litigation (see Table 1.1). Each form creates a distinctive politics. Of the four types, discouragement and management efforts have been the most visible, garnering the most media attention—and the most hyperbolic rhetoric. Yet as I argued in the introduction, replacement efforts and the battles they create expose more fully the roots of America's distinctively court-centered public policy style because they represent more fundamental attacks on litigation as a problem-solving device.

The Partisan Politics of Discouragement

Discouragement reforms take the most familiar and straightforward route to limiting litigation: they aim to discourage plaintiffs from bringing lawsuits. They do this by making lawsuits either harder to bring, harder to win, or less rewarding for the plaintiff. The politics of discouragement is similarly straightforward. Groups aligned with plaintiffs fight groups aligned with the defendants. Discouragement battles are thus highly partisan, with most Republicans on the antilitigation side and most Democrats lined up with the plaintiffs. These are struggles over distributional justice—who gets what—with dollars and the resources of the judiciary at stake. Proponents do not typically question the utility of litigation itself but argue that plaintiffs with weak claims are abusing the legal system.

The most prominent of all discouragement efforts, indeed of all antilitigation efforts, is the tort reform movement. A "tort" is an injury. Plaintiffs in tort cases seek monetary compensation for their injuries, punishment for their injurers, and some reassurance that injury-producing conduct will be deterred. The tort reform movement argues that the liability system is out of control, swollen with ridiculous claims, and that the jury system has in effect produced a lottery. Tort reformers promote an array of reforms aimed at making tort litigation less enticing for plaintiffs: barriers to filing a claim, an expansion of defenses, and limits on the amounts and types of awards. With a broad base of support

Table 1.1. Types of Antilitigation Efforts

	Discouragement	Management	Replacement	Resistance
Strategy	Discourage potential plaintiffs	Make disputing more efficient, less adversarial	Replace litigation with another problem-solving mechanism	Stop the creation of new forms of litigation
Examples	Caps on damages, restrictions on *habeas corpus*	Arbitration, mediation, uniform codes	No-fault systems, bureaucratization of child support, expert panels	Opposition to the ADA, children's rights, patient's bill of rights
Key Interest Groups	Business, professional, attorney, consumer, civil rights, public interest	Attorney and judicial groups	Business, professional, attorney, consumer, civil rights, public interest	?
Level of Conflict	High	Low	Mixed	?
Level of Partisanship	High	Low	Mixed	?

among business and professional groups, the tort reform movement has been churning tort law now for more than two decades.

The tort reform movement is a huge political enterprise. Nearly every large company, trade association, and professional group is involved at some level. Since the drive for tort reform began in the 1970s, these groups have become more and more organized, creating coalition organizations to coordinate their activities. The American Tort Reform Association (ATRA) helps coordinate and publicize state tort reform efforts. ATRA's membership includes Fortune 100 corporations, professional groups, insurers, small companies, nonprofit organizations, and a few units of government. ATRA serves as a clearinghouse for a network of forty state groups, providing them briefing materials, model bills, polling research, witnesses, and speakers and publishing several periodicals that cover their efforts. ATRA's publicity efforts are considerable, with press briefings, television and radio commercials (featuring Jack Kemp and George McGovern), a documentary (hosted by Walter Cronkite), an in-flight video, a website featuring "loony lawsuits," posters, pamphlets, and bumper stickers.[33]

For a time the largest coalition in the national tort movement was the Product Liability Coordinating Committee (PLCC), which at one point had an estimated budget of $3 million and a membership of 700,000 businesses and trade associations, including the Business Roundtable, the Chamber of Commerce, the National Association of Manufacturers, and an estimated 60 percent of the Fortune 500 companies.[34] Since the defeat of sweeping product liability legislation in the late 1990s, the PLCC has become inactive, but there are several other national coordinating bodies. The Civil Justice Reform Group is a separate group of general counsel from sixty of the nation's one hundred biggest companies who channel funds to various antilitigation organizations.[35] The Health Care Liability Alliance campaigns for medical malpractice reform laws: the Coalition to Eliminate Abusive Securities Suits successfully lobbied in the 1990s to limit shareholder litigation against companies.

These groups are just the tip of the iceberg. Most tort reform activities are carried out by individual businesses, trade associations, and state tort reform organizations. The American Medical Association, for example, has crusaded for a variety of tort reforms over the past two decades. The U.S. Chamber of Commerce has made tort reform, especially legislation to restrict class action lawsuits, a priority. In 1998 the chamber created the Institute for Legal Reform, which has sponsored conferences and published reports on such matters as legal fees, product liability law, and judicial elections. Among businesses, one of the most active is Aetna, an insurance firm whose interest in civil justice litigation is considerable: it defends thousands of lawsuits each year. Aetna is a member of national tort reform organizations, but it has also conducted its own antilitigation lobbying and advertising campaigns. In addition, Aetna has funded academic symposia, conferences, and research on tort law at the Rand Institute of Civil Justice, the Brookings Institution, the Manhattan Institute, and the American Law Institute.[36] Although Aetna is unusually active, its antilitigation activities are hardly unique. Many companies and trade and professional associations fund antilitigation lobbying, advertising, and research. On the research side, they have helped fund a plethora of antilitigation research (see note 16). Add this to the efforts of the coalition organizations, and the tort reform movement seems quite formidable.

Yet tort reformers have been largely frustrated in their efforts in Congress. Their successes have largely come through state legislatures, and even there they have often been thwarted by judicial rulings overturning tort reform laws on state constitutional grounds. The tort reform movement may have had its greatest impact outside the legislative arena, where it has apparently persuaded judges and juries to be more skeptical about personal injury claims. Indeed, tort reformers have helped to reshape public discourse about litigation, undermining the heroic view of lawyers and lawsuits that has always competed in the American mind with more unsavory images of the legal profession. Thus tort reformers have made steady gains in the cultural war over litigation even as they have often lost particular political and legal battles.[37]

Federal tort reform efforts began with a Nixon administration report on medical malpractice litigation in 1973.[38] In the following years, the Ford, Carter, and Reagan administrations sponsored reports proposing antilitigation legislation.[39] Federal product liability legislation, first introduced in the mid-1970s, has over the years varied in content. The earliest bills sought to undo the strict liability standard that the California Supreme Court had first adopted; others have provided for caps on damages and expanded defenses. None of the bills has become law, despite strong support from Republicans and some Democrats. Until 1994 the Democrats' control of Congress and use of filibusters prevented any bill from advancing. After the "Republican Revolution" of 1994 the combination of Democratic opposition, the threat of filibuster, some defections

by Republicans, and Clinton administration opposition kept product liability bills from being enacted. The closest any of the bills came to passage was in 1996, when Congress failed to override a Clinton veto. The
George W. Bush administration's enthusiasm for tort reform has been
diminished by the Democrats' control of the Senate and perhaps by the
political fallout from the Enron scandal.[40]

Federal medical malpractice tort reforms have also failed to make any
headway, despite much discussion. Between 1990 and 1994 forty-six
medical malpractice reform bills were introduced into Congress, most of
them involving discouragement reforms.[41] There was some talk about
putting a cap on malpractice damages in the Clinton health care bill, but
ultimately the bill had only minor medical malpractice provisions.

Indeed at the national level, the tort reform movement has been able
to enact only relatively minor laws. These laws, passed during the Clinton administration, limited the liability of small airplane manufacturers,
restricted company shareholder lawsuits, immunized volunteers (but not
the organizations they volunteer for) from litigation, taxed tort awards
for emotional distress and punitive damages, protected those who donate
food to shelters from liability, capped tort liability for Amtrak at $200
million per accident, restricted medical malpractice claims against cruise
ship operators, protected producers of raw materials for medical products from some suits, and limited liability claims arising from the "Y2K"
computer scourge.[42] While the number of laws passed might seem
impressive, these measures were limited in scope and effect, relatively
small-scale victories scattered amongst a series of major defeats. Observers suggest several explanations for the failures of the federal tort
reform effort: conflicts among the business groups advocating the
reforms, concerns about federalism,[43] and most important of all, the
powerful opposition of plaintiff lawyer groups.[44] Whatever the reason,
the major legislative successes of the tort reform movement thus far have
come at the state level.

The first major wave of state tort reform was in the mid-1970s, when
medical malpractice insurers rapidly raised their rates and exited some
markets. The result was labeled a "medical crisis" in many states, with
doctors finding it difficult to get malpractice insurance. Some California
doctors even went on a brief strike to dramatize their plight.[45] Legislatures responded with a flurry of tort reforms. Between 1975 and 1978,
fourteen states passed laws encouraging arbitration, twenty-nine created
screening panels for lawsuits, twenty limited attorney contingency fees,

fourteen put monetary caps on damages, and nineteen restricted the collateral source rule.*

The second wave of tort reform, which commenced in the mid-1980s, was much broader, going beyond medical malpractice to all areas of personal liability. Here again a major stimulus was a rapid rise in liability insurance rates together with reports that day care centers, playgrounds, and other facilities were closing because of the lack of affordable insurance. Between 1985 and 1988 sixteen states capped "pain and suffering" damages, twenty-eight limited punitive damages, twenty restricted the collateral source rule, and thirty modified their joint and several liability rules. In 1986 alone, forty-one of the forty-six legislatures who met passed some type of tort reform.

After several years of relative calm, a third wave of tort commenced, possibly spurred by state-level Republican gains in the 1994 elections. In 1995 eighteen states passed tort reforms, including extensive reform packages in Oklahoma, Illinois, Indiana, and Texas.[46] Between 1995 and 1997 fourteen states limited punitive damages, thirteen modified their joint and several liability rules, and eight made significant changes in product liability law.[47]

Research suggests that some of the measures passed in the first two waves of tort reform, particularly the caps on damages, have modestly reduced lawsuits, damage awards, and liability insurance premiums. Many of the tort reforms, though, seem to have had little or no effect.[48] But even where the tort reform movement has fallen short in the legislatures, it may be having indirect effects on the judicial process. The data are far from conclusive, but there are indications that publicity about the "litigation explosion" may be changing the behavior and attitudes of judges and juries. Research has found that jurors firmly believe that there has been a "litigation explosion" and are deeply suspicious of plaintiffs in tort lawsuits.[49] Another study found a "quiet revolution" in products liability, with judges rolling back some of the litigious policies enacted in the 1960s, seventies and early eighties, possibly in reaction to the publicity generated by tort reformers. As a result of the shift in doctrine, plaintiffs are faring worse, and claims have been dropping.[50] Thus the gains of the tort reform movement may go well beyond the passage of legislation.

---

*The collateral source rule prohibits judges or juries calculating damages from considering how outside sources compensate victims for their injuries. Thus the possibility that a plaintiff might have health insurance and so might collect twice for her medical injuries cannot be considered. Some of the restrictions on the collateral source rule passed by the states automatically reduced awards by the amount collected from collateral sources; others allowed judges and juries to consider collateral sources in calculating damages.

Thanks to the enormous material interests behind it, tort reform dominates public discussion of litigation politics. But tort is just one area in which discouragement policies have been debated or enacted. Consider some other examples:

CRIMINAL JUSTICE   The chief antilitigation effort in criminal law recently has been the move to restrict *habeas corpus* lawsuits, which critics say give prisoners and death row inmates too many chances to appeal, resulting in long delays. In 1996, in the wake of the bombing of the Murrah Federal Building in Oklahoma City, President Clinton signed the Anti-Terrorism and Effective Death Penalty Act, which included a provision limiting death row inmates to "one bite of the apple," a single *habeas corpus* appeal. The Supreme Court upheld this statute against a constitutional challenge—a ruling in line with several previous Court decisions limiting the right to appeal.[51] A second law, also passed in 1996, the Prison Litigation Reform Act, seeks to discourage civil suits by prisoners and to reduce judicial control over the administration of correctional institutions. It requires prisoners to pay a fee when filing a civil suit and penalizes prisoners who file lawsuits deemed frivolous with the loss of "good time" credits toward early release from prison.[52] Thus Congress has attempted to discourage prisoner lawsuits, one the largest and fastest-growing categories of federal litigation.[53]

CIVIL RIGHTS   When the U.S. Supreme Court in 1989 released a string of rulings that had the net effect of discouraging plaintiffs in civil rights cases, Congress reacted with an encouragement law. The 1991 Civil Rights Act undid the Court's decisions but went beyond this to expand the use of jury trials and increase the kinds of damages available to plaintiffs in discrimination lawsuits. These changes have in turn generated a host of horror stories about discrimination litigation, and in Congress discouragement bills have been introduced to limit damages and institute a "loser pays" system in civil rights lawsuits.[54]

ENVIRONMENTAL POLICY   Many American environmental statutes allow citizens to either sue regulators for being too lax in their enforcement efforts or to bypass the regulators entirely and sue alleged polluters directly. The citizen lawsuit provisions have been criticized for misdirecting enforcement and for creating an undeserved windfall for environmental groups who win damages lawsuits.[55] Discouragement reforms that limit clean air and clean water lawsuits have, however, failed to attract much support. George W. Bush's proposal to limit the sweep of citizen lawsuits under the Endangered Species Act was predictably pilloried by environmental groups.[56]

ADMINISTRATIVE LAW Across many policy areas, including the environment, courts since the 1960s have played a major role in the administrative process. Those dissatisfied with an agency ruling found that they could flee to the courts for a second opinion. Critics argue that judges should not second-guess the decisions of agencies and that the process of litigation greatly hinders administrative regulation.[57] The struggle to discourage litigation has primarily been carried out in the courts, where the U.S. Supreme Court's decision in the 1984 *Chevron* case was seen as a signal to lower courts to grant more discretion to agencies. Whether the courts have taken the hint, and whether the Supreme Court itself has become more deferential to agencies, is unclear.[58]

FUNDING FOR LITIGATION One seemingly straightforward way to discourage litigation is to eliminate programs that fund lawsuits. Yet antilitigationists have been largely unsuccessful in this effort. For example, attempts to rid citizen lawsuits of attorney fee provisions have gotten nowhere. Funding for legal aid, however, was slashed after the "Republican Revolution" of 1994 and subjected to various restrictions.[59]

CIVIL PROCEDURE Perhaps the most obscure discouragement struggles occur over efforts to reform civil procedure. In fact, despite its musty image, federal civil procedure has in recent years been a quite contentious realm, with particularly heated debate over class action lawsuits. The animating principle of procedural reform in recent years has been to speed up processing of cases by limiting litigation. Reforms regarding class actions, frivolous cases, and discovery have all attempted to reduce litigation. Many of these reforms have, however, met with opposition, and some have been significantly modified en route to enactment, often because of opposition within the bar.

Discouragement efforts can result in significant reductions in litigation. Research suggests that caps on damages in tort litigation, for example, reduce both the number of cases filed and the size of damage awards.[60] But even where tort reform and other discouragement efforts succeed in reducing cases and damage awards, they do not fundamentally dislodge a system of social decision making based on the model of adversarial legalism. In the adversarial legal model, remember, issues are organized as disputes between parties, the parties have the burden of invoking and enforcing the rules, the decision makers are not tightly bound to a higher authority, and the rules themselves are constantly in dispute and evolving. Discouragement policies do not attempt to transform these fundamental aspects of American court-based public policy. Thus, despite the antilitigation rhetoric that accompanies them, discouragement efforts are not an attack on litigation as a problem-solving device. Discouragement efforts seek to lower the volume of litigation, not change the channel.

The Muted Politics of Management

Management reforms aspire to make the disputing process smoother and more efficient. They streamline disputing through techniques such as arbitration, mediation, conciliation, and various measures aimed at resolving issues with less conflict. By definition, management reforms are those that do not obviously favor plaintiffs or defendants; thus in this type of reform there is little conflict between plaintiff and defendant groups and low partisanship. The conflicts that do arise usually pit groups within the legal system against each other on matters either of philosophy or turf. In comparison with discouragement politics, which is often partisan and strident, management reforms typically generate little controversy outside the bar.

On the surface, management efforts seem far more radical than discouragement. Some proponents of management reforms envision a wholesale transformation of social disputing, remaking a process that has been formal and conflict ridden into one that is informal and problem solving. Others, less idealistic, simply see in management reforms a way to avoid the transaction costs associated with litigation. Whatever the vision behind them, however, management efforts are not an attack on the adversarial legal model that characterizes the American legal system. They are aimed simply at making the legal system work more smoothly.

One set of management efforts involves the assortment of procedural devices collectively known as "alternative dispute resolution." ADR is not a recent innovation. Jerold Auerbach has traced how various religious communities used mediation and arbitration in colonial America, and the history of these devices is older than adjudication itself.[61] Commercial arbitration became an important form of dispute resolution in the business world shortly after World War I.[62] But the shift toward alternative dispute resolution in the 1970s and 1980s was more broadly based.

ADR proponents are a varied bunch, from 1960s community activists to 1990s corporate CEOs. The only thing that truly unites the ADR "movement" is dissatisfaction with traditional litigation, and even this dissatisfaction takes different forms.[63] For many of the lawyers and judges at the Pound Conference, which provided a major stimulus to the ADR movement, the primary problem was an overload of the courts. Diverting some cases to other venues would protect the quality of traditional adjudication by keeping the courts from being overwhelmed with litigation.[64] Similarly, Christine Harrington, in her study of the ideology and practice of ADR, sees support for arbitration as arising from criticisms of courts as lacking the capacity to deal effectively with "low-level" disputes.[65]

But there are other themes in the move toward ADR, as well. Supreme Court chief justice Warren Burger, an antilitigation crusader, spoke at the Pound Conference of the "damaging excesses of the contentious spirit" and the need for lawyers to "fulfill their historic function as the healers of society's conflicts."[66] Burger's articulation of the value of healing and civic peace echoes in some respects the communitarian views of left-wing proponents of community mediation, who argue that indigenous forums offer a richer, less adversarial, and more particularized brand of justice. Beginning in the 1960s, they advanced community mediation as a form of community empowerment.[67] Much of the support for ADR, however, is based on far more prosaic concerns, principally cost and efficiency. ADR, proponents say, can resolve disputes in less time and with lower cost than traditional litigation.

ADR in its many forms is the most prominent of management efforts, but the category includes any reform premised on smoothing the disputing process, from community dispute centers that use mediation to resolve "low-level" disputes, to court-annexed arbitration programs, to "rent-a-judge" and other private dispute resolution services, to the many techniques used in workplaces to resolve complaints through "internal dispute resolution."[68] Some other forms of management include:

MANDATORY ADR   Most ADR programs are voluntary: both parties must choose them after a dispute arises. This is undoubtedly one of the main reasons they attract so little controversy. Mandatory ADR has, by contrast, proven highly controversial. Employment, consumer, and commercial contracts increasingly include provisions requiring arbitration of any disputes that might arise between the parties.[69] Critics say that the arbitration systems built into contracts are often biased against plaintiffs and that one should never be asked to sign away the "right to sue." To the extent that mandatory arbitration tilts to the benefit of defendants, it is really a discouragement reform in disguise, and the politics it creates looks just as partisan and fierce as the battle over tort reform. Bills to ban mandatory arbitration have been introduced in Congress, and legal challenges to these contracts continue.[70]

SETTLEMENT INCENTIVES   Some "fee shifting" proposals penalize parties who refuse an early settlement offer only to receive a verdict at trial that is similar or less favorable. Under these proposals, the refusing party is responsible for all the legal costs incurred by the offering party. Another way to encourage parties to resolve their cases more quickly and efficiently is to teach and encourage judges to "manage" their cases more aggressively.

SUBSTANTIVE EFFICIENCY REFORM   Perhaps the most common way to streamline disputing is to change the law under which disputes arise so as to make it clearer. Changes in statutory language can eliminate ambiguities and so limit litigation. Jeb Barnes, writing about the politics of bankruptcy reform, labels this "substantive efficiency reform." As Barnes suggests, this type of reform is commonplace; it occurs whenever legislators codify the law in order to clarify and standardize it, as with the Uniform Commercial Code.[71]

Management reforms can have a significant effect on the amount and intensity of litigation. But as with discouragement policies, management reforms do not generally dislodge a system of social decision making based on the model of adversarial legalism. Instead they diminish the scope of issues in dispute or nest an alternative set of procedures within an adversarial legal system. Some of the formalism and adversarialism of litigation can be reduced, but the bilateralism, privatism, decentralization, and fluidity characteristic of the adversarial legal model are all retained. Social issues are organized as disputes among private parties resolved by a relatively independent decision maker using an evolving set of rules. Thus although management reforms may streamline the process of settling claims, management is not the frontal attack on litigation that proponents sometimes claim.

The Complex Politics of Replacement

Replacement efforts, by contrast, do involve a radical transformation of social decision making. Replacement eliminates an entire species of litigation and substitutes some other problem-solving device. The dispute between plaintiff and defendant becomes a social problem to be resolved through various nonlitigious mechanisms, generally compensation funds, bureaucratic regulation, or decision making by experts; the aim is to eliminate the original judicial dispute. All the core attributes of the adversarial legal model—bilateralism, privatism, decentralization, and fluidity—are attacked in replacement schemes.

The central feature of replacement politics is the effort to bring together groups associated with both plaintiffs and defendants to support a mechanism to replace litigation. This difficult task is taken up by what John Kingdon has called a "policy entrepreneur," someone who tries to sell others on a favored solution to a social problem.[72] The pitch of the policy entrepreneur who retails replacement reforms typically features two selling points, lower transaction costs and greater certainty. Transaction costs can be reduced by cutting out the middleman, the lawyer, so that plaintiffs and defendants can jointly capture the fees that litigation would otherwise eat up. Certainty can be increased by eliminating some of the sources of dispute between the parties and by replacing juries and judges with more tightly bounded decision makers. This is an appealing pitch, but the odds are against the policy entrepreneur who peddles replacement reforms, simply because bringing together groups associated with plaintiffs and defendants is so difficult. The two sides usually share little except great distrust for one another, making any alliance in support of replacement reforms hard to assemble and easy to demolish. And any such alliance has a natural enemy: lawyer interest groups often vigorously oppose replacement reforms.

The classic replacement reform is a no-fault system. In no-fault systems, accident victims generally avoid the trouble of litigation because they do not have to make a tort claim against another party. Instead, they simply apply for compensation from their own insurer, the way a home owner collects after a fire. This, according to no-fault supporters, avoids both the uncertainties and the transaction costs associated with tort litigation. No-fault systems, whether funded by private insurers or by public agencies, socialize the cost of an injury, thereby eliminating one of the basic motivations for bringing a lawsuit.

In addition to no-fault systems, the replacement category also includes efforts to strip the judiciary of decision-making responsibilities and lodge them instead in some other body, usually a bureaucratic agency or a group of experts. Thus replacement is a broad category:

WORKERS' COMPENSATION   Workers' compensation laws, which spread through the states during the Progressive era, remain even today the most significant of all antilitigation reforms. Workers' compensation is the original no-fault reform. It replaced tort litigation with a system of employer insurance: instead of suing their employers for negligence, injured employees in a workers' comp system need only apply for compensation from the employer's insurer. Workers' compensation laws were supported by both labor and business groups. Each found the tort system unpredictable and wearisome and hoped that a social insurance scheme would be more efficient and equitable.[73] In practice, workers' compensation has not eradicated workplace injury litigation. Over time, workers' compensation systems have come to look more litigation-like, with lawyers playing a larger role, and the system itself has become a constant target of reform. Moreover, not all workers are covered by workers' compensation laws, and efforts to extend the system have been stymied. Even so, workers' compensation can rightly be considered the "mother of all antilitigation reforms": it is hard to imagine how the legal system would handle the volume of tort litigation that would undoubtedly move through the courts in the absence of a workers' compensation system.

SEPTEMBER 11 COMPENSATION   The latest replacement reform is the September 11th Victim Compensation Fund, enacted into law just eleven days after the terrorist attacks on the Twin Towers and the Pentagon. The fund provides both economic compensation and limited pain-and-suffering payments to those physically injured in the attacks and to the families of those killed. The fund is no-fault in that claimants need not prove, as they would in court, that some defendant (the airlines would be the most obvious choice) is liable for their injuries. The office of the special master, Kenneth Feinberg, decides the amount of compensation based on guidelines that the office developed. The special master's decision cannot be appealed, and those who apply to the fund give up their right to sue in court. (Fund claimants may, however, still sue Al Qaeda and Osama bin Laden, a right that Congress specifically granted after critics pointed out that the original September 11 law seemed to rule this out.) Those who forgo the fund can bring a personal injury lawsuit, but Congress has made this option less attractive: the airlines can be sued only up to the limit of their insurance coverage (about $6 billion total[74]), and other potential defendants—including the maker of the planes, the airports from which the planes took off, the city of New York, and the owners and operators of the Twin Towers—have been granted limited liability.

NO-FAULT AUTO INSURANCE   Proponents of no-fault auto insurance drew inspiration from workers' compensation and extended its logic to disputes over auto accidents. Starting with Massachusetts in 1970, twenty-four states adopted some form of no-fault auto insurance, and Congress came close to enacting a federal policy. Since 1975 the spread of no-fault auto insurance has largely been halted. Chapter 3 details one of the fiercest struggles over no-fault in recent years, over a series of legislative and ballot proposals in California.

OTHER NO-FAULT SYSTEMS   Besides automobile insurance, no-fault proponents can point to a few other relatively minor successes. Two states, Florida and Virginia, have adopted no-fault laws governing injuries to newborn babies, a reform motivated in part by what was called a medical malpractice insurance crisis in those states.[75] The Black Lung Benefits Act compensates coal miners for mining-related respiratory illnesses. The Radiation Exposure Compensation Program provides payments to those injured by exposure to uranium or to nuclear weapons tests. The Energy Employees Occupation Illness Program pays benefits to those who have developed cancer as a result of working for the Department of Energy. With the Price-Anderson Act, Congress created a partial no-fault system for "extraordinary nuclear occurrences," though the system retains aspects of traditional tort litigation.[76] Finally, there is a no-fault system for compensating children injured by vaccines, whose creation is the subject of chapter 4. No-fault systems have been proposed for nearly every major category of tort lawsuit, including those arising from medical malpractice,[77] the disposal of hazardous wastes,[78] and injuries due to products such as asbestos and cigarettes.[79] These proposals have, however, not gotten very far.

BUREAUCRATIZATION   Efforts to replace litigation with bureaucratic decision making have also encountered strong opposition. An attempt to create a federal bankruptcy agency to replace most bankruptcy litigation was rejected by nearly every major interested party.[80] A proposal to replace judicial determination of medical malpractice with an administrative system has not received much consideration, despite the American

Medical Association's endorsement.[81] Congress has, however, passed a series of laws that have bureaucratized the traditionally judicial process of determining and collecting child support payments.[82]

Unlike discouragement and management efforts, replacement proposals are a direct attack on litigious policies and the model of adversarial legalism. Replacement policies aim to uproot each of the elements of the adversarial legal model, usually substituting a scheme based on a bureaucratic model. The bilateralism and privatism of the adversarial legal model is eliminated; issues are no longer organized as disputes between parties. The decentralized decision makers who apply fluid standards in the adversarial legal model are replaced either by experts using their professional judgments or, more commonly, bureaucrats applying standardized rules. Because replacement reforms trade litigation for another problem-solving device, struggles over such reforms necessarily involve consideration of the strengths and weaknesses of the adversarial legal model. Thus battles over replacement reforms are the most theoretically significant of all antilitigation efforts.

The radicalism of replacement is limited, however, in two ways. First, American replacement reforms have typically been partial, allowing some types of litigation to continue. Even the most radical American no-fault auto laws, for example, allow lawsuits in cases of severe injury. Second, even the more sweeping replacement schemes are usually eroded over time. Phillipe Nonet's classic study of the workers' compensation program showed how what had been envisioned as a nonadversarial, bureaucratic program evolved into a much more formal, lawyer-driven process.[83] Creative lawyers can find ways in which to get around replacement schemes and bring lawsuits. Plaintiff lawyers, for example, have won the right to sue for some workplace injuries notwithstanding the barriers created by workers' compensation laws. Today, workers' compensation programs have drifted away from their bureaucratic design toward a more adversarial legal model. In the United States, with its aggressive and creative bar and a judiciary receptive to novel claims, the law never stands still, so that replacement systems are often eroded. Even so, replacement efforts remain the most fundamental of all attacks on litigation.

The Uncommon Politics of Resistance

Resistance efforts attempt to block the creation of new forms of litigation. Unlike the other three categories, this is a relatively uncommon occurrence. Laws that create new forms of litigation are often resisted, but rarely because of worries about the adversarial legal form of social decision making. To take a famous example, southern conservatives in the 1950s and 1960s resisted civil rights laws on many grounds, but doubts about the efficacy of an adversarial legal approach to the problem of racial justice were doubtless far down the list of their concerns. Because resistance efforts—those aimed directly against the adversarial legal model as embodied by the American legal system—are relatively uncommon, it is difficult to generalize about the politics they generate.

One might expect those who decry the "litigation explosion" to make strong efforts to halt the creation of new types of lawsuits. Yet new forms of litigation are constantly being born. Courts create new species of lawsuits simply by authorizing the novel claims of litigants. When, for example, a federal judge decided that bumped airline passengers could sue for damages, a new form of litigation came into being.[84] Of course, judges also routinely deny attempts to bring new kinds of claims like these.

Moreover, many new forms of litigation arise not from the judicial system but from legislatures. American legislatures often authorize new species of lawsuits. Consider just a few examples:

- The so-called "plant-closings" law, enacted during the George H. Bush administration, gives employees and their unions the right to sue companies who fail to give sixty days' notice of an impending layoff.

- Landlord-tenant laws enacted by several states allow families to sue landlords who fail to remove leaded paint from apartments.[85]

- Drug dealer liability laws passed in several states grant individuals, including drug users, the right to sue dealers for the damage their drugs create.[86]

- The 1993 Violence against Women Act created a new right to sue in federal court for various acts of discrimination. (This provision was subsequently struck down as unconstitutional by the Supreme Court.)

Of course, not all efforts to create new rights to bring lawsuits are successful; some become objects of controversy. For example, a bill granting landowners the right to sue for compensation when federal environmental laws diminish the value of their property was stalled in Congress in

1995, though several states have passed similar laws. President Clinton's attempt to create a new right for parents to sue employers who discriminate against them foundered in Congress.[87] In the most prominent of all resistance struggles, policy makers have been wrestling over a "patients' bill of rights," a law that would make it easier for patients to sue HMOs in disputes over medical treatment. Not surprisingly, the HMOs have strongly opposed this proposal.

Even when efforts to create new forms of litigation do encounter opposition, the focus is typically on the goals of the law, not the mechanism of litigation itself. Environmentalists, for example, oppose the landowner rights laws not because they have a particular aversion to litigation but because they fear that such laws will cripple environmental regulations. Opposition to new forms of litigation rarely centers on concerns about litigiousness, and it is even rarer for an opponent to counterpropose a nonlitigious mechanism for realizing the same goal. Thus the resistance category is surprisingly small.

One case that clearly fits within the category is resistance to "children's rights." Some supporters of children's rights, notably Hillary Rodham, favored granting children legal representation in divorce proceedings and even envisioned lawsuits aimed at overturning laws and policies that discriminated against children.[88] Critics argued that giving children the right to sue could create legal chaos and that the interests of children could be better served in other ways. The critics have thus far prevailed. Indeed, even the American Academy of Matrimonial Lawyers—a group seemingly well positioned to benefit from the expansion of children's rights—has adopted guidelines that generally disapprove of giving children legal representation during divorce.[89]

As this example indicates, not every proposal to extend legal rights to new groups comes to fruition. Laboratory monkeys, after all, have yet to receive legal representation, despite the pleadings of animal rights activists.[90] American policy makers occasionally conclude that not every social problem has a litigious solution. Still, there are many more instances of creation than of successful resistance, an observation that is in itself theoretically significant. At a time when so many voices have risen up against litigiousness, how can new forms of litigation be created without much opposition? That question is addressed in the next chapter, on the creation of the Americans with Disabilities Act. In any case, resistance efforts, though theoretically significant, play only a small part in the attack on litigation.

DEFENDERS OF LITIGATION

My brief review of some discouragement, management, replacement, and resistance efforts suggests the formidable array of forces aligned against litigious policies. Business and professional interests constitute the main political actors in the attack on litigation, but antilitigation reformers range across the ideological spectrum, from conservative politicians such as Dan Quayle to left-wing proponents of community mediation.

The defense of litigation, by contrast, is a task performed mostly by those on the left side of the American political spectrum, a fact that suggests the role of litigation in American politics. As in other economically advanced nations, the left in the United States has struggled in recent years to defend the welfare and regulatory state from attack. But in the United States the left has had an additional task: defending legal rights and litigious policies. Indeed, when forced to choose, American liberals sometimes pick litigation and legal rights as a mechanism for realizing their policy goals over regulation and bureaucratic welfare approaches, a choice in keeping with the antistatist tendencies of all sides in American politics. Judicially enforced rights are a means by which liberals can promote public action on social problems without seeming to augment "government."

This ideological outlook has a correlate in the political base of the left within the United States. In many Western democracies, lawyers work primarily within the state; law is conceived as "the profession of the state." Dietrich Rueschmeyer concludes that because of this, the bar in nations such as Germany has a "civil service orientation." But in the United States the bar is not so closely tied to the state; lawyers are more closely allied with their clients, and to a large extent the bar divides politically along the lines of its clientele.[91] As a result, the Democratic party has become the party of plaintiff lawyers—attorneys who specialize in bringing lawsuits, particularly on behalf of individuals—and the plaintiff bar has become a significant source of campaign finance for the Democrats. Moreover, the Democratic party is the home of public interest lawyers, who see litigation as a tool by which to change society. Public interest lawyers have had prominent roles in most left movements within the United States. The feminist, consumer, environmental, and civil rights movements all have had lawyers in leadership positions and have used legal rights as a primary tool in their struggles. Thus prolitigation lawyers have become an important part of the Democratic party, and the defense of litigation has become a significant enterprise of the left.

Academics

Prolitigation forces have a helpful, though underutilized, base in academia. Academics, for example, effectively counterpunched against the claims of Dan Quayle and the antilitigation researchers on whom he has relied. Marc Galanter, a law professor at the University of Wisconsin, has become a kind of one-man litigation "truth squad," demonstrating that many of the figures widely quoted by tort reformers—that the United States has 70 percent of the world's lawyers or that tort litigation costs $300 billion annually—are vast exaggerations that were more or less made up.[92] These figures still find their way into the media,[93] but Galanter and several other sociolegal researchers have managed to draw attention to some of the defects in the tort reformers' case. Within academia, and particularly among those who most closely study tort law in action, Galanter's critical view of the tort reform movement prevails. Galanter and his fellow critics are hardly unalloyed devotees of the tort system, but they find little evidence for claims of a "litigation explosion," and they dismiss the lawsuit horror stories regularly generated by tort reformers as unrepresentative anecdotes. In the broader public debate, though, Galanter and other academic tort reform critics are outfinanced and often outgunned. Their research typically appears in specialized academic publications and is only occasionally discussed in the popular media. Moreover, there is no prolitigation think tank to rival the likes of the Manhattan Institute's Center for Legal Policy, which supports the research of Walter Olson and Peter Huber, the "intellectual gurus of the tort reform movement," as the Washington Post once put it. Even so, defenders of the tort system have plenty of academic research to draw on to support their position.[94]

Tort is not the only field where academics are highly critical of antilitigation efforts. Alternative dispute resolution has been subjected to a torrent of criticism by sociolegal scholars,[95] and prolitigation academics are still active in fields such as the environment, civil procedure, and administrative rule making. One law professor, Owen Fiss, goes so far as to take an unfashionable stand "Against Settlement," and another, Judith Resnik, even casts a critical eye on efforts by judges to expedite the settlement of cases, seemingly one of the most innocuous of all the antilitigation schemes.[96]

Lawyer Interest Groups

Having some academics and some facts and figures on one's side is nice, but in American politics it is of course much more important to have interest group support. The problem for defenders of litigation is that the constituency most affected by many antilitigation reforms is amorphous: people who in the future will want to litigate their disputes. Those people do not know they are members of such a group, so one cannot expect any help from them. Those who have already litigated their disputes are not likely to organize either. The problem of undermobilization is particularly acute in areas where plaintiffs are likely to be "one-shotters"— fields such as tort and civil rights, in which litigation is usually a once-in-a-lifetime experience for the plaintiff.[97] Who would represent such an unorganized constituency?

One answer, of course, is lawyers. Like many defendants, some lawyers are "repeat players," who are regularly involved in litigation and thus have a strong incentive to get involved in litigation politics. Then too, lawyers may be inclined by their socialization into the profession to be supportive of litigation as a means of resolving disputes.

Thus lawyers groups are central figures in many antilitigation battles. The American Bar Association and its state analogues, the main organization of lawyers in the United States, is active on many fronts. On one hand, the ABA opposes federal tort reform, no-fault auto insurance, limitations on *habeas corpus*, restrictions on damages in civil rights cases, limits on citizen lawsuits, and many other antilitigation proposals. The ABA has also retained a long-standing concern with access to justice, supporting increased funding and expansion of the judiciary and defending legal aid to the poor. On the other hand, the ABA has been a strong promoter of alternative dispute resolution and has also supported changes in civil procedure designed to speed the processing of cases. The ABA has more than a third of the nation's one million attorneys as members, but that size can be a hindrance. Some antilitigation issues cause splits within the ABA among plaintiff and defense lawyers. Moreover, the ABA gets involved in a vast array of issues, some of them having little to with the practice of law. No more than 10 percent of its $1.5 million lobbying budget is devoted to antilitigation legislation.[98]

In the high-stakes tort reform debate, the ABA is a small player. On tort issues the preeminent attorney group is the Association of Trial Lawyers of America (ATLA), along with its state affiliates. ATLA is an organization of plaintiff lawyers who have an intense interest in stopping tort reforms. Thus the association's fifty-six thousand members support a larger lobbying budget than the ABA's, nearly $2.4 million in 1999. ATLA also has one of the wealthiest political action committees in the nation, contributing more than $2.6 million in the 1999–2000 election cycle; the ABA has none.[99]

ATLA's political activities have grown as the litigation debate has developed. The group began in 1946 as an organization of attorneys concerned about the lack of effective representation of injured laborers in the workers' compensation system. Shortly afterwards, the group expanded to include the whole of personal injury law among its concerns.[100] The plaintiff bar at the time was disrespected, disorganized, and often overpowered by better-financed, better-researched defense lawyers. ATLA, led by Melvin Belli, set out to raise the standards of plaintiff lawyers through diffusion of knowledge of and technique in tort advocacy. The association became an increasingly sophisticated forum for information sharing among plaintiff lawyers across the nation.[101] Until the 1970s ATLA had little to do with legislative politics; until 1972 it didn't even have an office in Washington, D.C. But when Congress seemed about to enact no-fault auto insurance legislation, ATLA mobilized, hiring expensive lobbyists, creating its own political action committee, and eventually moving its whole operation to the capital.[102]

Beginning with the no-fault fight, ATLA developed a disciplined legislative strategy. It stuck to bread-and-butter issues, focusing almost exclusively on tort reform. One of the association's chief arguments against tort reform was that the common law, including tort law, was a matter for judges, not the legislature and certainly not the Congress. Given this position, there was no reason for ATLA to support even favorable legislation. Thus ATLA had no "positive" agenda; it worked solely to block legislation.

With a relatively small membership and a poor public image, ATLA chose an insider approach to influencing Congress. By cultivating relationships with legislators, especially Democratic leaders on relevant committees, the organization could usually stop tort reforms from reaching the floor. The chief method of cultivation was the use of campaign contributions. ATLA's political action committee doled out millions of dollars each year, but even more money was given by individual plaintiff lawyers. ATLA didn't attempt to take on the tort reform movement with a public campaign, nor did it get involved with other issues, despite pleas from the rank and file. The architects of ATLA's strategy reasoned that, given the image of lawyers, those moves would do more harm than good, since "if the lawyers get out front, everyone beats them up." Thus they employed a "no-see-um" approach.[103]

State-level plaintiff lawyer organizations have adopted variations on this approach, with less success. Plaintiff lawyers give millions to Democratic state legislators, making them one of the top cash constituencies of the party. Outnumbered by the conglomeration of business and professional interests on the other side, the state plaintiff lawyer associations rely on their tight relationship with the Democrats, their network of well-organized lawyers (adept, after all, in persuasion), and especially the structure of American legislatures, which creates many opportunities to block bills. At times the plaintiff lawyers have been forced into the electoral arena by ballot initiatives, where these assets have dissipated. When they have lost, the plaintiff lawyers have increasingly turned to state courts, which have overturned dozens of tort reform laws based on state constitutions.

The one advantage the plaintiff lawyers have always retained is their intensity of interest in tort reform, which has allowed them to compete politically with much more numerous and well-funded business and professional interests for whom tort is just one of many issues. Plaintiff lawyers enthusiastically defend their work. They see themselves as "equalizers" who roam through American society looking for injustice, taking the side of victimized individuals against large, uncaring institutions and in the process making a lot of money. Plaintiff lawyers are mavericks who, as one of them put it, "personify the American Dream."[104] Unlike other attorneys, plaintiff lawyers make money only if they win their cases for clients, but the rewards of success can be high: the standard contingency fee is one-third of the damages awarded. Though many plaintiff lawyers struggle to survive in the profession, the most successful among them—who have reaped the rewards of class action lawsuits against the makers of asbestos, cigarettes, and other products—take in millions of dollars each year and so are highly motivated to defend their way of life. One oft noted example is William Lerach, a specialist in shareholder torts, whose firm in 1995 had about 250 pending lawsuits alleging more than $10 billion in damages. Lerach has contributed heavily to ATLA and other groups that oppose tort reform, hosted fundraisers for Democrats including President Clinton and Vice President Gore, and given hundreds of thousands of dollars to legislators both in Congress and in the state of California, at one point running afoul of federal limits on campaign contributions.[105] (Nonetheless, a law aimed squarely at Lerach's business, shareholder lawsuits against companies, was enacted during the Clinton administration, albeit over Clinton's veto.)

ATLA's insider strategy meant that for years it channeled resources toward campaign contributions and high-priced lobbyists, spending comparatively little for research or advertising. ATLA funded a few studies of tort law through the Roscoe Pound Foundation, which also conducts seminars and conferences, some of them on antilitigation issues. A Pound-funded seminar series, for example, brought state supreme court and appellate judges together for a forum on state constitutional rights.[106] ATLA also made contributions to the Brookings Institution and the Rand Institute for Civil Justice. Overall, though, ATLA's research funding amounted to only a fraction of that provided by the tort reform movement. Nor did ATLA create advertising campaigns to counter those of Aetna and the other tort reform proponents. While Ralph Nader and several consumer groups took on the tort reformers in the media, ATLA preferred to work quietly through congressional leaders.

ATLA's strategy was undeniably successful in blocking federal tort reform legislation. Until the fall of 1994 the association could credibly claim that it had never been beaten in Congress. Reader's Digest hyperbolically acclaimed ATLA as "America's Most Powerful Lobby."[107] Even today there are only minor blemishes on ATLA's record in Congress. The downside of ATLA's strategy, however, was that the lawyers seemed to be losing the battle of public opinion, and with it the hearts and minds of juries and judges. Detractors argued that in the long run the association would also lose with legislators. ATLA's strategy was controversial with its closest allies in the tort reform debate, public interest and consumer groups.[108] Nader urged ATLA to become more of a grassroots, public organization—in other words, to become more like the public interest groups he had founded.[109]

In 1994 ATLA moved modestly in this direction as Linda Lipsen, former lead lobbyist for Consumers Union, replaced Alan Parker, one of the architects of the ATLA strategy, as public affairs director. Under Lipsen the association has on occasion adopted a more public stance, with television and newspaper ads to counteract those of the tort reform groups. ATLA helped organize a coalition of opponents of tort reform called Citizens Allied for Safety and Accountability, which included unions and feminist groups.[110] State-level plaintiff lawyer organizations have even renamed themselves to reflect a closer alliance with consumer groups: the California Trial Lawyers Association is now the Consumer Attorneys of California. Further, ATLA has moved beyond its long-standing strategy of playing defense and has gone on the attack, lobbying heavily for a new litigious policy, the patients' bill of rights. Nonetheless, ATLA has not become the forceful public advocate for the tort system that Nader and other consumer activists had hoped would emerge. The organization still emphasizes the "inside" game over the "outside" game.

This characterization is underscored by the plaintiff lawyers' latest and perhaps most effective tactic in the tort reform battle: in a series of cases, plaintiff lawyer organizations have argued before state courts that tort reforms violate state constitutions. These lawsuits, employing a variety of legal theories, have brought major victories in Ohio, Illinois, Indiana, Florida, and Oregon, where state courts have overturned important tort laws on state constitutional grounds. Altogether, from 1990 to 2000 there were at least forty-eight state court decisions holding tort reform laws unconstitutional.[111] The genius behind the plaintiff lawyers' move to state courts is that, because state supreme courts are final in matters of state law, their decisions are immune from review by (more conservative) judges in the federal judiciary.

In fact, the only way tort reformers can overcome unfavorable state judicial rulings is by replacing the judges, a possibility that has made judicial elections—a surprisingly common mechanism for picking supreme court judges—the new battleground in the tort war. From 1994 to 2000 the amount of money contributed to state supreme court candidates more than doubled, from about $21 million to over $45 million. State supreme court candidates who raised money in 2000 averaged $430,000 in contributions, at least half of which has been identified as coming from business and legal interests. These numbers, though, hide an important fact: almost all of the contributions were concentrated in just a few states—Alabama, Illinois, Michigan, Mississippi, Nevada, Ohio, Texas, and West Virginia—that feature high-profile judicial struggles over the tort system. Indeed, Alabama alone recorded more than $13 million in contributions in 2000. Beyond their contributions to candidates, business and plaintiff-lawyer groups in four tort battleground states—Ohio, Alabama, Michigan, and Mississippi—also bought their own television ads to participate directly in the election. In Ohio, where the supreme court had recently struck down a comprehensive tort reform law, business interests—in particular, the U.S. Chamber of Commerce and Citizens for a Sound Economy—dominated the ad war, spending nearly $2 million in direct advertising against $1 million spent by plaintiff lawyers and their labor union allies. Ohio viewers saw a total of more than twelve thousand television ads costing more than $5 million; many of the ads were devoted to criticizing or defending the judges' votes on civil liability issues. Thus ATLA's move to state courts has transferred much of the energy in the litigation debate–and loads of money—from legislative and ballot struggles to judicial campaigns, in the process transforming the politics of state supreme courts.[112]

ATLA is the giant among plaintiff lawyer groups, but there are plenty of more specialized associations that from time to time become active in antilitigation issues. State-level workers' compensation plaintiff lawyer groups focus on workers' comp reform bills but often work closely with the trial lawyer organizations. The Academy of Rail Labor Attorneys guards against changes in the railroad employee tort system, while the National Employment Law Association fights for the rights of employees in lawsuits over discrimination, wrongful termination, and benefits.

The voice of the civil defense bar in antilitigation politics is, in contrast to the plaintiff side, muted. There are many civil defense groups that lobby at the state level, but the only civil defense interest group with a Washington office is Lawyers for Civil Justice. LCJ, which generally takes antilitigation positions, has neither the political action committee nor the big lobbying budget of ATLA. In recent years it has concentrated much of its money on class action reform and conflicts over civil procedure, though it participates in the full range of tort reform issues.[113] Either because they lack the large incentives of the plaintiff lawyers or because they have ambivalent attitudes toward antilitigation efforts, defense lawyers are far less mobilized than their courtroom adversaries.

Aside from tort, lawyer groups seem to have the most influence in the more technical antilitigation struggles, for instance, those over civil procedure, which fail to attract many nonlegal interest groups. Where many interests get involved, as in the battle over the patients' bill of rights, even the ABA is just one among many groups, with no special claim to influence. Still it is rare to find an antilitigation battle in which lawyer groups do not participate in some way.

Ralph Nader and Public Interest Liberalism

Aside from lawyers, the chief defenders of litigation are representatives of public interest liberalism. As Michael McCann has argued, litigation is a primary strategy of the public interest movement, the assortment of environmental, consumer, and citizen action reform groups that grew up in the 1960s and 1970s. Reversing the view of their ancestors, the New Deal liberals, for whom courts were bastions of reactionary conservatism, public interest reformers argued that courts were needed to check the abuses of both government and corporate bureaucracies. The public interest reformers used the federal courts to gain access to political power, invigorating judicial review of administrative agencies and exercising rights of citizen enforcement of environmental laws. Thus the public interest movement was behind many of the litigious policies adopted in the 1970s.[114]

Ralph Nader, the most influential leader of the movement, exemplifies its prolitigation aspects. Though he is most widely known today for his role in the 2000 presidential election, in the comparatively obscure world of litigation politics he is a giant. Nader has long been the most outspoken defender of litigation in America, regularly flagellating the tort reform movement in the media and providing a one-man cheering squad for tort law, the jury system, and plaintiff lawyers. Nader disparages all the major antilitigation proposals, from no-fault to ADR to tort reform. He sees these efforts as part of an attempt by corporate interests to subdue courts, the one institution in American government that he believes business does not yet fully control. Traveling from state to state, Nader has for years campaigned against antilitigation proposals with florid rhetoric and a stream of statistics.[115] He has criticized law professors who have turned against the tort system, calling them "empirically starved" and attributing their turnaround to an interest in consulting for "perpetrators."[116] He has spoken at conventions of plaintiff lawyers, chastising them for their willingness to "cut a deal with the likes of Aetna" on tort legislation and exhorting them to "fight the good fight" against tort reform.[117]

For years critics charged that Nader's unequivocal prolitigation stance reflected the funding he received from plaintiff lawyers. The criticism began in the mid-seventies, when Nader appeared to waffle on the issue of no-fault auto insurance just as one of his organizations received a check from ATLA. (The check was never cashed.)[118] In fact, Nader and the consumer groups he established *were* generously supported by plaintiff lawyers for many years—until the election of 2000, when Nader's candidacy for president enraged ATLA's leadership. ATLA had strongly supported Al Gore, fearing the election of George W. Bush, a proud tort reformer. Plaintiff lawyers blamed Nader for helping to tip the election in favor of Bush and excoriated him as, in the words of one, "a victim of his own ego." They pulled funding from Nader-associated consumer groups such as Public Citizen, the Aviation Consumer Action Project, and the Center for the Study of Responsive Law. Nader had once been acclaimed at ATLA conventions as a hero; now he "might need some protection" were he foolish enough to show up, according to Fred Baron, ATLA's president in 2001.[119] For his part, Nader argued that Gore was hardly a great friend of tort law, having surrounded himself with tort "deformers," including Gore's running mate, Joe Lieberman, who had often crossed party lines in the Senate to vote for liability reform laws. Nader criticized the plaintiff lawyers for timorously clinging to the Democratic party, which he charged had failed to stand up in defense of tort law and had often betrayed plaintiff lawyers. Further, Nader insisted that the funding pullback was no great loss for him or consumer organizations.[120]

The long-term consequences of the rupture between Nader and the plaintiff lawyers for the litigation debate are, at this point, hard to assess. There is, however, no chance that Nader will change his tune about the virtues of tort law or about litigation more broadly, for these themes go to the heart of his political philosophy. The hallmark of that philosophy is a deep distrust of both corporate and government bureaucracies. Indeed, though he does not use this language, Nader has developed a strong defense of the adversarial legal model of decision making as against the bureaucratic model. In the adversarial legal model, remember, social issues are organized as disputes between parties, and the decision makers (judges and juries in the American system) are not tightly bound to a centralized higher authority; the rules the decision makers use are themselves constantly in dispute and evolving. This contrasts with the bureaucratic model, in which low-level workers in a hierarchical system apply fixed rules laid down by their superiors. Throughout his career, Nader has demonstrated a pervasive skepticism of the bureaucratic model as embodied in both government and corporate organizations, and a corresponding love for the fluidity and unpredictability of adversarial legalism as embodied in the American legal system. Nader's first crusade, to improve the safety of American automobiles, resulted in an array of new regulations governing automakers to be administered by the National Highway Traffic Safety Administration (NHTSA). But almost from the moment NHTSA began dealing with the new regulations, Nader soured on the agency. It is a pattern he has repeated throughout his career; Nader vilifies even those federal agencies his movement helped to create. Indeed Nader's antipathy toward bureaucracies can be seen in the unstructured way he manages his own organizations. One of his chief goals is to make sure that "the evils of bureaucracy do not afflict us."[121]

Nader indicts bureaucracies on several counts. First, government bureaucracies are always vulnerable to capture by corporate interests, a phenomenon that Nader says he first witnessed with NHTSA. Second, bureaucracies corrode the moral sensibilities of those who work within them, because bureaucrats can always blame the organization or its rules for their conduct. This makes it hard to hold bureaucrats accountable for what they have done. Third, bureaucrats become distracted from their mission and worry more about their own security and comfort than doing their job well. "The greatest prejudice of a bureaucrat," Nader says, "is a vested interest in the job."[122] For Nader, organizations are always perilous to the human spirit, always tending toward rigidity and decay, a view that makes social change through bureaucratic regulation profoundly problematic.

But for everything wrong with bureaucracies, Nader sees something right with courts—and adversarial legalism. Bureaucracies are staffed by bureaucrats, with all their vested interests; courts are staffed by juries, ordinary citizens whose connection to the organization ends when they finish their deliberations. Bureaucracies are slow to consider new issues, Nader argues, but the common law is constantly in a state of adjustment. Nader sees the "grandeur of the civil justice system" in "its incredible adaptability," which puts it at "the cutting edge of social and technical change." Bureaucracies quickly fall under the sway of powerful interests; courts give the individual a chance to take them on. "Where else," Nader asks, "can a person without any money take on General Motors?" Finally, bureaucracies reward plodding bureaucrats, while courts reward plaintiff lawyers, who heroically risk everything to confront corporate evil. "It's amazing that lawyers who labor for the victims and only get paid when they win and not when they lose, are always on the defensive," he says.[123]

Nader believes that corporations fight so ferociously against litigation precisely because it disrupts their bureaucratic routines. Corporations, he claims, can easily adjust to the relatively small flow of money they pay out in tort lawsuits. What bothers them, Nader argues, is the unpredictability of the legal system, its threat to dig deep into their decision-making processes and expose their wrongdoing.[124] Corporations crave predictability because it gives them control. "They want to know exactly what their exposure is, what their risk is," Nader says, "so they can translate it into the cost of doing business and reduce forever any kind of deterrent, any kind of unpredictable sting in their pocketbooks."[125]

Given this analysis, it is not surprising that Nader disapproves even of antilitigation reforms favored by some liberals, for example, no-fault systems. No-fault, Nader argues, bureaucratizes the tort system. The dangers of no-fault, Nader claims, are illustrated by the workers' compensation system, which is staffed by risk-averse lawyers and so stands still, taking many years to recognize new and important dangers such as workplace chemical exposure. The common law, Nader claims, will always move much more quickly than a bureaucratized system.[126]

Nader's antibureaucratic impulses are, of course, in line with the deepest traditions of American political thought. Indeed Nader's view of *government* bureaucracies is largely shared by his conservative critics. Nader's turn to the courts, like that of many liberal activists, is rooted in the combination of an intense desire to change society and a particularly American distrust of government. Litigation seems to offer a way out of this dilemma. Thus for Nader, as for the public interest movement generally, antilitigation proposals are anathema.

Consumer Groups

Besides ATLA and Nader, the chief lobbyists against federal tort reform have been consumer groups, particularly Public Citizen, Consumers Union, the Consumer Federation of America, the National Insurance Consumer Organization, Citizen Action, and the U.S. Public Interest Research Group. Consumer groups are also active in state-level tort reform battles. Vastly outfinanced by their business opponents, they nonetheless can be found wherever civil liability is an issue.

Although plaintiff lawyers and consumer groups are for the most part united on antilitigation issues, there were divisions even before Nader's recent fall from plaintiff lawyer grace. Nader and Public Citizen have attacked bans on lawyer advertising and laws barring nonlawyers from performing routine legal tasks. Consumer groups, along with Nader, have criticized the trial lawyer associations for occasionally compromising on state-level tort reforms. The California "Napkin Deal," in which trial lawyers conceded several reforms, was a particularly galling example. In addition, some consumer groups have supported no-fault auto insurance, while those in the Naderite wing of the consumer movement opposed it. (Chapter 3 tells the story of the Napkin Deal and the no-fault struggle that followed it.) There is also a consumer group organized specifically to protest the high costs of legal services—HALT, an acronym for Help Abolish Legal Tyranny. The activities of HALT, however, are an exception to what has been a generally warm relationship between consumer and plaintiff lawyer groups.

Other Liberal Groups

ATLA and the consumer organizations occupy the front lines in the tort battle, but other liberal groups are also involved from time to time in antilitigation struggles. Environmental public interest groups defend citizen suit provisions. Civil rights groups defend antidiscrimination laws and sometimes speak up in debates over civil procedure. Public interest groups generally oppose attempts to eliminate attorney fee provisions.

There has been less participation—and sometimes even opposition—from other members of the liberal coalition. Unions, for example, have been relatively uninvolved in tort battles in Congress. Opponents of tort reform have attempted to bring previously uninvolved groups, particularly unions and feminist organizations, into the debate. Nonetheless, the defense of tort litigation has remained a task performed almost solely by consumer and lawyer groups.

The Democratic Party

The groups that defend litigation from attack are mainly aligned with the Democratic party. Thus it is not surprising that when antilitigation legislation is opposed, the opposition usually comes from Democratic legislators. In Congress and in state legislatures, battles over tort reform, civil rights, and criminal procedure occur generally along party lines, with some defection on both sides.

The final chapter of this book includes a study of congressional votes on litigious policies during the 104th Congress (1995–96), the first House controlled by Republicans in forty years. This session featured debate over a broad range of antilitigation and prolitigation measures, including bills to limit criminal appeals, attorney's fees, Clean Water Act and racial discrimination lawsuits, and tort litigation involving faulty products, stock market fraud, and medical malpractice. Each vote was largely along party lines, and on all but two of the votes—involving Republican proposals to create new rights to sue over environmental regulations—the Democrats took the prolitigation side. This pattern recurs throughout the litigation debate: where litigious policies are defended in politics, it is usually Democrats who are doing the defending.

Judges

Prolitigationists sometimes find support among judges, particularly at the state level. Although many judges have embraced aspects of the antilitigation message and have become involved in ADR and other management reforms, others resist these measures, particularly those that encroach on the independence of the judiciary. Further, whereas some judges have cut back on tort doctrines, giving defendants more chance to prevail, many others have struck down *legislative* tort reform as unconstitutional. Indeed, as noted above, state judicial decisions have become a primary weapon of plaintiff lawyer groups in their struggle against tort reform. Thus state courts have become key allies for those favoring litigious policies.

The U.S. Supreme Court, in contrast, has repeatedly sided with antilitigation forces during William Rehnquist's tenure as chief justice. In rulings on standing,[127] judicial review of administrative agencies,[128] class actions,[129] expert testimony,[130] limitations on *habeas corpus*,[131] and the constitutionality of citizen lawsuits against states,[132] the Rehnquist Court has upheld laws or promulgated decisions that discourage litigation. The Court has struck down lawsuits under the Violence against Women Act and has restricted the range of lawsuits under a series of civil rights laws including the Age Discrimination in Employment Act and the Americans with Disabilities Act.[133] In tort the Court in *BMW v. Gore* for the first time struck down a personal injury liability verdict as unconstitutionally excessive.[134] In another case, *Honda v. Oberg*, the Court overturned an Oregon law limiting the ability of judges to review jury awards of punitive damages.[135] These decisions, according to former solicitor general Walter E. Dellinger, reflect "the Court's strong distrust of the private litigation process."[136] As Lori Johnson has argued, one subset of these antilitigation decisions—the rulings on federalism—may also reflect some justices' concerns about protecting the federal judiciary from overload. The justices have voiced these concerns in testimony before Congress, in public speeches, and within the federal judiciary's own policy-making body, the Judicial Conference.[137] In any case, the Court has emerged as a major source of support for antilitigation forces.

THE FOCUS OF THIS STUDY

As this review indicates, a formidable array of interest groups, scholars, and public officials are fighting over lawsuits and litigiousness across many policy realms. The balance of this book, however, focuses on just three cases drawn from the panoply of antilitigation efforts I have described.

How can three cases represent such a diverse assortment of struggles? The answer is obvious: they can't. Representation, however, is not the purpose of what social scientists sometimes call the "small-*n* case study method." Instead, small-*n* analysis (in this study *n* = 3) allows the researcher and reader to evaluate theories by probing a few carefully selected cases in great depth. The small-*n* method is particularly appropriate when, as in this study, the central issues have not been studied before. In such a situation, lacking a base of well-developed theory and empirical research, it makes little sense to proceed to large-*n* statistical tests of data abstracted from the cases. With in-depth case studies, both researcher and reader can investigate more fully the events, beliefs, and institutions that shape outcomes and through this process carefully develop theories to explain these outcomes.[138]

Successful small-*n* research requires careful selection of cases. My case selection is guided by several criteria.[139] First, *this study is confined to cases of serious legislative antilitigation efforts.*[140] A book that attempted to cover all judicial or contractual efforts to limit litigation would be endless. After all, many (maybe even most) lawsuits ask for an interpretation of a rule that creates new opportunities for litigation or ends old ones. The universe of judicial struggles over litigation is therefore astronomical. Similarly, private sector initiatives to limit litigation—for instance, through mandatory arbitration contracts—are ubiquitous. But beyond the need to pick from a limited universe of cases, my focus on legislative cases rests on their theoretical value. Legislative cases best reveal the institutional, cultural, and political sources of support and opposition to litigation in the United States. This is because legislative politics involves (1) broad participation of interest groups at varying levels of mobilization, (2) publicly available records of deliberation, and (3) extended articulation and debate about public values. Exploring the roots of the distinctively American preference for litigation demands an examination of both the ideas and the interests that support or oppose litigious policies, and legislative struggles are far more helpful in this regard than court decisions or contractual agreements.

Second, *the cases are drawn from the replacement and resistance categories of antilitigation efforts.* As I've suggested, these categories offer the most theoretically interesting of all antilitigation struggles because they pose the starkest choice between litigation and other modes of problem resolution. Only resistance and replacement efforts attack the core attributes of the adversarial legal model, its bilateralism, privatism, decentralization, and fluidity. Thus only by studying resistance and replacement efforts are we likely to answer most directly the question of why American policy makers choose—or choose to limit—litigious policies.

Third, *in each case the policy outcomes are compared to those in other economically advanced nations.* My primary explanation for the prominence of litigious policies in the United States rests on aspects of American political culture and governmental structure that distinguish it from many other nations. Cross-national comparisons help us think through this explanation. Although this study does not provide detailed comparisons, it does suggest general patterns and in so doing gives a sense of the range of policy approaches among advanced economies.

Finally, *the cases vary in outcome.* In a small-n study it is particularly important to study cases in which the outcomes differ in order to gain insight as to what exactly is causing what. The three cases include (1) an unsuccessful attempt to stop a new form of litigation, the Americans with Disabilities Act; (2) an unsuccessful attempt to reform an old source of litigation, auto accident personal injury law; and (3) a successful attempt to reform litigation over vaccine injuries, the Vaccine Injury Compensation Act. The case studies begin with the birth of a litigious policy, the Americans with Disabilities Act.

CHAPTER 2

THE CREATION OF A LITIGIOUS POLICY

The Americans with Disabilities Act

The problems of people with disabilities are immense. Americans with disabilities are the largest and poorest of all minority groups in the United States. For most, welfare payments or support from a family member is the chief source of income. Fewer than one in three has a job, though most say they would like to work. Thirty percent of people with disabilities say they have encountered job discrimination. In 1998, 34 percent had an income of $15,000 or less, compared to only 12 percent of the nondisabled population. One-fifth had not completed high school, more than twice the proportion among the nondisabled. People with disabilities are more socially isolated than the nondisabled, joining clubs and visiting friends and family less often. They are less likely to go to a restaurant, see a movie, or attend a sports event. Not surprisingly, they are less satisfied with their lives than the nondisabled, and a majority of them believe that their disability has prevented them from realizing their full potential in life.[1]

Estimates of the size of the disabled population vary. The most prominent figure cited by disability activists is 43 million; another, more conservative estimate is 36 million.[2] According to even the lower numbers, at least one of eight Americans is disabled, which means nearly everyone has a disabled relative or friend. The magnitude of these estimates may seem surprising until one realizes the range of people considered "disabled." The word *disability* groups together people with very different life histories. It camouflages the differences between, say, a truck driver with a back injury and a quadriplegic who has had limited mobility since birth, or an elderly woman with a heart condition and a schizophrenic teenager. One could argue that lumping together people of such diverse fates disguises the complexity of their problems.

And there is yet another level of complexity. As is often noted, the category of disabled is, like all categories, socially constructed and thus changes over time.[3] At one point in Western society, to be mentally ill was to be morally deficient; at another it was a sign of demonic possession. The line between the disabled and the nondisabled is constantly being tinkered with. Even today it is not clear that Americans have decided on which side alcoholics, or diabetics, or obese people belong. In addressing the problems of "disabled" people one is dealing with a moving target.

The most significant recent attempt to respond to the problems of people with disabilities in the United States is the Americans with Disabilities Act (ADA). Passed in 1990 by a wide margin in Congress and signed by an enthusiastic President Bush, the ADA prohibits discrimination against disabled people in a wide range of activities. It requires employers to provide "reasonable accommodations" to disabled employees and to treat disabled and nondisabled job applicants equally.[4] It mandates that all new equipment and facilities for public transportation be accessible to people with disabilities and requires some alterations of existing facilities. It commands that nearly all public facilities, from bars and bowling alleys to parks and zoos, be made as accessible as is "readily achievable" and that new facilities be designed to be accessible unless it is "structurally impracticable" to do so.[5] The ADA gives people with disabilities the right to sue employers and managers of public facilities who fail to live up to its provisions. Employers found guilty of discrimination can be made to provide back pay, attorney's fees, and in some cases punitive and compensatory damages. Managers of public facilities can be sued to force them to open their facilities and, where there is a pattern of violations, can be fined and required to pay damages.[6]

The ADA was criticized by conservatives as a "lawyer's employment act" that would result in extended and expensive litigation.[7] Yet the ADA was fostered by two Republican administrations. Nurtured in a federal commission appointed by Ronald Reagan, it was enthusiastically endorsed by George H. Bush. On this bill militant disability activists, conservative Bush and Reagan administration officials, and civil rights groups found common ground. Although there was extensive haggling over the details of the ADA, few quarreled with its central tenet: that the problems of people with disabilities stem largely from discrimination and that the best way to remedy this is by giving them the right to sue.

The ADA is, in my terms, a litigious policy, and the effort to stop its enactment fits into the resistance category of antilitigation efforts. The story of the ADA, though, can also be described as a kind of replacement effort in reverse. In replacement efforts, remember, reformers attempt to substitute some mechanism, usually a welfare or regulatory program, for litigation. In this case, the ADA's proponents sought to do the opposite: to move disability policy from an emphasis on welfare to a focus on legal rights and thus from a bureaucratic model of policy implementation to an adversarial legal model. In a period when politicians were castigating litigation as wasteful, needlessly adversarial, and out of control, disability activists were embracing legal rights as a solution to their problems, a step beyond the welfare and rehabilitation programs that had dominated disability policy.

This movement—from "needs to rights," as some have characterized it—was never really resisted. Concerns about litigiousness were expressed throughout congressional consideration of the ADA. Business leaders worried that the vague mandates of the ADA would result in expensive and unpredictable jury verdicts. And yet what stands out about the case is how little opposition there was to a potentially important source of litigation. The Bush administration made one major discouragement effort, an attempt to limit the kinds of damage awards people with disabilities could collect in their lawsuits, but this failed. Aside from the attempt to limit remedies, however, no one opposed the notion that people with disabilities would be best served by the chance to litigate their grievances. With a few minor exceptions, no one questioned the premises of the ADA or tendered alternatives to it.

To understand why something did not happen is an inherently difficult enterprise. Explaining nonevents—why, to use an inevitable social science cliché, a dog doesn't bark—is much trickier than explaining events, such as why your dog growls at your neighbor. Fortunately the case of the ADA does not constitute a pure nonevent. The main source of opposition to the ADA, after all, was concern about the potential for litigation it could generate, a concern expressed throughout the bill's congressional consideration. Only the next step—a sustained critique of the ADA, or a well-developed alternative—was missing.

Moreover, in the case of the ADA there are plenty of clues along the way to help explain why the opposition was so muted. To uncover these clues, however, one needs to understand the sources of support for the disability rights movement, both among disabled activists and among liberal and conservative politicians. That is why this case study begins not with congressional consideration of the ADA but far before, at the dawn of the disability movement in the late 1960s. The fate of the ADA antilitigation effort can only be explained through an examination of the origin and history of the disability rights idea.

There are two parts to this explanation. First, I trace how a diverse cast of characters—disability activists, congressional liberals, Reagan and Bush administration officials, civil rights leaders, and business groups— all came to accept the proposition that disability was a matter of civil rights. Second, I seek to understand why none of these groups quarreled with a second proposition, that the way to protect these rights was through litigation. The widespread acceptance of the second proposition is particularly puzzling given the steady stream of antilitigation talk in American culture and politics in the 1980s and 1990s. Indeed, some of the most strident antilitigation rhetoric came from the same Bush administration that so strongly supported ADA. What made litigation such a tempting policy choice for both Bush officials and disability activists? The answer begins with the rise of the disability movement in the late 1960s.

THE RISE OF THE DISABILITY MOVEMENT

Until the 1960s disability policy centered on welfare and rehabilitation programs and institutionalized caregiving. With the important exception of blind and deaf people, few publicly challenged discriminatory attitudes or architectural barriers, and the rhetoric of disability rights was mainly confined to academic treatises.[8] Disability politics was mostly animated by the nondisabled, especially physicians, rehabilitation therapists, and other service providers. The main ideal of disability policy was charity: disability was an unfortunate condition, and society had an obligation to extend a helping hand to the afflicted.

The politics of disability, however, was changed forever by the rise of a new generation of people with disabilities in the 1960s, the result of improvements in medical technology, the polio epidemic of the 1950s, and the Vietnam War. The new generation was larger, better educated, and perhaps as a result, more determined than its predecessors. The younger generation of people with disabilities formed a growing constituency for new thinking about disability.

The demographic change in the disabled population was reflected in a transformation of disability politics that began in the late 1960s. Until then disability politics was dominated by organizations of rehabilitation providers, especially the National Rehabilitation Association (NRA) but also various research and service associations such as the National

Paraplegia Foundation. The politics of disability often centered on the intricacies of the federal rehabilitation program, and NRA was a powerful player in this arena. Another set of participants was parent groups, formed partly out of frustration with the services provided by disability professionals. Groups such as the National Association for Retarded Children and the Muscular Dystrophy Association, focused on service provision and were not heavily involved in politics. A final set of groups—sometimes called "consumer" groups—were run by people with disabilities themselves, the consumers of disability services. Before the 1960s these groups, such as the National Association for the Deaf and the National Federation of the Blind, were usually limited to one category of disability and rarely worked on political goals that stretched across disability categories.[9]

In the late 1960s a new generation of consumer groups arose, more varied, more militant, and more ecumenical, branching out across disabilities. Starting in centers of radical political activity, especially Berkeley, California, and New York City, groups such as Disabled in Action, the United Handicapped Federation, SO FED UP (Students Organization for Every Disability United), MIGHT (Mobility Impaired Grappling Hurdles Together), and WARPATH (World Association to Remove Prejudice against the Handicapped) spread throughout the nation. These groups rejected charity and traditional rehab therapy as fatally paternalistic. Advancing slogans like "You've given us your dimes, now give us our rights!" they demanded more power for people with disabilities to control their own lives.[10]

The Independent Living Movement
The focus of the new wave of disability activism in its first years was the creation of independent living centers. The independent living centers were a reaction to the limitations of the vocational rehabilitation system, which disability activists had experienced firsthand. Vocational rehabilitation programs had aimed from their beginnings in the 1920s at getting their clients into the job market as efficiently as possible. Vocational rehabilitation directors justified their programs with cost-benefit statistics showing that they more than paid for themselves in increased tax revenues from gainfully employed people with disabilities. Thus the bureaucratic imperative within the program was to make people employable at the lowest cost. Because the rehabilitation programs generally had far more applicants than they could serve, they "creamed"—taking the younger, the whiter, and the less disabled and rejecting the rest.[11]

Vocational rehabilitation programs had little use for people with severe disabilities, who were deemed unemployable. Moreover, oriented as they were to job placement, the programs paid little attention to the myriad other basic life problems disabled people faced. Surmounting architectural barriers, finding and paying for personal attendants, arranging accessible transportation, and dealing with the various welfare bureaucracies were all areas in which the rehabilitation programs were useless. Independent living centers were places where these kinds of needs could be met. As people with disabilities gathered at the centers, attracted by the array of services provided, they became forums for discussion and headquarters for political activism.

Many disability activists in the independent living movement's first wave embraced a radical critique of the ideology of rehabilitation. The critique grew both out of personal experiences with rehabilitation professionals and exposure to various currents of thought in the 1960s and 1970s. In an influential analysis of the ideological origins of independent living, Gerben DeJong describes the movement as a response to what he and other observers have called the "medical model" of disability. In the medical model the physician is the expert who uses his knowledge to make decisions for the patient. The patient is expected to fulfill what Talcott Parsons called the "sick role." The patient is exempted from normal social activities and responsibilities and from blame for his or her illness. In exchange, the patient is obligated to define his or her condition as undesirable and to follow the doctor's advice to get well. People with disabilities, DeJong argues, often fell into a variant of the sick role, the impaired role, in which the patient gives up the hope of recovery but continues life as a dependent, relieved of all normal responsibilities of life.[12]

Unlike medical rehabilitation, vocational rehabilitation at least attempted to restore some of those responsibilities, but it also tended to reinforce the belief that the problem of disability lay with the individual. According to the precepts of independent living, this belief in itself limited the lives of the disabled. The advocates of independent living redefined success for the disabled. Instead of "fitting in" by learning to overcome their disabilities, the independent living philosophy stressed that people with disabilities should control their own lives as much as possible. Independent living was premised on the belief that success for disabled people was more a matter of changing attitudes and removing barriers than rising above one's physical condition.

Thus, as DeJong puts it, rehabilitation was part of the problem, not the solution.[13] Accordingly, independent living centers aimed above all to remain independent of disability professionals—physical therapists, occupational therapists, vocational rehabilitation counselors, even doctors. One of the leaders of the disability movement, Ed Roberts, was proud of the fact that he seldom went to a doctor.[14] Instead, services were to be controlled by people with disabilities themselves. Independent living centers strongly favored in-home personal attendants hired by the disabled themselves over services provided by nurses in institutional settings. People with disabilities, according to the independent living philosophy, should be treated as capable adults, not sick children.

The disabled leaders of the independent living movement rejected the idea that employment and independent living were separate tracks. Further, they objected to the traditional rehabilitation measure of success, the "closure" of cases. Independent living centers, they argued, should have continuing relationships with disabled people, not a predetermined endpoint. The disabled advocates feared that the bureaucratic mentality of vocational rehabilitation, which stressed closing cases once clients met specific goals, would be transferred in a new guise to the independent living centers.[15] For their part, the rehabilitation establishment criticized the independent living centers' fuzzy goals and lack of accountability.

This argument would haunt the independent living movement at a crucial point. Faced with chronic funding shortages, the independent living centers tried to get a small slice of the federal rehabilitation budget. In 1972 their supporters succeeded in attaching an amendment to the omnibus Rehabilitation Act, which authorized funding for the vocational rehabilitation program. But President Nixon criticized the bill for adding new welfarelike programs and commissions that would "serve only to dilute the resources of the vocational rehabilitation program and impair its continued valuable achievements in restoring deserving American citizens to meaningful employment."[16] After two vetoes, Nixon signed the Rehabilitation Act in 1973, after Congress deleted, among other items, the independent living center funding.

THE RISE OF DISABILITY RIGHTS

In the midst of this painful defeat, another provision of the Rehabilitation Act passed by almost unnoticed. This provision, called Section 504, was to become the catalyst for a new emphasis in the disability movement on disability rights.

Ideas about disability rights had been floating around even before the changes in disability politics in the late 1960s and early 1970s. Academics such as Jacobus ten Broek, a professor of law who was blind, had written articles exploring the application of rights concepts to people with disabilities.[17] Moreover, litigation in the areas of deinstitutionalization, patient rights, and education of the disabled had invoked rights concepts. Two important lower federal court decisions even entertained the possibility of considering disability a special "suspect" or "semisuspect" category under the Equal Protection Clause of the U.S. Constitution, thus according people with disabilities the same constitutional rights extended to blacks and women.[18]

For many in the disability movement, however, disability rights were a somewhat abstract idea compared to the basic existential issues raised by the independent living movement. Although historical accounts generally treat the independent living movement as almost synonymous with the disability rights movement, some participants see the two as distinct. Independent living leaders such as Lex Frieden had always been concerned about discrimination against people with disabilities, but in the early 1970s their efforts were focused on the practicalities of running the independent living centers, especially funding. Only with the arrival of Section 504 did rights come to the forefront of the disability movement.[19]

Section 504

The genesis of Section 504 has been traced to James Pedley, a young legislative aide to Charles Vanik, an Ohio member of Congress. Vanik had become interested in the problems of employment discrimination and transportation accessibility faced by people with disabilities. Pedley suggested to his boss that the handicapped should be protected from discrimination through civil rights legislation, just as minorities and women were. Vanik decided to introduce a bill to amend the Civil Rights Act of 1964 to include people with disabilities. Vanik also got Hubert Humphrey to introduce the bill in the Senate, but it ended up stalled in the Judiciary Committee.[20] Committee members were apparently concerned that opening up the Civil Rights Act to amendments could prove disastrous, and so were not willing to let the bill advance.[21]

What happened next is somewhat murky. According to one account, the staff of the Senate Subcommittee on the Handicapped was meeting on revisions to the markup of the 1972 Rehabilitation Act when someone suggested adding a disability rights provision modeled after Title VI of the Civil Rights Act. The provision would protect people with disabilities from discrimination by the federal government and by businesses and institutions receiving federal funds. This suggestion was incorporated into the bill.[22] Another account suggests that it was Humphrey who suggested the change and got the subcommittee to adopt it.[23] In either case, the provision was added with little fanfare. It sailed through the Senate, survived conference committee, stayed in the bill through both Nixon vetoes, and become law with almost no discussion of its merits.

Section 504 was a deceptively simple statement. It held that "no otherwise qualified individual in the United States . . . shall, by reason of his handicap, be excluded from participation in, be denied the benefits of, or be subjected to discrimination under any program or activity receiving Federal assistance."[24] Nothing in the Rehabilitation Act suggested how this statement was to be implemented by the executive branch. Was it merely an expression of aspiration? A blueprint for governmentwide antidiscrimination rules? An invitation to people with disabilities to sue government-funded agencies that discriminated against them? In drafting a committee report on the original bill, the staff of the Senate subcommittee created some legislative history to flesh out the meaning of 504. It suggested that 504 was intended to be treated just like the Civil Rights Act, with regulations and penalties for noncompliance. The conference report was accepted without debate.

In developing this legislative history, the staff was aided by lawyers in the Office of Civil Rights of the Department of Health, Education, and Welfare (HEW). The subcommittee staff in turn worked to make sure that the writing of Section 504 regulations ended up the responsibility of the civil rights office.[25] The choice of the civil rights office was significant because the office was filled with lawyers extremely sympathetic to rights-oriented policies and distrustful of governmental actors. As one observer has suggested, 504 might have become a wholly different animal, far more hortatory in design, had it ended up in the hands of another possible venue, the Rehabilitative Services Administration, a bastion for the traditional rehabilitation model of disability policy.[26] In contrast, the civil rights office had no background in disability issues but much experience enforcing civil rights actions against recalcitrant government officials. This orientation pushed the civil rights office in drafting 504 regulations toward vigorous measures and far-reaching rules. For example, the office downgraded cost considerations in designing the regulations because, it argued, civil rights shouldn't be balanced against cost. The civil rights office believed that the costs of compliance with the regulation were likely to be exaggerated by opponents, just as southerners had exaggerated the costs of complying with desegregation orders.[27] The regulations the civil rights office wrote prohibited discrimination against people with disabilities, including a requirement that employers provide "reasonable accommodation" to disabled workers. This meant that physical barriers and unequal access to facilities were for the first time made a civil rights violation.

As 504 advanced through the administrative process, word filtered through the disability movement. In the spring of 1975 the Office of Civil Rights completed a draft of the 504 regulations, but the secretary of health, education, and welfare, David Matthews, stalled on enacting them. There the matter stood until 1977, when the Carter administration took over and Joseph Califano became HEW secretary. When Califano also seemed to stall, disability activists held a wheelchair parade in front of his home and later sat in at Califano's office overnight. A day of protest was held in several cities across the nation. The center of action was California, where the West Coast wing of the disability movement, led by Judy Heumann, conducted a twenty-eight-day sit-in at the San Francisco federal building. With more than a hundred people with disabilities, many in wheelchairs, sitting in and some going on a hunger strike, Califano relented and signed the regulations.

It is an exaggeration to say that the controversy over the 504 regulations created the disability rights movement, but as Richard Scotch has argued, the controversy did greatly strengthen the movement. First, as part of the effort to implement 504, disability groups for the first time received government funding. Some of this money was used to demonstrate against the same agencies that were handing it out.[28] The Disability Rights and Education Defense Fund (DREDF), which started life as the legal arm of the Berkeley Center for Independent Living, received several grants to help implement 504. This money was spent to train disabled people to assert their rights.[29] But perhaps more important than the funding was the example of the protests, which brought people of different disabilities together for a common goal. People with a wide range of disabilities—deafness, blindness, cerebral palsy, spinal cord injury, mental retardation, mental illness, and others—joined the protests.[30] Until the 1970s groups representing any of these disabilities, when politically active at all, had worked on their own, and the staggering differences among them had seemed larger than their common interests.[31] In a fight over disability rights, however, they became joined. Thus the protests over 504 attained for the disability movement the same kind of significance that the Montgomery bus boycott had for the civil rights movement or the Stonewall riot had for the gay rights movement.

The Rights Model

In the aftermath of the Section 504 controversy, a "rights model," or as some put it, a "minority model," of the situation of people with disabilities emerged in the writings of disability activists and their academic sympathizers. These writings echoed the themes of the independent living movement but moved beyond its focus on the critique of traditional rehabilitation programs. The theorists of the rights model were influenced most by the civil rights movement. Some of the leaders of the disability movement had begun their activities in politics through their involvement in civil rights efforts; others had simply grown up watching the movement on television. The proponents of the rights model drew strong parallels between disabled people and racial minorities. The rights model would become the philosophical cornerstone of the ADA.

The essence of the rights model is the contention that people with disabilities are oppressed more by society than by their disabilities. "The general public does not associate the word 'discrimination' with the segregation and exclusion of disabled people," wrote Robert Funk, the first director of the DREDF. "Historically the inferior economic and social status of disabled people has been viewed as the inevitable consequence of the physical and mental differences imposed by disability."[32] According to the rights model, however, every building with narrow hallways, every sidewalk curb without a "cut," every subway without an elevator, and every elevator without braille buttons is an act of discrimination against the disabled. Separate transportation, separate housing, and separate educational programs are acts of segregation comparable to Jim Crow laws that divided blacks from whites before the civil rights movement. Frank Bowe, the first executive director of the American Coalition of Citizens with Disabilities (ACCD), compared the historical oppression of blacks to the legacy of oppression of people with disabilities:

> The tragedy is that for two hundred years disabled people have not been asked about their needs and desires. Buildings went up before their inaccessibility was "discovered"—and then it was too late. During America's periods of greatest growth, when subways were constructed, television and motion pictures produced, telephone lines laid, school programs designed, and jobs manufactured, disabled people were hidden away in attics, "special" programs and institutions, unseen and unheard. Day by day, year by year, America became ever more oppressive to its hidden minority.[33]

Society allows physical and social barriers to exist because of pervasive prejudice against disabled people, the argument goes, just as Jim Crow laws were allowed to exist because of white racism. Of course, where racism is often overtly hostile to blacks, prejudice against people with disabilities is often more tender, usually taking the form of pity. But pity can be even more damaging than hatred. Many see disabled people as "childlike, helpless, hopeless, nonfunctioning and noncontributing members of society" who are not expected to lead normal lives.[34]

This attitude is reflected, according to the rights model, in the way government chooses to aid people with disabilities. Instead of spending money on services to help them become more independent, the government devotes nearly all its disability budget to welfare payments: "It looks as though the federal government prefers to keep disabled people down than help them up."[35]

Paternalism toward people with disabilities is also reflected, according to the rights model, in private charity efforts, particularly telethons. Hence, proponents of the rights model condemned an effort many thought the hallmark of goodwill, the Jerry Lewis Muscular Dystrophy Telethon. Evan Kemp, Jr., a disability rights leader who himself had muscular dystrophy, argued that the telethon depicted disabled people as poor, suffering children whose lives were hopeless in the absence of a cure. In the effort to arouse pity, Kemp wrote, Lewis had reinforced "stereotypes that offend our self-respect, harm our efforts to live independent lives and segregate us from the mainstream of society." Kemp, whose own parents had helped to create the telethon, called on Lewis to show disabled people "working, raising families and generally sharing in community life."[36] Similar criticism moved the Easter Seal and United Cerebral Palsy telethons to drop the pity approach and turn in the direction disability activists recommended.[37]

If, as proponents of the rights model asserted, the fundamental problem for people with disabilities was discrimination caused by prejudice, the solution was for people with disabilities to claim their rights. The arrangement of society to suit only the nondisabled violated basic norms of freedom and equality. Thus people with disabilities should treat barrier removal and other modifications not as a privilege conceded to them but as a right that had been denied, an injustice to be rectified. One proponent of the rights model suggested that an undue emphasis on social service programs could delay the removal of barriers.[38] The act of demanding rights would also undermine the paternalistic way people saw a person with disabilities: "How can we keep alive our vision of him as the helpless victim of a handicapping condition when he is putting together a political organization and agitating for change?"[39]

The rights model, then, entailed political action based on a radical reconceptualization of the disabled person's role in society. On its face it hardly seemed the stuff of Republican politics. Yet in the 1980s many elements of the rights model came to be accepted by Reagan and Bush administration officials. This acceptance paved the way for the ADA.

How Conservatives Embraced the Rights Model

After the exhilaration of the battle over Section 504, the disability movement faced a backlash in the late 1970s and early 1980s. The transportation industry fought against Section 504 regulations that mandated full accessibility of buses and trains, winning a U.S. Court of Appeals decision that struck down the regulations as beyond 504's scope.[40] Stories in the media emphasized the high costs of complying with 504 regulations and in some cases the absurdity: a small town in Iowa with a population of less than five hundred was reportedly told to spend $6,500 for a ramp to make its library accessible, though no one in the town used a wheelchair.[41] The victory of Ronald Reagan, with his call for getting government off the backs of the American people, seemed to presage further setbacks. As part of his crusade against regulation, Reagan appointed Vice President George Bush to head his Task Force for Regulatory Relief. Two of the task force's early targets were Section 504 and the Education for All Handicapped Children Act.[42]

These threats mobilized the disability rights movement. In 1981 DREDF expanded beyond its Berkeley base to create a Washington office staffed by Robert Funk and Pat Wright, who devoted their efforts to fighting the proposed revisions. They were joined by Evan Kemp, director of the Ralph Nader–backed Disability Rights Center. One of DREDF's first moves was to send a memo to people with disabilities publicizing the administration proposals. (The mailing list for the memo was composed of names collected during the HEW-funded workshops on Section 504.) The memo "got the community up in arms," and the administration was deluged with letters.[43] Another large batch of letters came from parents of disabled children, opposing the administration's proposal to change the Education for All Handicapped Children Act. The heavy protest demonstrated to the task force the political muscle of the disability movement.[44]

The disability rights advocates also began meeting with C. Boyden Gray, Bush's legal counsel. Kemp happened to have become friends with Gray years before, and he set to work to "educate" Gray, who had known little about disability policy before coming to the task force.[45]

What Kemp, along with Wright and Funk, taught Gray was an understanding of the rights model of disability congenial to a conservative Republican's worldview. Kemp told Gray that disabled people didn't want the paternalistic heavy hand of government doling out welfare to them. The disability regulations were not handouts, Kemp argued, but accommodations made so that people with disabilities could become independent and support themselves with jobs. Kemp contended that the costs of the Section 504 accommodations were minimal compared to the heavy costs of welfare spending on people with disabilities. The disability rights advocates reinforced this message about paternalism and independence by inviting Gray and Bush to visit independent living centers and meet with disabled people.[46]

These efforts paid off. On March 21, 1983, Bush announced in a letter sent to leaders of disability groups that the administration would not try to change Section 504.[47] The administration also dropped plans to alter the education regulations. Although these moves did not end the conflicts between the Reagan administration and disability advocates, the long-term effects of the episode turned out to be powerful. Disability rights leaders found in Gray "the strongest advocate we have ever had in any administration," as one put it.[48] Gray would demonstrate his newfound commitment to disability rights during the development of the ADA. Kemp, meanwhile, formed a relationship with Bush that continued far past the controversy over 504. During the balance of the Reagan administration, Bush asked Kemp for his help in drafting speeches on disability issues. In 1987 Bush recommended Kemp for a seat on the Equal Employment Opportunity Commission; in 1989, as president, Bush would name him the EEOC's chair. Perhaps most important, Bush and Gray came to accept key elements of the rights model. For Gray the fight over 504 was a turning point in the Bush administration's support of ADA: "It all germinated back in that time."[49]

The National Council on the Handicapped

Meanwhile, in a far more obscure corner of the Reagan administration, another group of conservative Republicans also came to embrace the rights model. The National Council on the Handicapped, created during the Carter administration, had kept a very low profile during its first few years. But in 1984 Congress asked the council to produce a report "analyzing Federal programs and presenting legislative recommendations to enhance the productivity and quality of life of Americans with Disabilities."[50] That report, created by a council dominated by conservative

Reaganites, became a blueprint for the ADA. Reagan had replaced nearly all of the Carter appointees on the council with his supporters, mainly conservative Republicans. Several had been fund-raisers for Reagan in the 1980 presidential campaign. It might have seemed at first glance a rather unlikely group of disability policy innovators, but that impression would have overlooked the unique qualities of some of its more forceful members.

Among them was Justin Dart, Jr. The son of a rich and very conservative businessman, Dart had been struck with polio at the age of eighteen. After graduating from college, Dart became a successful businessman in Japan. He gradually became interested in disability policy through his sponsorship of athletic events for the disabled. What finally brought Dart into the disability movement, though, was a visit to Vietnam as an observer for the World Congress on Disability in 1967. Conditions for people with disabilities in Vietnam were generally horrible, but one moment in particular struck him. At an institution for children with polio, he found a shed with a tin roof and a concrete floor where children with bloated stomachs and matchstick arms were left to die in pools of urine and feces. At one point during Dart's tour a girl reached her arms out to him, as if hoping that he would save her. Dart realized that the owner of the facility was being paid simply to hold the children until their deaths and then to bury them. Sickened by a feeling that he had not done enough, that his philosophy of life had been shallow, that he had been "a counterfeit saint," Dart returned to Japan, folded up his businesses, and went to live with his wife in a remote area in the Japanese mountains for six years to contemplate his life.[51]

By the 1970s, when he returned to the United States, Dart had transformed from Great Society liberal into Reaganite conservative—and from businessman to disability activist. Dart's work on disability policy in his home state of Texas convinced him that the disability movement needed to make civil rights its priority. Rehabilitation programs, education, and residential institutions had been substantially improved, and some significant, though limited, civil rights laws had been passed. But public knowledge of these changes and full implementation of the laws had lagged. Laws such as 504 left vast gaps because 504 and the other provisions of the 1973 Rehabilitation Act covered only government institutions or businesses and institutions receiving federal funds.

Perhaps more important, attitudes had not changed. Individuals such as Franklin Roosevelt had proven time and again the capabilities of disabled people, but this lesson had not sunk in. "The basic assumption of inequality remained intact," Dart concluded. "The great majority of people with severe disabilities remained isolated, unemployed, impoverished and dependent."[52] The main problem for people with disabilities, Dart believed, was that "we were considered subhuman," as his experience in Vietnam vividly illustrated. A comprehensive civil rights law would be a way to "establish the fact that we're human beings."[53]

Dart had been deeply impressed with the impact of the 1964 Civil Rights Act. He had attended college in the segregated South and had even started a college civil rights group—which attracted all of five members. "I would have bet every penny I had that I would never see the day when integration was accepted."[54] Civil rights laws, he believed, were a powerful way to change American attitudes: "To Americans, total equality is a sacred concept of transcending power and majesty. 'We hold these truths . . .' and 'I have a dream . . .' are far easier to communicate than partial rights and particular services.[55] Thus Dart decided to devote his life to passing a comprehensive civil rights law for people with disabilities.

When Dart was appointed to the National Commission on the Handicapped in 1981, he was able to put his views into action. Realizing that he had to create a constituency for a comprehensive civil rights bill, Dart used his own money to travel from state to state, meeting disability leaders and building support for the civil rights approach. In these meetings he developed a statement on disability policy stressing the need to promote independence and maximize productivity among people with disabilities. The statement included a recommendation that "Congress and the Executive branch should act forthwith to include persons with disabilities in the Civil Rights Act of 1964, the Equal Opportunity Act of 1972 and other civil rights legislation and regulation." In 1983 Dart persuaded the council to endorse and publish this statement as a "National Policy for Persons with Disabilities."[56]

Together with Sandra Parrino, the council's chair, Dart worked to make a rights law part of the council's agenda. They hired Lex Frieden, a leader in the independent living movement, and Robert Burgdorf, Jr., a prominent disability rights lawyer, as staff for the council. Burgdorf had produced the first legal textbook on disability law and had represented plaintiffs in Section 504 cases for several years. In 1983 he had collaborated on a report for the U.S. Commission on Civil Rights that reviewed the state of disability rights law and some of the complexities of Section 504, particularly the "reasonable accommodation" provision.[57] A year later, Burgdorf collaborated on an article recommending that Congress use its commerce power to write a civil rights bill for disabled people. The article was unique in that it recommended a stand-alone bill rather than an amendment to the Civil Rights Act of 1964.[58]

Once the council began to discuss civil rights, it soon became clear that the idea resonated even with the council's conservative members. All of them had close experience with disabled people and so could relate to cases in which a disabled person had been discriminated against unfairly. Dart organized town meetings at which council members met with disabled people across the country; discrimination and the need for a civil rights law were common themes at the meetings. Moreover, Dart's message of independence for people with disabilities was one the Reaganites on the council appreciated. Burgdorf pointed out that most of the $60 billion spent annually by the federal government was going to welfare programs; only about $3 billion was used to help disabled people become productive and independent. The council members, Burgdorf says, saw civil rights "as simply a way to get from a society that takes care of people with disabilities to a society that tries to help people become productive and mainstream."[59] Civil rights ended up at the top of the council's agenda.

The council agreed with Dart that a comprehensive civil rights bill for people with disabilities should be created, one that would go beyond Section 504's narrow coverage of federal governmental institutions and groups receiving federal funds. Burgdorf recommended a stand-alone bill rather than an amendment to the 1964 Civil Rights Act, and this was accepted by the council. There was discussion about whether the Reagan administration would appreciate such a sweeping recommendation but no serious disagreement on the merits of the idea.[60]

In 1986 the council produced its report, *Toward Independence.* The tone of the report can best be summarized by its epigraph, a quotation from Theodore Roosevelt: "Our country calls not for the life of ease, but for the life of strenuous endeavor."[61] The report adopted many of the precepts of the rights model of disability but refracted them through the prism of Reaganite conservatism. For instance, the report stresses the costs to the government of federal welfare programs for the disabled, which "are premised upon the dependency of the people who receive benefits."[62] The introduction to *Toward Independence* quotes approvingly a United Nations report that concluded that "more people are forced into limited lives and made to suffer by . . . man-made obstacles than by any specific physical or mental disability."[63] The council then warns that, unless structural and attitudinal barriers to disabled people are reduced, the costs of services and care for the disabled will "mush-room" with the aging of the baby boom generation.[64] Thus concern about the personal costs of discrimination was mixed with a call for fiscal prudence.

Unlike the theorists who developed the rights model of disability, the writers of *Toward Independence* avoided putting the situation of disabled people into the context of earlier struggles by blacks and women. The historical precedent of the civil rights movement is never mentioned. Indeed, except in referring to the titles of particular laws, the report avoids the use of the term *civil rights* altogether. Instead the report stresses "equality of opportunity," "dignity," and most of all, "independence." (*Independence* is used twenty-one times in the first fourteen pages of the report.) "Equality and independence," the report argues, "have been fundamental elements of the American form of government since its inception."[65] *Toward Independence* quotes a Ronald Reagan speech on disability policy: "By returning to our traditional values of self-reliance, human dignity, and independence, we can find the solution together. We can help replace chaos with order in Federal programs, and we can promote opportunity and offer the promise of sharing the joys and responsibilities of community life."[66] The title of the report was taken from Reagan's speech, in which he declared, "We must encourage the provision of rehabilitation and other comprehensive services oriented *toward independence* within the context of family and community."[67] Thus the report embraced the rights model's critique of dependency-inducing effects of traditional disability policy but left out its emphasis on the societal oppression of people with disabilities.

Although its analysis of disability was conservative, the recommendations of *Toward Independence* were sweeping. Foremost was the endorsement of a comprehensive equal opportunity law for people with disabilities. The law's coverage would be even wider than traditional civil rights laws. Duties under the law, the report concluded, should include removal of architectural, transportation, and communication barriers.[68] The law should be administratively enforced but should include a private right of action in federal court and fines for violators. The report also urged changes in social security laws to allow people with disabilities to keep their benefits when they earn income and to require the assessment of each recipient to see whether he or she is capable of work. The transportation section of *Toward Independence* embraced the "full accessibility" approach the Reagan Administration had opposed as exorbitant and inefficient;[69] the housing section recommended amending the Civil

Rights Act of 1968 to bar discrimination against disabled people by land-lords. The council also urged fuller funding for independent living cen-ters, extension of the Education for All Handicapped Children Act to twenty-one-year-olds, and demonstration project funding of personal assistants for severely disabled people.

Dart worried that the Reagan administration would repudiate the report. But after meeting with Bradford Reynolds, Reagan's assistant attorney general for civil rights, Dart found that the administration intended to endorse it,[70] albeit blandly and broadly.[71] To help build the case for an antidiscrimination law, the council commissioned a survey of people with disabilities to document their living conditions and attitudes. Among the findings was that only one-third of disabled people held jobs but two-thirds of all unemployed disabled people wanted to work. The study also concluded that disabled people were more socially isolated, less educated, and more unhappy with their lives than other Americans.[72] These conclusions would be cited constantly in the debate over the ADA.

Frustrated with congressional inaction on their proposal, the council voted in 1987 to draft a disability rights bill based on the outline in *Toward Independence*. Council leaders shopped the bill around to sym-pathetic members of Congress, particularly Lowell Weicker in the Senate and Tony Coelho in the House, both key disability advocates. In January 1988 the council published its follow-up to *Toward Independence,* titled *On the Threshold of Independence.* The report included the first version of the Americans with Disabilities Act.[73] Later that spring, after negotia-tions with disability groups, Weicker, followed by Coelho in the House, introduced the first version of the ADA into Congress.[74]

ENACTMENT OF THE ADA

Weicker and Coelho introduced the bill mainly for symbolic reasons. There were hearings late in the fall, but no serious action was ever con-templated. Yet the draft did have an important effect: during the 1988 presidential campaign, George Bush endorsed the bill in concept. In his presidential nomination acceptance speech at the Republican national convention, Bush pledged that "I'm going to do whatever it takes to make sure the disabled are included in the mainstream." Since his expe-rience with Reagan's Task Force on Regulatory Review, Bush had become a disability rights believer and had continued to use disability rights activist Evan Kemp as an advisor. Moreover, Bush was influenced by another group of Reagan appointees, the Commission on the Human Immunodeficiency Virus Epidemic. Bush said he was "very much persuaded" by the AIDS commission's conclusion that discrimination against people with HIV should be made illegal, and its endorsement of the ADA as a vehicle for this.[75] Bush's stance was reinforced after the 1988 election. A pollster for Louis Harris and Associates estimated in a letter to the president that up to half of Bush's four-million-vote margin in the election had come from disabled voters who had switched from the Democratic party to Bush.[76] This estimate was circulated in the White House and became a point of pride for C. Boyden Gray, who had pushed to make disability rights a priority in the Bush administration.[77]

Bush's endorsement of the ADA before the election set the tone for the legislative struggle that ensued. When Bush took office, he was committed to passing the bill, and there was little or no public opposition within the White House. "Shut up and get on with it was the attitude," according to one top Administration official.[78]

ADA in the Senate

Tom Harkin, chair of the Subcommittee on the Handicapped (later renamed the Subcommittee on Disability Policy), and Ted Kennedy, chair of the Education and Labor Committee, became the prime movers of the ADA in the Senate. They determined early on that the first version of the ADA, based largely on the National Council on the Handicapped proposal, would have to be extensively revised.[79] The Reagan-appointed conservatives on the council had approved a surprisingly radical measure. Dubbed the "make the world flat" bill, the first version of the ADA would have required all buildings to be made accessible within five years unless doing so would fundamentally alter the nature of a program or threaten a company's existence.[80] This "bankruptcy" provision, among others, would have to be modified, the senators decided, if the bill was to stand a chance in Congress.

In January of 1989 a core group of disability activists and Senate staff members began revising the bill.[81] The group adopted a strategy that would become a primary theme in the debate over the ADA. The ADA's first version used language from the regulations and case law that had been developed in Section 504 enforcement. In employment cases, for example, employers were required to provide "reasonable accommodation," the same phrase used in 504 employment cases. But in many respects, such as the infamous "bankruptcy" provision, the first draft deviated significantly from 504. Robert Silverstein, staff director of the Senate Subcommittee on Disability Policy, argued that the ADA should as much as possible draw language and concepts from the enforcement of Section 504. As a result, the group changed the bankruptcy provision so that a company would have only to prove that a modification entailed an "undue hardship"—the same defense businesses used in Section 504 cases. Instead of mandating "flat earth" modifications to existing buildings, changes would be required only if "readily achievable," again language from case law over 504. The use of this language was meant to reassure anxious members of Congress that the ADA was simply an extension of Section 504 and that years of experience with the 504 language would guarantee the ADA's smooth implementation. As one participant said, "Every time we departed from 504, we had to have a damn good reason to do so, and one that was politically viable."[82]

Proponents of the ADA enlisted many organizations to endorse the bill, but the most important allies for the disability lobbyists were civil rights groups. Pat Wright, the head of DREDF and the primary strategist among the disability activists, had nurtured the relationship between disability groups and civil rights groups for years. In 1981 DREDF had called a conference of civil rights leaders, ostensibly to have them share expertise on political action with disability rights lobbyists. Ralph Neas, executive director of the Leadership Conference on Civil Rights, suspected an ulterior motive: "What [DREDF was] doing was making all of us a captive audience and educating us with respect to disability rights."[83] Shortly afterward the Leadership Conference, a lobbying coalition of all major civil rights groups, decided that disability was indeed a civil rights issue. Neas cannot remember any public debate within the Leadership Conference about whether disability rights was a civil rights issue.[84]

The Leadership Conference first worked with the disability lobby on the 1984 Voting Accessibility Act.[85] Civil rights and disability groups became true coalition partners, though, in the struggle over the Civil Rights Restoration Act. The act aimed to reverse the Supreme Court's 1984 decision in *Grove City College v. Bell*,[86] which held that a university could violate Title IX antidiscrimination rules in one program but continue to receive federal funds for other programs. The same day the Court applied similar reasoning to Section 504.[87] The logic of the two decisions also applied to several other antidiscrimination laws. As a result, a coalition of groups representing women, racial minorities, the elderly, and people with disabilities came together to support the Restoration Act. The coalition stuck together even when conservatives specifically attacked the disability provisions.[88] The groups bonded further during the fight over the Fair Housing Amendments Act, which included a provision protecting disabled people from discrimination. Thus civil rights groups had become an important resource for the disability rights lobby. During debate over the ADA, disability leaders relied on the Leadership Conference's extensive experience with Congress and its access to members.[89]

The ADA began life in Congress with many advantages—chief among them, broad bipartisan support and an enthusiastic president. The one major obstacle was the opposition of business groups, but this turned out to be surprisingly limited. In some areas, principally public transportation and food service, major controversies erupted over the bill's requirements. But on the general issue of disability discrimination, most business groups adopted the premises of the ADA and acquiesced in it from the beginning. The National Association of Manufacturers, the Chamber of Commerce, the Labor Policy Association, and the American Society of Personnel Administrators—the big business groups most involved in the ADA—worked to smooth the bill's edges rather than oppose it fundamentally. Among large-scale general business groups, only the National Federation of Independent Businesses (NFIB) and National Small Business United, both representing small business owners, opposed the ADA outright, and only the NFIB developed any kind of a critique of the rights model of disability.[90] As an NFIB official said, there was an "awfully meager alliance" of business groups against the ADA.[91]

One reason for business acquiescence of the ADA was that many larger corporations had learned to live with disability rights requirements because they were federal contractors and subject to 504; they did not fear the bill's impact. Many companies were probably concerned about the bad publicity that would result from opposing a bill to help people with disabilities. Finally, business interests accepted the ADA's premise that disabled people were a minority group deserving civil rights protections.[92]

The business community's approach was also tactical. As the Senate was revising the ADA, the Bush administration let it be known that it was committed to passing the bill. Although the administration would work with business groups to address their concerns, it would not support outright attempts to block the ADA.[93] The Bush administration's position meant that attempts to defeat the bill faced long odds. Consequently the vast majority of groups tried to modify rather than defeat the bill. In a memo to other business lobbyists, a Chamber of Commerce official concluded that bipartisan support for the ADA, together with President Bush's endorsement, "adds up to almost certain passage in one form or another." The memo invited the business lobbyists to join a working group "whose goal would be to help fashion legislation so that it is acceptable to the business community while addressing the needs of the disabled."[94] This was the posture of most business groups throughout congressional consideration of the ADA.

The business lobbyists' top priority was to limit the awards that ADA plaintiffs could win in court. Under the Civil Rights Act of 1964, plaintiffs in employment discrimination cases were eligible to win an injunction giving them back their jobs, back pay, and attorney's fees. Racial minorities, however, were not limited to the remedies in the 1964 Civil Rights Act. They could also sue under Section 1981 of the 1866 Civil Rights Act, a law that had collected dust on the books until it was revitalized during the modern civil rights movement. Section 1981 allowed injunctive relief, back pay, and attorney's fees, but it also gave plaintiffs the right to collect pain-and-suffering and punitive damages. These extra provisions created the possibility of very large verdicts—and made it easier for prospective plaintiffs to find lawyers willing to represent them. Women and religious minorities, not covered under Section 1981, were limited to the rewards of the Civil Rights Act of 1964.

The revised version of the ADA gave disabled plaintiffs in employment cases the same remedies as those in Section 1981. In cases involving discrimination in public accommodations, the remedies were tied to those available through the 1988 Fair Housing Amendments Act, which also made plaintiffs eligible for a full range of damages. For the business groups this was anathema; they feared a litigation explosion. Business groups were particularly fearful because under Section 1981 juries would decide discrimination cases, and it was expected that in jury trials people with disabilities would make extremely sympathetic plaintiffs. The threat of punitive damages in such cases inspired misgivings. Business lobbyists also complained that language in the ADA—"reasonable accommodation," "undue hardship," and "readily achievable"—was so vague as make compliance with the bill a guessing game and the jury trials a lottery. The uncertainties created by a regime of adversarial legalism—fluid and unpredictable interpretations of legal language made through the decentralized decision making of jurors—loomed large in the fears of business groups.

The Bush administration took up the business groups' demands in negotiations with Senate leaders. Attorney General Richard Thornburgh outlined the administration's view in testimony before the Senate Subcommittee on the Handicapped on June 22, 1989, a month after introduction of the revised ADA bill. Thornburgh pledged the administration's support for a comprehensive civil rights bill, but he urged that remedies and enforcement mechanisms in the bill should parallel those in the 1964 Civil Rights Act. Because "we are a litigious society," Thornburgh said, the administration was "merely making a plea for the tried and true remedies." The changes Thornburgh advocated eliminated the use of juries and the possibility of punitive or pain-and-suffering damages in ADA lawsuits. In addition, Thornburgh urged that the language of the bill parallel Section 504 as much as possible and that compromises be made to protect small businesses and transit systems.[95]

Soon after Thornburgh's testimony, Harkin and Kennedy made a deal with the Bush administration. The essence of the deal was a trade on remedies. The senators agreed to cut back the scope of the remedies in exchange for a broader range of coverage than in previous civil rights laws. Remedies and enforcement procedures for employment discrimination in the ADA were tied to those in the Civil Rights Act, as the administration wanted. The only remedy available to those bringing public accommodations lawsuits was an injunction. This would make accommodations lawsuits much less attractive to plaintiff lawyers, who would not be able to collect a contingency fee based on monetary damages. The compromise included, however, a provision authorizing the attorney general to seek monetary damages on behalf of individuals harmed as a result of a "pattern or practice" of discrimination and to mete out fines of $50,000 for a first violation and $100,000 for additional violations.[96] In exchange, the senators got broader coverage of businesses than in the Civil Rights Act. The 1964 act covered only restaurants, stores, gas stations, hotels, motels, theaters, and other places of entertainment. The revised bill expanded this to include a long list of businesses and institutions. Pharmacies, a major interest for people with disabilities, were included, along with such venues as lawyers' offices, zoos, homeless shelters, and golf courses.[97]

Bolstered by the administration's endorsement, the ADA reached the Senate floor three months later, on September 7, 1989. Harkin introduced the bill as a "landmark statement of basic human rights" that would also "help strengthen our economy and enhance our international competitiveness."[98] These two themes—rights and economic productivity—dominated the debate. Concerns about the cost to business were expressed by a few Democrats, but the only outright opposition to the bill came from a handful of conservative Republicans. The ADA passed the Senate on a vote of 76 to 8.

The Remedies Fight in the House

Steny Hoyer, a Maryland Democrat, was assigned by the House leadership to refine the details of the ADA with Steve Bartlett, a Texas Republican. Bartlett, an ADA supporter, attempted to find a way to rectify the myriad complaints of business groups. These groups were particularly critical of what they considered vague language in the bill. Bartlett was sympathetic to business complaints but also frustrated by the inability of some business groups to offer constructive alternatives.[99] Some of the proposals offered by NFIB were deemed politically infeasible. For instance, NFIB suggested that a "reasonable accommodation" in employment should cost no more than a certain percentage of an employee's wages. Bartlett opposed a ceiling on the cost of accommodations, however, because it could easily become a floor—employers, he feared, would spend up to the ceiling in order to put to rest fears of litigation. Moreover, such a ceiling was unacceptable to House Democrats and disability groups.[100] Similarly, NFIB's suggestion that businesses with fewer than fifteen employees be exempted from the public accommodations section of the ADA was rejected out of hand.

After several months of negotiations, Bartlett and Hoyer produced a draft that made several concessions to business groups, including a longer phase-in for small businesses, deference to employers' job descriptions in defining the "essential functions" of a job, and coordination of complaints filed under both the ADA and Section 504. The compromise also included language requiring courts to consider "site-specific factors" in determining whether an accommodation would create an "undue hardship" for an employer or whether it was "readily achievable." This meant that a court would decide whether an accommodation in a chain restaurant was an undue burden based on the financial condition of the particular location rather than the chain as a whole. Though slowed, the bill seemed to be moving ahead steadily.

Then an old issue resurfaced: remedies. In February of 1990 Senator Edward (Ted) Kennedy and Representative Augustus Hawkins introduced a bill amending the 1964 Civil Rights Act. The bill was designed to reverse six Supreme Court decisions on civil rights issues but also included a provision expanding the remedies available to plaintiffs under the Civil Rights Act. The Kennedy-Hawkins bill would have allowed plaintiffs in Civil Rights Act cases to collect compensatory and punitive damages. In addition, the bill allowed both defendants and plaintiffs to demand jury trials.[101] As part of their deal with the White House, Kennedy and Harkin had tied to the ADA the same remedies and procedures as in the Civil Rights Act. Thus, if the amendments to the Civil Rights Act proposed by Kennedy and Hawkins were adopted, ADA plaintiffs would also be eligible for expanded remedies and jury trials. For the Bush administration, this changed the rules of the game. The limitations on remedies the administration thought it had negotiated earlier would be stripped away by the Kennedy-Hawkins measure. Accordingly, Thornburgh sought to delete from the ADA the reference to the Civil Rights Act of 1964, pleading that his original deal included only limited remedies.[102]

Not surprisingly, those who had worked on the Senate side of the deal saw things differently. The point of the deal, they argued, was that ADA plaintiffs should be governed by the same set of remedies given other minority groups. If Congress chose to grant expanded remedies to women, religious minorities, and racial minorities, logic dictated that people with disabilities should get them too.[103] Democrats in Congress, along with disability and civil rights groups, insisted on retaining the reference to the Civil Rights Act.

When the ADA reached the House floor, one of the last remaining issues was an amendment to restrict its remedies. In introducing the amendment, Wisconsin Republican F. James Sensenbrenner urged his colleagues to respect the terms of the deal and argued that, because the ADA was a new type of legislation, it should be treated differently from the Civil Rights Act. Most businesses had little experience with disability discrimination laws, Sensenbrenner argued, so the possibility of compensatory and punitive damages awards and jury trials "raises the stakes much higher without any corresponding increasing benefit to the disabled." Moreover, expanded remedies should be provided only after a thorough examination of the effects; Congress had not considered expanded remedies in the committee process on the ADA and was not likely to give them much thought during debate over the Kennedy-Hawkins bill.[104]

Democrats who opposed the Sensenbrenner amendment had a simple response: people with disabilities should be treated the same as other oppressed groups. California Democrat Don Edwards charged that the amendment "provides for a two-tier system, where women and minorities get a better break than persons with disabilities."[105] Colorado

Democrat Pat Schroeder summed up the logic of this view when she argued that "there are no rights without remedies"; thus "you have lesser rights if you have lesser remedies."[106]

Kansas Democrat Dan Glickman, in contrast, de-emphasized the importance of remedies, arguing that "rights and remedies are not the same thing" and that "a court of law should be the place of last resort, not first resort, to enforce civil rights." Glickman had added an amendment to the ADA urging that parties use arbitration instead of litigation to settle disability rights claims. Yet Glickman also argued that people with disabilities should not be locked into a weaker set of remedies. The argument over remedies, Glickman said, should be dealt with later, during consideration of the Kennedy-Hawkins bill.[107] Glickman's view prevailed: the Sensenbrenner amendment was defeated 192 to 227. The vote split mostly along party and ideological lines, with Republicans supporting the amendment 146 to 24 and Democrats opposing it 46 to 203; conservative southern Democrats provided 36 of the 46 Democratic votes in favor. Aside from these conservative southerners, the Bush administration was unable to attract enough Democratic party defectors to limit remedies.

The House vote on the full bill was not nearly so close, 403 to 20. A conference committee of House and Senate representatives charged with reconciling differences between the two chambers' versions of the bill became locked in struggle over the Chapman amendment, a provision enabling employers to remove persons with contagious diseases, including AIDS, from food-handling positions. In the end, however, the Chapman amendment was narrowly defeated, and both House and Senate passed the reconciled bill. With Evan Kemp and Justin Dart at his side, President Bush proudly signed the bill into law on July 26, 1990.

Remedies and the Civil Rights Act of 1991

The enactment of the ADA left the issue of remedies unresolved. Democrats in Congress had beaten back attempts to detach people with disabilities from remedies available through the 1964 Civil Rights Act. The pending Kennedy-Hawkins bill proposed to expand those remedies to allow plaintiffs in discrimination lawsuits to collect both pain-and-suffering and punitive damages. Remedies, however, became a secondary issue in the debate over the bill. Republicans, led by President Bush, focused on a provision that would have reversed a Supreme Court decision and reimposed a requirement that defendants in civil rights cases prove that employment practices that resulted in racially "disparate impacts" were a "business necessity." Bush and the Republicans claimed that businesses would sidestep this requirement by developing quotas to ward off discrimination lawsuits. Calling Kennedy-Hawkins a "quota bill," Bush vetoed the 1990 Civil Rights Act. An effort to override Bush's veto failed in the Senate by one vote.

The following year congressional Democrats reintroduced the bill. After a complex series of negotiations and some softening among Republicans in Congress on the bill, President Bush signed a compromise measure. The Civil Rights Act of 1991 for the first time allowed both pain-and-suffering and punitive damages but capped them in proportion to the size of the business involved. For employers of between 14 and 101 workers these damages could not exceed $50,000. The upper limit, for employers of more than 500, was $300,000. A special provision in the bill barred damages in "reasonable accommodation" cases under the ADA or the 1973 Rehabilitation Act if the defendant demonstrated a good-faith effort to comply. Nonetheless, the bill's passage meant that plaintiffs in ADA employment cases were eligible both for a jury trial and an expanded range of remedies, just as Republicans and business groups who supported the Sensenbrenner amendment had feared. The only major attempt to curb the litigious design of the ADA had largely failed.

EXPLAINING THE LITIGIOUS OUTCOME

Here we return to the question posed at the beginning of this chapter: why was there no effective counterattack against the fundamentally litigious design of the ADA? This in turn raises related questions: why did so many disparate groups, from Reagan and Bush administration officials and business lobbyists to civil rights leaders and disability activists, all come together behind the ADA? Why did the Bush administration support a new source of litigation, even while fighting changes to other civil rights laws on the basis of their litigation-creating potential? Why didn't business groups unite to stop a potentially costly new law?

One simple answer to these questions is that, paradoxically, people with disabilities are a uniquely powerful force—or at least, a group uniquely difficult to challenge. Disabled people are diffused throughout society, among Democrats and Republicans, rich and poor. Every politician who worked on the ADA, from George Bush down, could point to a close friend or relative with a disability. Probably every person in America can make a similar claim, if one takes the 43-million estimate seriously. Further, everyone faces the possibility of becoming disabled, particularly in old age. The result is that disabled people enjoy a level of sympathy far beyond other minority groups. Moreover, although the paternalism and pity many feel toward people with disabilities may ultimately be harmful, as disability advocates argue, it also has political benefits. The vast majority of Americans believe that disabled people are blameless victims and deserve help, whether through public or private charity. This fact about disability politics helps explain why the ADA passed through Congress so quickly and why so few spoke up against its basic structure. It is not good publicity to fight with disabled people. All those involved in the ADA, even business groups, had a strong incentive to keep their reservations to themselves.

But these unique aspects of disability politics do not by themselves explain the ADA's passage. If politicians want to be seen as doing "good things" for people with disabilities, the question remains why they did this particular good thing rather than another. They could instead have simply increased funding for rehabilitation or raised the monthly welfare payments that many disabled people received. Perhaps more to the point, they could have adopted the many recommendations of the National Council on the Handicapped that went beyond the ADA—increased funding for personal assistants, for example—which were largely ignored. The simple inclination to be nice to people with disabilities, then, does not explain the move toward disability rights.

Indeed, the view that of disability groups are uniquely politically powerful is highly misleading. Politicians can say, and have said, "no" to disabled groups. At the federal level many of the disability movement's demands have gone largely unheeded. The greatest victories of disability advocates have come through rights-oriented laws, particularly the ADA, Section 504, and the Education for All Handicapped Children Act, but also the Fair Housing Amendments Act of 1988 and the Civil Rights Restoration Act of 1988. Thus we need to know what has been so singularly attractive about the rights model of disability. Why didn't anyone step forward to challenge it? Here again there is a fairly obvious answer: perhaps the model is unchallengeable simply because it fits reality so well. Perhaps the problems of people with disabilities really are so like the problems of racial minorities that potential critics just don't have any plausible argument against the model.

Certainly the power of the rights model was demonstrated at every step in the disability movement. The civil rights movement was an inspiration for many early disability activists. They saw the discrimination and stigmatization that African Americans had suffered as a mirror of their own oppression and hoped that political action would achieve for them the same gains blacks had made. But the civil rights acts were also an easily grasped model for policy makers. The genesis of Section 504, after all, was a legislative aide's suggestion that disabled people could simply be added to the Civil Rights Act of 1964. That suggestion was taken up by Hubert Humphrey, one of the authors of the civil rights laws in Congress. Section 504 of the Rehabilitation Act was given teeth when the Office of Civil Rights in HEW wrote the regulations for it. Lawyers in the office relied on their experiences with implementing civil rights laws.

The analogy to the civil rights movement loomed large in the debate over the ADA. Sandra Parrino's statement on the first day of congressional testimony on the ADA was often quoted in the debate: "Martin Luther King had a dream. We have a vision. Dr. King dreamed of an America 'where a person is judged not by the color of his skin, but by the content of his character.' ADA's vision is of an America where persons are judged by their abilities and not on the basis of their disabilities."[108] Many of those testifying in favor of the ADA cited terrible stories of discrimination, anecdotes that harkened back to the days of Jim Crow. A young woman with cerebral palsy was barred from going to a movie theater.[109] Undertakers refused to embalm a baby who had died as a result of AIDS.[110] Tony Coelho, the member of Congress who first introduced the ADA in the House, told of nearly being driven to suicide by the discrimination he faced after he was diagnosed as having epilepsy.[111] People with disabilities sent Congress thousands of "discrimination diaries" documenting prejudice they had experienced in everyday life. These stories reinforced the notion that bias against disabled people was much like bias against racial minorities. In addition, the strong support of civil rights groups in the debate over ADA implicitly established the parallels between the two movements. And when Republicans sought to distinguish disabled people from other groups covered in the Civil Rights Act, the prevailing argument was that people with disabilities should be treated like any other minority group. To put them in a separate category, it was argued, would demean their struggle and make them second-class citizens. The power of the civil rights analogy was demonstrated continually during the debate over the ADA.

It is not surprising that the civil rights analogy was widely accepted, because there is much truth in it. But it is also problematic in many respects, confusing at least as much as it clarifies. Consider some of the fairly obvious ways in which the analogy misleads.[112]

DISCRIMINATION ALLOWED   There *are* some rational bases for discriminating against people with disabilities. As one report put it, "knowing people's sex, race, national origin, religion, or age does not allow us to judge their abilities to perform tasks or engage in activities. Knowing their handicaps may give pertinent information about their individual functional abilities."[113] Blind people can't be cab drivers, mentally retarded people can't be college professors, people with severe mobility impairments can't be professional football players. Thus disability rights laws, unlike other civil rights laws, must allow for many kinds of discrimination.[114]

INDIFFERENCE TO ATTRIBUTES   In civil rights law one preeminent (though sometimes controversial) criterion is what has been called color blindness: one must not let a person's skin color affect how one treats that person. (The controversial exception to this, of course, is affirmative action.) In the case of disability rights, indifference to the attributes of the individual is not always a goal. Indeed in many cases it is a violation. Under the ADA an employer who hires a person with AIDS and does not take into account his or her needs in designing a work schedule may be considered guilty of discrimination. A school may be required to give learning-disabled people more time on tests, blind people braille readers, and deaf people sign language interpreters. Because each disability is unique and because each setting provides different obstacles to people with disabilities, there can be no simple criterion of nondiscrimination. Further, whether one intends to discriminate is often irrelevant.

ACTION REQUIRED   A kind of "affirmative action" is required in many cases, not as a remedy for past injustice but as a means of equal treatment. Employers and managers of public facilities must be prepared to spend money—sometimes a lot of money—to fulfill the dictates of disability rights. These affirmative obligations are by far the most controversial aspect of disability laws.

A MOVING CATEGORY   As noted at the beginning of this chapter, disability is a category constantly in flux: drug addiction, for example, was once considered a moral failing, but under the ADA it may be considered a disability. Partly because of this, it is not at all clear, even among people with disabilities, who is considered disabled. In the 1986 Harris survey commissioned by the National Council on the Handicapped, half of those defined as disabled by the surveyor said they did not consider themselves "a disabled or handicapped person."[115] Of course the categories *black* or even *woman* have been contested, but they rarely reach this level of dissensus. The difficulty that courts have had in determining just who counts as "disabled" under the ADA illustrates just how slippery the category has proven in practice.

LITTLE IN COMMON   Because *disability* is such a sweeping category, disabled people don't have much in common. True, African Americans vary widely in their experiences, but the vast majority at least have recognizably dark skin and a parent who identified himself or herself as African American. Consider some of the conditions lumped together as "disability": mental illness, deafness, AIDS, drug addiction, paraplegia, cancer, lower back injury, epilepsy, blindness, and arthritis. People with disabilities aren't linked by some kind of common "disabled culture," nor do they have a common history. Most disabled people do not have disabled parents, and most disabled people were not born with their disabilities.[116]

NO FIXED MEMBERSHIP   It would be unusual for a white person to become black, and it is difficult for a man to become a woman. (People sometimes "pass," of course.) Disability, however, is a category many people join or leave during their lives. An illness can be cured; technology can transform one's condition. And as some people with disabilities have put it, all the rest of us are merely "TABs"—temporarily able-bodied. Disability is a club with constantly changing membership.

One might expect that these important disanalogies would have been discussed extensively in the debate over the ADA. In fact, there was remarkably little criticism of the rights model, not in the National Council on the Handicapped, which first proposed the ADA, not in the Bush White House, not within the business community, and not in all the congressional deliberations over the ADA. Even outright opponents of the ADA tended not to reject the fundamental assumptions of the rights model.[117] If, as I have argued, the civil rights model is not unimpeachable, why was it not impeached?

A second, related question is why no one considered a nonlitigious method of vindicating disability rights. If the civil rights model meant that people with disabilities were to use the same mechanisms for improving their lives as minorities and women, litigation may have seemed an obvious choice. Yet in fact, some of the most important civil rights laws rely on bureaucratic rather than litigious mechanisms. The most consequential law in the campaign to desegregate schools was Title VI of the Civil Rights Act of 1964, which authorized federal bureaucrats to cut off federal education funds to schools that had not desegregated. Title VI was included in the Civil Rights Act precisely because civil rights activists despaired at the inability of litigation to achieve desegregation.[118] Moreover, many of the civil rights laws passed during the modern civil rights movement require those who complain of discrimination to use bureaucratic mechanisms first to resolve their grievances. Litigation, at least in theory, is just one of several tools. Thus the link between civil rights and litigation is less necessary than many suppose.[119]

The ADA itself contains a mixture of bureaucratic and litigious mechanisms. It too requires those who would litigate over employment discrimination to file first with the EEOC. Indeed, the text of the ADA is mostly a set of instructions to bureaucrats about how to implement various provisions. Yet no one would deny that the provisions allowing private parties to litigate their disputes are at the center of the ADA, as they were at the center of debate over the bill. Moreover, it is through litigation that the exact nature of the ADA's requirements is being spelled out: court interpretations of the law trump agency interpretations, so that the implementation of the ADA is ultimately in the hands of judges.

One could imagine, as an alternative to private litigation, the creation of an OSHA-like agency with rules on access and inspectors to enforce them. In some nations accessibility regulations are enforced without private litigation. But no one discussed a purely bureaucratic alternative to the ADA, not in the council that first proposed it, not among disability activists who championed it, not in the Bush White House, not within the business community, and not in all the congressional deliberations over the bill. If, as chapter 1 suggests, litigation has become such a controversial choice, why was it so easily chosen in this case?

Common Explanations

Some common explanations for America's distinctively litigious policy style aren't supported by the case of the ADA. Commentators often point to the predominance of lawyer interest groups in American politics as an explanation for the place of litigious policies in the United States. As chapter 1 suggested, lawyer interest groups, particularly the plaintiff lawyers' group, ATLA, are politically active and influential on some issues. There is no evidence, however, that lawyer interest groups had much of an impact on the outcome in this case. ATLA did not participate and took no position on the ADA. The ABA supported the ADA, but no one I interviewed nor any documentary sources mentioned the bar's participation as significant.

Another, related claim is that America favors litigious policies because it has so many lawyers in policy-making positions. Compared to other nations, the United States does have a disproportionate number of lawyers in its legislatures.[120] But the high percentage of lawyers in policy-making roles is significant only if lawyers act differently from non-lawyers. The history of the ADA reveals no clear differences in the predicted direction: many nonlawyers were crucial to the development of the ADA, and some lawyers in Congress were among its sharpest critics. The first disability rights law, Section 504, was initiated first by the ideas of a legislative aide, then proposed by a member of Congress (Vanik) who was a lawyer, then apparently put into the 1973 Rehabilitation Act by Hubert Humphrey, a nonlawyer. Justin Dart, Jr., who crusaded for disability rights, was a nonlawyer. The rights-oriented regulations for Section 504 were drawn up by lawyers in the civil rights office but were supported by many nonlawyers. Robert Burgdorf, the ADA's first drafter, was a lawyer, but none of the members of the National Council of the Handicapped who approved Burgdorf's draft were lawyers. In Congress the leading proponents of the ADA—Harkin, Weicker, and Kennedy in the Senate, Coehlo and Hoyer in the House—were all lawyers. But so were the people who worked most to narrow it—Hatch in the Senate, Bartlett and Sensenbrenner in the House. There seems to be no clear difference between lawyer and nonlawyer involvement in the disability rights movement in general or on the ADA in particular.

Such observations are, however, unsatisfyingly fuzzy. Perhaps the best way to see whether there is a difference between lawyers and others, at least in Congress, is to perform that political science standby, the roll call test. In the case of the ADA the votes on passage were lopsided and so do not provide a good test. There was, however, a key vote on an issue of great concern to critics of litigiousness—the House vote on the Sensenbrenner amendment restricting the remedies available under the ADA. In Table 2.1 we see the roll call vote divided by JDs (people holding law degrees) and non-JDs. The uncontrolled raw vote has a higher percentage of JDs voting for the litigious policy, but when controls for party are introduced there is no difference.* This suggests that lawyers and non-lawyers did not think differently about the issues of litigation involved. In the ADA case, there was no evidence that lawyers made a difference.

*The same thing happened when I defined lawyers more narrowly, as those who had practiced in some area of law for three years or more prior to serving in Congress.

Table 2.1. Lawyers and Nonlawyers in Congress
Vote on Restricting Remedies in the ADA

	Total		Republicans		Democrats	
	JD	Non-JD	JD	Non-JD	JD	Non-JD
Oppose	58%	51%	14%	15%	81%	81%
Restriction	(109)	(120)	(9)	(16)	(100)	(104)
Support	42%	49%	86%	85%	19%	19%
Restriction	(80)	(114)	(56)	(90)	(24)	(24)

SOURCE: Roll-call data gathered from *Congressional Quarterly*; educational data from biographies in Michael Barone and Grant Ujifusa, *The Almanac of American Politics* (Washington, D.C.: National Journal, 1988 and 1990). Members with LL.M.'s were counted as JDs. Members not voting and not paired were excluded from the analysis.

Another explanation for the distinctively litigious American policy style concerns Americans' propensity for thinking in terms of rights. In this view Americans are so imbued with rights thinking that they naturally tend to formulate issues in terms of rights, without much consideration of the appropriateness of this formulation. The formulation of issues in terms of rights leads in turn to a reliance on litigation to vindicate rights. "Rights talk" did seem to be a powerful force in this case. Whereas disability had previously been seen as a problem to be solved through rehabilitation and welfare payments, the disability rights movement successfully reformulated it as a civil rights issue. Once this reformulation occurred, rights talk seemed to have an almost talismanic power, moving conservatives, business interests, and just about everything in its path to accept a major new piece of disability rights legislation.

And yet there is something deeply unsatisfying about ascribing the outcome in this case to a generalized power of "rights." Not every rights claim, after all, wins out in American politics. The "welfare rights" movement struggled for years to establish a minimum income as a right and failed miserably. Many rights claims that are accepted in other nations—rights to medical care, housing, and a basic standard of living—have been rejected in the United States. If disability activists had asked for a right to twenty-four-hour personal assistants, or to expanded welfare programs, or to employment on demand, they doubtless would have found that the power of "rights" in the United States has serious limits. So instead of ascribing the outcome in this case to the power of rights talk, we need to ask what it was about the particular brand of rights talk employed by disability activists in this case that made it so powerful.

Once again, we must ask what it was about the civil rights model of disability—with its analogy to the civil rights movement and its emphasis on
equal rights litigation—that made it so readily accepted.

The ADA and the Constitutional Theory

The Constitutional Theory suggests an answer to this question: disability
activists, conservative Republicans, and the others who played a role in
the ADA's enactment were responding to incentives created by the American constitutional tradition. Remember that I posited three incentives
that lead activists to create litigious public policies. By lodging implementation of policies in courts, activists can (1) insulate the policy from enemies (the insulation incentive); (2) do good things for constituents without drawing on the budget (the cost-shifting incentive); and (3) gain
power over the actions of states and localities (the control incentive).
Each of these incentives is illustrated by the story of the ADA. Consider
first the cost-shifting incentive, which is most obvious.

THE COST-SHIFTING INCENTIVE   The ADA offered both disability activists
and their conservative Republican supporters a chance to do something
good for disabled people without expanding the federal budget. There
are some minor tax credits and deductions for organizations and individuals who comply with the ADA, but for the most part it is an unfunded
mandate, a set of commands to states, localities, businesses, and nonprofit agencies unaccompanied by grants or subsidies. The ADA, like
other rights laws, allowed politicians to claim credit for helping a constituency while pushing the costs onto others, at a time when other types
of governmental actions were limited by tight budgetary constraints. This
explains why the disability movement has been so successful in winning
passage of rights laws yet relatively unsuccessful in enacting other measures: rights laws cost next to nothing for those who pass them. Indeed,
the ADA was sold as a way to *reduce* governmental expenditures by getting people with disabilities off welfare. For the Bush and Reagan officials
the ADA was a kind of welfare reform. Their view is a familiar one: welfare programs, where most of the disability dollar is spent, reduce people
to dependency and waste taxpayers' money. Thus supporters of the ADA
could argue that theirs was a vote for both civil rights and fiscal rectitude.

THE INSULATION INCENTIVE   Because rights laws like the ADA impose
costs on many private and public organizations, their enforcement can be
expected to arouse opposition. If the rights law is being enforced by an

agency, a political attack on the agency may develop. In a separation-of-powers system, interest groups opposing enforcement can pressure either the executive or legislative branch, which can then pressure the agency. For disability rights activists—and the policy makers who align with them—the danger is clear: the agency may redirect enforcement of the law into directions they oppose or curtail enforcement altogether. This is why it is so important to have judicial enforcement as a backup. Courts are relatively independent of the political pressures that affect agencies. At the very least, if a provision for court-based enforcement is in the law, the activist will always have an opportunity to enforce the law him- or herself, by bringing a lawsuit. Thus proponents of disability rights laws should be expected to favor court-based enforcement in order to insulate the law from enemies.

The case of the ADA offers no direct evidence that the desire for insulation was behind the ADA's litigious design, simply because no nonlitigious alternative was ever discussed. But the case offers considerable indirect evidence that the insulation incentive was at work. When asked why no one considered a purely bureaucratic mechanism for enforcing the ADA, participants in the bill's creation offered no clear answer. Several of the disability activists mentioned the deficiencies of previous administrative mechanisms in disability policy. The Architectural Barriers and Transportation Compliance Board, for example, was widely criticized by disability advocates as underfunded and ineffective. Bureaucratic enforcement of Section 504 was similarly considered, as one disability rights supporter put it, "at best lethargic and at worst ineffectual."[121] Given this history, one can imagine the reaction of disability activists to anyone who suggested putting ADA enforcement entirely in the hands of bureaucrats.

But far more important than specific enforcement experiences was the broadly antibureaucratic, antiwelfare ethos of the disability rights movement, which militated against agency enforcement. The hallmark of the rights model, after all, is the profound distrust of government programs. The political power of the rights model stemmed largely from its critique of the welfare state as dependency inducing, a critique that was compatible with the ideology of the disability groups and with Reagan and Bush officials. Disability activists shared the ambivalent attitude toward government of most left-liberal reformers of the 1960s and 1970s, but for the disability activists this ambivalence was powerfully supplemented by their own negative experiences with government bureaucracies. The activists were, as people with disabilities, dissatisfied consumers of government services. Indeed the first major incarnation of the disability movement, the independent living movement, arose out of a radical critique of traditional governmental approaches to disability. A new program that relied on bureaucrats was precisely what disability activists were trying to move beyond.

On the other side of the ADA coalition, the Reagan and Bush administration officials would have been the last to suggest a purely bureaucratic remedy, especially the creation of a new disability agency. The National Council on the Handicapped reports that advocated ADA were full of antibureaucratic rhetoric. Their purpose was to move disabled people "toward independence" and away from reliance on government.

Given this background, supporters of the ADA across the political spectrum feared what unchecked agency enforcement would do to the ADA. Disability activists, given their background and previous experiences with bureaucracies, feared lax enforcement; Republicans could fear overly aggressive enforcement. Both sides had reason to prefer that courts have a hand in implementing the ADA. It should be no surprise, then, that the designers of the ADA made sure that it could be enforced through courts.[122]

THE CONTROL INCENTIVE   The litigious design of the ADA gave disability activists and their supporters a way to supervise the actions of states and localities, a crucial goal for the disability movement. The ADA regulates nearly every local government unit in the nation, with particularly detailed control over transit agencies. During debate over the ADA, a struggle developed over the design of local transit systems, which has been a preoccupation of disability policy for more than a quarter century and a major arena for conflict under the ADA's predecessor, Section 504.[123] Similarly, concern about the accessibility of local government facilities has been a major impetus for other disability rights laws. The 1975 Education for All Handicapped Children Act (now called the Individuals with Disabilities Education Act) mandates that local school districts offer a "free, appropriate" education to disabled children. The 1986 Voting Accessibility Act requires election officials to ensure that people with disabilities can vote. Indeed, few of the facilities to which disabled people want access are under the direct control of the federal government.

Before the ADA, most states had disability rights laws of some kind, but the laws varied tremendously in their scope and enforceability.[124] Section 504 imposed nationwide standards but was limited in coverage to agencies receiving federal funds. The ADA strengthened and expanded the scope of 504's mandates and—through its litigious design—gave proponents a mechanism for enforcing its commands. Without a litigation mechanism, the only way that the federal government could impose disability mandates on states and local governments was through conditions on federal aid. Other than through "bribing" states and localities, it is questionable whether an agency could enforce rules against localities without a litigious mechanism. Indeed, it was in part the need to gain power over the racist policies of states and localities that led to the passage of federal civil rights law, the model for disability rights laws.[125] In both cases federalism posed an unpleasant obstacle for activists that was overcome through the use of litigation.

The case of the ADA, then, helps to explain why litigious policies are so appealing, even to politicians who campaign against litigiousness. In a federalist separation-of-powers system, litigious policies offer a way to (1) push costs onto others, (2) insulate policies from enemies, and (3) control the activities of states and localities. And in a nation highly distrustful of government, litigious policies provide a mechanism for addressing social problems without seeming to expand the state.

The Failed Antilitigation Effort

The antilitigation side in this case had to contend with all three of the incentives specified by the Constitutional Theory. But it also had a major advantage: rather than trying to pass a bill limiting litigation, antilitigationists in this case simply had to stop a new policy from being enacted. Generally in American politics it is much easier to block a new policy than it is to enact one. The many "veto points" in American government make politics a much more comfortable occupation for goaltenders than for goal scorers. In the case of the ADA, however, once the disability rights idea caught on, antilitigation forces were in deep trouble.

One problem for the antilitigation effort was that all the dangers of the ADA that opponents conjured were purely speculative. Business interests warned of the uncertainty and high transaction costs of a system of implementation by lawsuit, but they had no data on which to base these warnings. Similarly, though small business groups could speculate that the ADA might destroy some companies, supporters had a ready response, arguing that the implementation of the analogous 504 law had been relatively smooth and painless. Indeed, ADA proponents often argued that the costs imposed by the ADA would be more than made up by the increased productivity generated by getting people with disabilities into the workforce.

The main weakness in the antilitigation effort in the ADA case, though, is that business groups offered no nonlitigious alternative to the ADA. Business groups complained about the vagueness of the bill's provisions yet offered piecemeal and unsatisfactory solutions. The business groups' criticisms never reached the fundamental assumptions of the rights model or the ADA's emphasis on court-based enforcement. It was up to ADA opponents to offer a replacement reform—a nonlitigious mechanism that would support the goal of freedom and independence for people with disabilities—but nothing like this was ever suggested.

Instead, business groups fought a discouragement battle in which they attempted to limit the rewards available to plaintiffs under the ADA. They made the remedies issue the centerpiece of the antilitigation effort. The discouragement struggle pitted business interests, the Bush administration, and congressional Republicans against disability groups, the civil rights lobby, and Democrats. The Bush administration was at a disadvantage in such a fight because, try as it might, it could not credibly threaten to veto the entire ADA on this one objection. For one thing, the objection—about the scope of remedies—was in some respects a phantom, since the expanded remedies would not materialize until the passage of amendments to the Civil Rights Act. But more important, the administration and its allies were caught in a contradictory stance. They had to argue that people with disabilities did not deserve the same protections afforded other minority groups. Yet in supporting and promoting the ADA, the administration had embraced the rights model, with its explicit analogy between disabled people and African Americans. On the key House vote the administration's antilitigation argument attracted Republicans but failed to gain the support of enough Democrats to prevail. As chapter 1 suggested, discouragement struggles are usually partisan, and in this case the business–White House–Republican alliance was simply outnumbered in Congress. Thus even on the more limited discouragement effort, the antilitigation forces largely failed.

Comparisons

American disability activists have attempted, with increasing success, to export the disability rights model to other nations, but nowhere has disability policy become as litigious as in the United States. Since the creation of the ADA, Australia, Canada, Britain, Ireland, New Zealand, Israel, and Sweden have all enacted laws that give individuals with disabilities the ability to bring discrimination claims. Compared to the ADA, however, these laws typically feature weaker penalties, less extensive accommodation requirements, and most important, greater use of commissions and other nonjudicial governmental agencies rather than courts. Stanley Herr's cross-national study of nondiscrimination policies finds "a striking convergence in the development of high-profile disability rights commissions, armed with governmental powers and public funds" to combat disability discrimination.[126] In the United States, by contrast, the main governmental body charged with enforcing the ADA, the Equal Employment Opportunity Commission, has been criticized as woefully underfunded and thus unable to fully investigate more than a fraction of claims that come to it, much less to move beyond complaint handling and actively order changes that would improve life for people with disabilities.[127] Because unsatisfied EEOC complainants can easily move on to the federal courts if they wish, courts have taken center stage in ADA enforcement. The Supreme Court has been particularly active, in one crucial case overriding the EEOC's own interpretation of the law.[128] Overall the record of ADA plaintiffs in court has been dismal, a fact that has surprised and saddened disability advocates.[129]

Frustration with court-based ADA enforcement led Herr, a disability activist, to suggest that Americans might learn something from the nonlitigious ways in which other nations are implementing discrimination policies.[130] It seems unlikely, however, that the activists who fought for the Americans with Disabilities Act would favor the kind of government-run, conciliation-focused systems used by some nations with disability nondiscrimination laws. Sweden provides an instructive example. Sweden's 1999 law outlawing discrimination in employment is administered by the Office of the Disability Ombudsman. Complainants have their claims investigated by staff in the ombudsman's office; if the claim is found to be meritorious, the office attempts conciliation between the complainant and employer. This parallels the American system, in which complaints of employment discrimination must first go to the EEOC. The difference is that in Sweden, unlike the United States, such complaints almost never end up in court, for reasons that are easily understood: Sweden, like most nations, has a "loser pays" rule that makes unsuccessful plaintiffs liable for the legal fees paid by defendants. Further, the Swedish law has comparably meager remedies, with no provision for punitive damages and limited pain-and-suffering awards. In 2001 the ombudsman's office filed its first disability discrimination lawsuit. The case concerned a church that had declined to hire a man as a part-time church janitor, allegedly because he was hard of hearing. The ombudsman and the church settled before trial for about $3,500, an amount that would be considered less than a pittance in the American legal system. (The ombudsman had asked for about $5,000.) Awards like this practically guarantee that Swedes with disabilities will rarely litigate their claims. Instead, Sweden's law is likely to be implemented almost entirely through the ombudsman, as well as through trade unions, which are empowered to represent disabled employees in any grievance.[131]

Variations on the Swedish approach to disability discrimination may soon become common in continental Europe. In 2000 the European Union (EU) enacted an "Equal Treatment Directive" requiring its fifteen member nations to establish laws against discrimination in employment and vocational training on the basis of race, sexual orientation, religion, age, or disability. The directive does not, however, require that these laws create a private right of action in court. Member nations have until 2006 to decide how they will structure their disability nondiscrimination enforcement systems; they can choose any combination of judicial and administrative remedies.[132]

As the example of the EU directive suggests, the influence of the rights model is growing throughout the world. Yet it is important to remember that at the national level, the traditional welfarist approaches to disability are still dominant. In continental Europe and in Japan the primary government policy for promoting the employment of people with disabilities remains the quota system. Quota laws require employers to hire a certain percentage of workers who have been registered by the state as disabled. In practice the quotas are underenforced and the targets unmet, yet national-level disability organizations often favor retaining them.[133] The German quota system sets a 6 percent target for employers with more than sixteen employees; employers who fail to reach the target must pay a special "compensation contribution" each month for every unfilled place in the quota.[134] In her study of Japanese disability politics, Katharina Heyer finds that the quota system remains firmly in place, despite the formation of a disability rights movement heavily influenced by the United States.[135] Many advanced economies also provide wage subsidies to employers who hire people with disabilities; some nations provide personal assistants and technical aids to disabled employees to keep them in the workforce. Finally, in all nations, even the United States, rehabilitation, caregiving, and welfare programs remain central aspects of disability policy.[136]

Nevertheless, the United States has made the sharpest turn away from a welfare model of disability toward a rights model, and the biggest jump into litigating disability issues. Both these moves—the turn from welfare to rights, and the use of courts to enforce those rights—reflect the incentives created by the American constitutional tradition. By adopting the rights model, and tapping courts to implement the model, American disability activists were able to demand public action on their concerns without putting a strain on the federal budget or relying on a new bureaucracy.

But more than that, disability activists were able to ask for help without seeming helpless. The essence of disability activists' struggle has been to show that people with disabilities are not needy, pitiable creatures. Yet demonstrations of need are the typical way in which groups ask for governmental resources. For the activists, demonstrations of need were part of the problem, not the solution. That is why they despised the well-intentioned ministrations of Jerry Lewis, the muscular dystrophy telethon leader. The rights model allowed disability activists to ask for resources without emphasizing their neediness. They took advantage of the magical element of rights: a need, something you beg to have fulfilled, can be turned into a right, something that is your due. Expressing a need seems to infantilize the needer; claiming a right seems adult and dignified. Thus rights were made to order for the American disability movement.

CHAPTER 3

A FAILED ANTILITIGATION EFFORT

The Struggle over No-Fault Auto Insurance in California

In a purely quantitative sense, anyone intent on limiting litigation in the United States might sensibly begin not with asbestos, or cigarettes, or breast implants but with the mundane car accident. From fender benders to multicar catastrophes, millions of Americans crash their vehicles each year. Roughly four million of them are injured, and according to one estimate, about two million seek compensation through tort litigation.[1] Motor vehicle accidents account for the lion's share of cases in the personal injury tort system in the United States. About two-thirds of all claims, three-quarters of all lawyer's fees, and three-quarters of all payouts in the personal injury liability system arise from auto accident cases.[2]

If the car accident is the classic source of personal injury litigation, then no-fault auto insurance is the classic replacement reform. In the traditional liability system, accident victims get compensated when they make a claim that some other person caused the accident.[3] This claim is typically made against the other person's insurer. In the jargon of insurers, the traditional system is a *third-party* system, in which the person compensated is not the insured (the first party) but the person the insured hurt (the third party). No-fault, by contrast, is a *first-party* system, because the injured person applies to his own insurer for compensation. As the name implies, this system eliminates the central issue in tort lawsuits—fault—because the injured party receives compensation whatever the cause of the accident, even if the driver bumbled into the accident by himself.[4] No-fault auto insurance is thus a replacement reform in which a first-party insurance system replaces personal injury lawsuits. (The only remaining source of dispute is the insurance contract itself, which can be the subject of litigation between insurer and insured.)

No-fault systems in the United States typically offer a kind of bargain between insurers and consumers. For their part, consumers are asked to forgo pain-and-suffering claims, which compensate for the mental anguish or loss of the enjoyment of life's pleasures they have endured as a result of an accident. Insurers, on their side, promise that claims for economic losses (usually lost wages and hospital bills) will be handled relatively quickly because issues of fault do not have to be considered. Finally, in a no-fault system the insurer compensates for all economic losses, not just the ones caused by someone else's negligence. The goal is a more routinized, less variable, hence more rational and efficient compensation system.

The politics of no-fault differs in one crucial respect from the last chapter's subject, the politics of disability. The story of the Americans with Disabilities Act demonstrated how the elements of the constitutional tradition—federalism, separation of powers, judicial independence, and antistatism—steered activists toward a litigious approach to the problems of disabled people. The role of the constitutional tradition in no-fault politics is much more subtle: it plays no direct part in the battles but instead shapes the kinds of replacement schemes that are considered. The effect of the constitutional tradition can be seen when we compare American auto accident compensation systems to those of other advanced economies. In most nations compensation for accident injuries is provided chiefly by government programs, especially national health insurance and social security, sharply limiting the role of tort liability. A tort lawsuit, when it is brought, is usually restricted to the costs of an accident that have not been compensated by other sources. The net effect is that accident compensation in most nations comes primarily from a government-funded no-fault system.[5] The politics of accident compensation thus mostly involves reforms in government programs.

Proposals to reform auto accident compensation in the United States are, by contrast, overwhelmingly concerned with private insurance. And this, according to the Constitutional Theory, is no accident: by designing their proposals as private insurance schemes, American no-fault proponents have avoided the major barrier to replacement reforms, the constitutional tradition and the incentives it creates. Instead of expanding the role of government in accident compensation, American no-fault proponents merely ask for a change in the way private insurers—already a part of the tort system—do their business. The incentives that make litigation so attractive to activists thus become irrelevant.[6] Private insurance schemes are an appealing alternative to both litigation and government programs. Hence it is not surprising that private insurer no-fault has been the most successful replacement reform in the United States.

Yet even private no-fault campaigns are fraught with difficulties, as the story of the battle over no-fault auto insurance in California suggests. This chapter analyzes the debate over no-fault in California in the late 1980s and 1990s. California's struggle over no-fault is particularly interesting because it involved both a legislative battle and ballot measures. The ballot measures stimulated widespread debate over the merits of no-fault, a rare example of a public discussion of the costs and benefits of litigation. The legislative battle produced a fascinating split in the Democratic party. In both arenas no-fault proponents mounted a formidable offensive. One of the ballot campaigns was at the time the most expensive in California history, and the legislative effort was headed by a savvy politician who assembled a remarkable coalition of interest groups in support. Yet in the end the drive for no-fault failed miserably: the traditional tort litigation system remained quite firmly in place. Thus the California case illustrates some of the major obstacles to replacement reforms.

Fear and loathing of government often dooms government-based replacement schemes, but as California no-fault proponents found, fear and loathing of insurers can just as easily imperil insurer-based schemes. Indeed, if litigation seems an adroit way of controlling governmental abuses, it can seem an equally apt way of keeping insurers in line. Thus in no-fault battles, attitudes toward insurers become just as consequential as attitudes toward government are in other antilitigation struggles. In California, the lousy image of auto insurers became a major stumbling block for no-fault proponents.

The insurers were far from the only problem. Remember that, to achieve their goals, replacement reformers must create a coalition between groups associated with both plaintiffs and defendants. Reformers must convince both sides that they will benefit by an alternative system that squeezes out the middlemen, the lawyers. This is a difficult task, because groups aligned with plaintiffs and those aligned with defendants rarely have much in common except distrust for each other. In such an environment it is easy for opponents to sow doubts about the replacement scheme, and in California, no-fault opponents, especially consumer activists allied with Ralph Nader, did this expertly.

One of their most effective arguments used the theme of individual responsibility, always potent in American politics. As its name implies, no-fault is premised on the view that the problem of accident injuries is best solved not by punishing individuals but by pooling the risk of accidents through an efficient insurance system. The no-fault idea is contro-versial, in part because it seems to neglect the individual dimension of the problem: the person who causes the injury appears to get away with his or her misdeed.[7] Opponents of no-fault seized on this point and used it throughout their campaign.

But beyond all these problems for no-fault supporters, there was one obstacle that loomed largest of all: the vigorous opposition of the state's plaintiff lawyers. In the previous chapter, on the development of the ADA, the lawyer groups were marginal players. As the chapter suggested, there are many public policy realms in which lawyer groups are unim-portant. But within one fairly narrow sphere—legislation affecting per-sonal injury law—lawyer groups can be quite active, as this case demon-strates. It is an exaggeration to say, as one participant in the no-fault battle claimed, that in this case it was "trial lawyers versus the universe," but however one analyzes the lineup, in the end the plaintiff lawyers played a major role.

THE RISE—AND SLUMP—OF NO-FAULT

The no-fault idea originated fairly soon after cars became speedy and prevalent enough to do serious damage. In 1925 Judge Robert Marx pro-posed a no-fault system modeled after workers' compensation. In 1932 Columbia University's Commission to Study Compensation for Auto Accidents recommended a no-fault system based on the workers' com-pensation model, with benefits paid out on a schedule according to the injury. This recommendation failed to stimulate legislation, however. The report was heavily criticized by both the insurance industry and bar associations, and while four U.S. states considered no-fault, only the Saskatchewan province of Canada adopted it, in 1946.[8]

Interest in no-fault heated up with the 1965 publication of Robert Keeton and Jeffrey O'Connell's *Basic Protection for the Traffic Victim*. Keeton and O'Connell contended that the liability system then in place was an irrational system for compensating victims. Many of the injured, they argued, received no compensation at all because the litigation process was layered with obstacles to recovery. Those with the severest injuries usually received only a fraction of their losses. Meanwhile some with minor injuries were overcompensated because insurance companies preferred to settle small cases rather than go to court. The liability sys-tem, the authors charged, "provides too little, too late, unfairly allocated, at wasteful cost, and through means that promote dishonesty and disrespect for law."[9] The two professors examined empirical data on the recovery of accident victims, criticized previous no-fault proposals, and advanced their own plan.

It was one of Keeton's former students at Harvard Law School, Michael Dukakis, who turned what was an academic blueprint into the first American no-fault law. Dukakis was a state legislator in Massachusetts with firsthand experience with the limits of the tort system: he had litigated accident cases himself and found that the process, with its propensity for fraud and abuse, was "awful." When Dukakis found out about the Keeton plan, he got together with his old teacher and developed a no-fault bill. In 1970 Dukakis ushered his bill through the legislature, despite opposition from both trial lawyers and the insurance industry.[10] No-fault suddenly became a "hot" policy, with twenty-four states adopting it in the next six years.

This seeming success belied the fact that many of the no-fault laws differed considerably from the prototype developed by Keeton and O'Connell. The professors' original plan was designed to slash fault-based litigation, but many state legislatures created no-fault systems that allowed lawsuits to flourish. In fact, ten no-fault states, as well as the District of Columbia, currently have no restrictions on lawsuits at all. In these *add-on* states, the no-fault system exists side by side with the traditional tort system. In add-on states some accident victims can collect no-fault payments for their economic damages and then use the tort system to sue for pain and suffering. This violates a basic trade-off in Keeton and O'Connell's concept. As in orthodox no-fault, costs are higher because everyone, even negligent drivers, collects. But add-on states also have high costs from pain-and-suffering claims. Thus it is no surprise that add-on states have higher than average premiums and are often considered failures by policy analysts and reformers.[11]

Another seven states and Puerto Rico allow lawsuits when medical damages reach some dollar level, restricting victims otherwise to compensation from their own first-party insurance. These *monetary threshold* states vary in the dollar level chosen, from $2,000 in Kansas, Massachusetts, and Puerto Rico to $5,000 in Hawaii. The monetary threshold system creates a perverse incentive to incur medical costs to get above the threshold, and it is a rather unimaginative accident victim who cannot find $2,000 of medical treatment. A 1985 study by the U.S. Department of Transportation (DOT) concluded that three out of eight states with *low* monetary thresholds were "out of balance," meaning that no-fault insurance premiums in those states cost more than a traditional liability policy would have cost. Those states on the upper end fared somewhat better, with only one out of four in the DOT study considered out of balance.[12]

When no-fault opponents want to skewer the system, they typically point to the experiences of low-monetary-threshold and add-on states. No-fault proponents like O'Connell consider them pale imitations of true no-fault. Supporters invariably point instead to the three *verbal threshold* states, Michigan, New York, and Florida. In these states only people with exceptionally severe injuries can file a lawsuit. Michigan, for example, requires that the injury must result in "death, serious impairment of body function, or permanent serious disfigurement." Most analysts conclude at the very least that the verbal threshold states have held their premium costs below those of comparable states; they also appear to pay victims faster, at a lower transaction cost.[13] But at the same time the verbal threshold approach involves the most radical shift from the traditional tort liability system.

Two states, Pennsylvania and New Jersey, have recently switched from other forms of no-fault to join Kentucky in the latest fashion in auto insurance, the *choice* system, advocated by O'Connell as a compromise measure. In a choice system, drivers opt for either no-fault insurance or the traditional liability system. Those choosing no-fault give up the right to sue for pain and suffering except when their injuries exceed some threshold. O'Connell has advocated choice as a compromise measure and in the late 1990s persuaded Congress to hold hearings on a national choice law, though the effort has failed to go any further.

Indeed, aside from the attention given to choice systems, the no-fault movement has waned since its rise in the 1970s. A national no-fault bill was beaten back in Congress in the mid-1970s, and no state has adopted no-fault since then; three have repealed it.[14] What seemed at one point to be a national no-fault wave has crested and receded.

No-fault had several sources of support during its boom in the early 1970s. First, no-fault was favored by "policy wonks" in both government and the media who saw it as a way of rationalizing the personal injury system. They agreed with O'Connell and Keeton's argument that the traditional tort system was a lottery and that no-fault's promise of prompt full payment for economic damages was a fair exchange for giving up pain-and-suffering claims in most accidents. Second, no-fault was a bipartisan policy. Although Democrats like Dukakis and Coleman Young of Michigan were high-profile no-fault promoters, Republicans also proved supportive.[15] Third, no-fault eventually developed significant, though not unanimous, backing from insurance companies, who generally favored it because it reduced the uncertainties created by large pain-and-suffering awards to defendants and helped to stabilize the insurance system. Finally, no-fault was strongly supported by consumer groups and some unions, particularly at the national level.

But no-fault attracted considerable opposition, mainly from lawyer interest groups. Because auto accidents are such a common source of litigation, they are a major source of revenue for plaintiff lawyers. No-fault reduces opportunities for litigation by limiting pain-and-suffering damages and legal wrangling over fault. Thus it directly affects the livelihood of the plaintiff bar.[16] Hence the plaintiff bar has a strong incentive to organize politically against no-fault. As discussed in chapter 1, it was the threat of a national no-fault auto insurance system that mobilized the plaintiff lawyers in the Association of Trial Lawyers of America, turning a politically quiescent trade association into a major Washington lobbyist. ATLA played a key role in the defeat of national no-fault in Congress, and its state affiliates had a powerful impact on state-level no-fault battles.[17] Jeffrey O'Connell, one of the "fathers" of the no-fault concept, has argued that the no-fault slump can be blamed on "a small group of self-interested professionals who see a serious threat in the passage of tougher no-fault laws."[18] Even in states where no-fault was passed, opposition by plaintiff lawyer groups led to watered-down versions of no-fault such as the add-on and low-monetary-threshold systems, which many no-fault proponents condemn.

NO-FAULT IN CALIFORNIA

The California legislature rejected several versions of no-fault in the 1970s.[19] But unlike the rest of the nation, California experienced its greatest no-fault battles in the late 1980s and early 1990s. These battles grew partly out of a series of celebrated incidents in California politics.

By the mid-1980s auto insurance in California was a pressing concern. Rates surged 12 percent each year between 1982 and 1986; many drivers were going without insurance.[20] Policy makers responded by proposing regulations on California's auto insurance industry. But more attention was given to controlling the costs of other forms of liability insurance. Liability insurance rates for all kinds of activities, not just driving, zoomed in the mid-1980s, creating a wave of state tort reform. California had participated in the first wave of tort reform in the 1970s by enacting a law that greatly restricted medical malpractice lawsuits. In the mid-1980s the state once again joined the tort debate.

In 1986 California tort reform groups put forward a statewide ballot initiative eliminating joint and several liability for pain-and-suffering damages. Joint and several liability is the rule that allows a plaintiff to sue and collect all damages from any party who is responsible for an injury, even if the party's share of the blame is small. Under the rule, plaintiffs can go after "deep pockets" defendants, those who can pay big claims, even if they were not the primary cause of an injury. The proponents of Proposition 51, which they called the "Deep Pockets" initiative, argued that local governments often ended up footing the bill for accidents, diverting tax dollars from worthier causes.

The threat posed by Proposition 51 drew the California Trial Lawyers Association into a ballot battle for the first time. CTLA had been established in the late 1960s as a traditional trade association, conducting workshops and distributing newsletters about the craft of plaintiff advocacy, but the 1975 passage of medical malpractice reform had stimulated the group to become more active politically. CTLA created a political action committee and hired lobbyists; by the late 1970s it was a powerful player in California politics. Relatively small in size, with a membership of around five thousand, CTLA nonetheless had significant resources. Its lobbyists were renowned as among the best in Sacramento, and in the 1980s its political action committee was regularly among the top ten in total donations among interest groups in California.

In 1980 CTLA's influence rose with the ascension of Willie Brown, a strong supporter of the plaintiff lawyers, to the speakership of the California Assembly. Brown liked to say that his close relationship with CTLA stemmed from his own experiences as a lawyer in the 1950s, when he found San Francisco corporate law firms unwilling to hire a black man. He ended up doing street law, defending prostitutes and working for his local church.[21] After being elected to the assembly, Brown saw his practice transformed by the acquisition of powerful corporate clients. But Brown harkened back to his days as a street lawyer and may have felt a kinship with the membership of CTLA, who practice one of the least prestigious forms of law. In the legislature, Brown earned a reputation as a brilliant strategist, keeping the assembly in line with an array of carrots and sticks. As speaker, Brown decided for himself who would chair assembly committees and, when provoked, would strip rebellious assembly members from their committee assignments. With a big campaign organization, a large staff, and influence over many sources of campaign finance, Brown had many weapons at his disposal in making friends and punishing adversaries.[22] CTLA was among his top allies.

Thus CTLA had an intimidating reputation in the legislature. An initiative campaign, however, was new for CTLA. Moreover, stopping Proposition 51 was no simple matter: the groups behind it were well organized to take advantage of public anger over rising liability insurance costs. Although the plaintiff lawyers mounted a $5 million campaign against it,[23] Proposition 51 passed by a wide margin.

The Napkin Deal

For plaintiff lawyers Proposition 51 was an alarming defeat. Not only were they beaten, but they had also exhausted themselves financially in the process. At the height of a nationwide wave of tort reform, they envisioned a series of other tort measures coming at them from all quarters. Frightened by the prospect of a cascade of tort reform initiatives, the plaintiff lawyers moved to make peace with all the forces aligned against them.[24]

CTLA held a series of meetings with its potential adversaries, first, officials from local and state government who had been behind Prop. 51, then with all the major interest groups involved in liability issues—the Association of California Insurance Companies, the Association for California Tort Reform, the California Medical Association, and the California Chamber of Commerce. State senator Bill Lockyer worked as a broker for the various sides. Lockyer had taken an interest in medical malpractice issues and had begun by trying to bring doctors and lawyers together, but his efforts had expanded to encompass a wide variety of tort issues.[25] In a series of meetings, Lockyer, with help from Brown, persuaded the parties to agree to a civil liability reform bill that raised statutory limits on contingency fees on malpractice cases, made it harder to obtain punitive damages in personal injury lawsuits, and exempted "inherently unsafe" products (tobacco among them) from liability lawsuits. Meeting in a well-known Sacramento Chinese restaurant, Frank Fat's, to celebrate the proposed law, the groups decided to sign a "nonaggression pact" in which all parties agreed to consult with each other before pushing for legislation or ballot initiatives on eleven different liability and regulatory issues, including no-fault auto insurance, for the next five years. The agreement was jotted down on a cloth napkin by Senator Lockyer, an episode that was memorialized as the "Napkin Deal at Frank Fat's" and even turned into a poster sold around the capitol. On the following day, September 11, 1987, a bill based on the agreement at Frank Fat's was passed by large margins in both houses of the state legislature and was later signed by the governor.

The Napkin Deal Unravels

To some consumer groups the Napkin Deal was nothing to celebrate. Public officials, they argued, had deferred to a roomful of private interests; the resulting agreement was turned into a bill with very little public input. Perhaps just as galling, no consumer group had been invited into the room. Consumer activists were particularly angered that the plaintiff lawyers, their traditional allies, had agreed to several concessions on liability law with no outside input.[26]

One of those consumer activists was Harvey Rosenfield, a Ralph Nader–trained organizer and leader of the group Access to Justice. Although the Napkin Deal had established a truce on auto insurance issues, neither Rosenfield nor the other consumer groups working on auto insurance were constrained by it. Soon after the Napkin Deal was worked out, Access to Justice announced it was filing a ballot initiative that would aggressively regulate the insurance industry and force it to cut automobile insurance rates by 20 percent.

Within a few weeks, Rosenfield's initiative unraveled the carefully constructed compromise among plaintiff lawyers and their enemies. Insurers, believing that they had to defend themselves against Rosenfield's initiative, drafted a competing initiative and promoted it as a better way to lower insurance rates. More than one hundred pages long, it dealt with many insurance issues, but its centerpiece was a plan for no-fault. Plaintiff lawyers claimed that the insurers, by creating the no-fault initiative, broke the Napkin Deal. Insurers argued that the pact allowed for the interests represented to defend themselves against outside initiatives, so that their response was fully within the limits of the deal. Whatever the case, the two sides, faced by the unwelcome intervention of a third, were not able to come together. After the insurers began to obtain signatures to qualify their no-fault initiative, CTLA struck back with its own initiative. An independent insurance group offered a fourth, and the insurers involved in the no-fault initiative offered a fifth. (See Table 3.1.) Despite months of negotiations aimed at reaching a second truce, the battle all feared came to pass—and no-fault suddenly became a major political issue.*

The Ballot Campaign

The Rosenfield measure, sponsored by the newly created coalition Voter Revolt to Cut Insurance Rates, became Proposition 103. In addition to

---

*Outside the automobile area, however, the truce did hold for the entire five-year period agreed to by the parties at Frank Fat's.

Table 3.1. 1988 California Insurance Propositions

	Prop. 100	Prop. 101	Prop. 103	Prop. 104	Prop. 106
Backers	California Trial Lawyers Association; Insurance Consumer Action Network	Coastal Insurance Co.; Assembly member Richard Polanco	Voter Revolt to Cut Insurance Rates; Harvey Rosenfield; Ralph Nader	Insurance industry groups	Insurance industry groups
Provisions	Reduce premiums; require 20% good driver discount; regulate insurance rates; prohibit plaintiff lawyer contingency fee limits	Reduce bodily injury and uninsured premiums 50%; limit pain and suffering damages; limit contingency fees	Reduce liability insurance rates 20%; require 20% good driver discount; regulate insurance rates; eliminate insurance industry antitrust exemption; create elected insurance commissioner; limit territorial rating	Create no-fault system; reduce medical, personal injury, and uninsured motorist premiums by average of 20%; limit plaintiff attorney contingency fees; preempt various insurance regulations; require ²⁄₃ vote of citizenry or legislature to amend	Limit plaintiff attorney contingency fees
Budget	$16 million	$5.5 million	$3 million	$55 million	$3.6 million
Vote in Favor	40.9%	13.3%	51.1%	25.5%	46.9%

the 20 percent mandatory rate cuts for auto, home, and commercial liability policies, 103 offered a 20 percent further discount for "good drivers," eliminated territorial pricing, created an elected insurance commissioner, and mandated rate regulation of the industry. The Voter Revolt
measure also removed the California insurance industry's exemptions
from antitrust and consumer laws, which allowed the companies to share
information and keep their finances secret. The measure backed by
CTLA, which became Proposition 100, was a milder (and, the trial
lawyers believed, better-drafted) version of 103. It did not, however, con-
tain 103's 20 percent general rollback provision. Another initiative,
Prop. 101, was backed by a single maverick insurance company and a
state legislator, who advertised it as a balanced measure that hit both
insurers and lawyers. The second insurance industry initiative, Prop. 106,
was aimed directly at plaintiff lawyers. It limited contingency fees for
plaintiff lawyers in personal injury cases.

The insurance industry's no-fault initiative became Proposition 104.
Compared to the average no-fault system, it had a tough verbal threshold
and relatively low coverage requirements. Under the plan, each driver
was required to carry first-party insurance for $10,000 in medical
expenses, $15,000 in wage losses, and $5,000 in funeral benefits. If costs
rose above the limits of the insurance, the victim could use the traditional
liability system. Pain-and-suffering lawsuits would, however, be limited
to cases of "serious *and* permanent" injury, which would have been the
toughest verbal threshold of all the no-fault states. Property damage from
collisions would be reimbursed under the old fault system. Benefit payments would have to be made within thirty days or insurers would pay
18 percent interest on overdue amounts. Disputes over claims would be
submitted to mandatory arbitration, with no provision for lawsuit.
Proposition 104 promised to cut the bodily injury, uninsured motorist,
and medical payment parts of auto insurance by an average 20 percent of
the price of the policy on the day after the election. Other parts of the
policy would not be restricted.

Prop. 104 went far beyond no-fault. In more than one hundred pages,
104 dealt with such controversial issues as sex differentials in insurance
pricing, the insurers' antitrust exemption, punitive damages against
insurers, contingency fees, competition from banks, and rate regulation.
Adding so many provisions to 104 may have cemented support for it
among insurers, but opponents criticized 104 as a wish list for the industry. This argument would be used throughout the 1988 campaign.

The underlying stimulus for the flurry of initiatives was deep public anger over rising automobile rates. California had the fourth highest insurance rates in the nation, with premiums averaging 40 percent more than the national average.[27] For middle- and lower-class families living in Los Angeles, auto insurance was a major cost. In Inglewood, a low-income suburb of Los Angeles, a minimum policy for a twenty-five-year-old driver with a clean driving history was $1,400 a year.[28] As a result, studies suggested that more than a quarter of California drivers went without insurance, further driving up insurance prices.[29] Thus car insurance was no abstract political issue for Californians—it hit them where they lived. Dick Woodward, the consultant hired by CTLA for the Prop. 100 campaign, found that, when he conducted focus groups on auto insurance, arguments broke out over who was to blame for the rates and he "almost had people coming across the table at each other." The public's fury shaped the ensuing campaign. "I'd never seen an issue as intense," said Woodward. "It was clear that there wasn't going to be a great deal of persuasion, because the environment was such that you weren't going to be able to convert a lot of people. So it became more a question of who to be against than what these things were going to do."[30] The public, Woodward believed, was searching for villains as much as solutions.

The insurers hired Clinton Reilly—like Woodward, a top campaign consultant in California. Reilly apparently determined that it was important to define the problem and steer the public's anger as soon as possible, for he began his advertising campaign in February, extraordinarily early for a November ballot measure. The first television commercials in the campaign presented vignettes about how rising insurance rates were affecting Californians. In one, an elderly couple talks about how the latest insurance bill will change their lifestyle. In another a child asks his teary-eyed mother, "What's wrong?" after she lingers sadly over her latest bill. In the middle of each scene a single word appears—"anger." As the campaign progressed, the ads began to explain the no-fault system and to make comparisons between California and successful no-fault states, chiefly New York.

Beginning in February Reilly also ran a series of four newspaper ads introducing the public to the no-fault concept. The first asked "Which Is Higher?" and posed the alternatives of "Mount Everest" and "Your Auto Insurance Bill." With Everest looming in the background, the ad laid out the theory of no-fault in two pages. It claimed that no-fault would solve

the problems of the current system, which "costs too much, delays legitimate payments to victims, rewards uninsured motorists, and allows
fraudulent claimants and lawyers to profit at the expense of facts of accidents." The ad compared the Prop. 104 plan to no-fault systems in New
York and Florida and even featured a chart adapted from a U.S. Department of Transportation study that praised verbal-threshold no-fault plans.

The most dramatic part of the 104 campaign, though, were the anti-
lawyer television commercials. In these, attorneys were portrayed as greedy,
tricky, and litigious, draining money away from clients and clogging up
the legal system with small cases. In one of the commercials a lawyer who
advocates settling an accident case is upbraided by his superiors. In
another a crestfallen client discovers that after the lawyer's 40 percent fee
is taken off the top, he gets less than he would had he settled earlier.
These commercials emphasized the excesses of the tort system, linked
them to lawyers, and suggested no-fault as an answer. Reilly was conducting what would become one of the best-funded state-level political
campaigns in American history. In making the lawyers the focus of his
attack, he chose an easy target. And with the vast majority of the state's
insurance companies fully behind 104, Reilly had an army of workers at
his disposal, as agents and brokers threw themselves into the campaign.

But from the start of the Prop. 104 campaign there were signs of trouble. Even after heavy advertising for the measure, Woodward's private
polling in May showed that 104 was only slightly above 50 percent
approval. This was a poor showing, especially coming before the plaintiff
lawyers had begun the bulk of their campaign.[31] Woodward's research
suggested that 104 was vulnerable to two lines of attack. First, the public
was concerned that no-fault fostered irresponsibility because it didn't
punish the driver who was at fault. Second, there was a deep public suspicion of the insurance industry, which effectively canceled out antilawyer
sentiment. In a public poll conducted in June, respondents were asked to
explain the high costs of the insurance system. Thirty-six percent blamed
lawyers and the legal system, but 45 percent blamed the insurers.[32]

The anti-104 forces began their television commercials with an ad
pushing the responsibility theme. In the lead commercial, a man walks
around a junkyard filled with wrecked cars:

> The insurance industry says it has a good idea. They call it no-fault insurance.
> Under no-fault, when a bad driver causes an accident, he doesn't have to pay
> for your damages. And his insurance company doesn't have to pay either. You
> have to try to collect the money from your own insurance company. Of course

your rates will have to go up. Because a bad driver is no longer responsible? Since when is that a good idea?

The rest of the commercials attacked insurers as greedy and arrogant. In one typical example a smug, well-dressed man, representing the insurance industry, tells what seem to be elected officials at a hearing that his industry makes massive profits, is completely unregulated, and pays no federal taxes. "How can you get away with that?" asks one of the exasperated officials. "Easy. We're insurance companies."

Whatever the effectiveness of Woodward's advertising, it was evident by the summer of 1988 that the Prop. 104 campaign had serious problems. The most fundamental was voters' deep skepticism about any idea backed by the insurance industry. Like lawyers, insurers were perceived as part of the problem, not part of the solution. A June poll asked voters about the various groups involved in the initiative campaign. The poll tested the level of support for an initiative if all that respondents knew was the group that sponsored it. A group described as consumer oriented or Ralph Nader led scored the highest. Insurance companies and trial lawyers were found at the bottom of the poll, trailing far below even the unpopular state legislature.[33] A later analysis suggested that the more the public knew about which propositions lawyers and insurers supported, the more likely it was to vote against them. In trying to sort out five complex initiatives on a very technical issue, many voters used their knowledge of the sponsoring groups as cues.[34]

The insurers' heavy financing of Prop. 104, though providing for an unprecedented level of advertising, itself became a major issue in the campaign. Ralph Nader, who made several well-publicized campaign swings in support of Voter Revolt's 103 initiative, constantly highlighted this aspect of the election. More than $55 million, nearly all from insurers, was spent in support of Proposition 104. Another $3.6 million in insurer money funded 106, and $15 million was used to oppose the trial lawyer–backed 100 and Voter Revolt–supported 103. The insurers' heavy spending obscured the huge (though comparatively paltry) sums spent by the trial lawyers. The trial lawyers' anti-106 and pro-100 campaigns spent $16 million, still more than any initiative campaign in California history up to that time.[35] Meanwhile the Voter Revolt 103 campaign somehow managed to scrape by on what in comparison seemed a shoestring $3 million budget.[36] Rosenfield and Nader never tired in noting this disparity, and much of the coverage of the campaign focused on the big spending of the insurers and lawyers.

Voter skepticism toward 104 was reinforced by its length and complexity. Insurance lobbyists later developed the dictum that you could tell whether a proposition was going to pass by how much it weighed.[37] Proposition 104 weighed a lot, and many of its provisions were vulnerable to attack. Critics, seizing on voters' distrust of insurers, called 104 a Trojan horse because of all the non-no-fault provisions.[38]

The election was nothing short of a disaster for the insurers. Prop. 104 was massacred, receiving only 25 percent of the vote. Meanwhile the proposition that insurers feared most, Voter Revolt's 103, was the only one of the five to pass. Observers suggest that a major source of 103's support was its elimination of territorial rating, which gave urban drivers the prospect of much-reduced insurance rates (and rural drivers the prospect of a huge increase). 103 won narrowly, losing in fifty of California's fifty-eight counties but proving very popular in the state's heavily populated urban areas, especially Los Angeles.[39] Thus the bill with the most stringent regulation of insurers, the Rosenfield-Nader–Voter Revolt Proposition 103, came out on top. A small consumer group with a comparatively tiny budget beat what was at the time one of the most massively financed campaigns in American history.[40]

No-Fault in the California Assembly

Proposition 104 suffered an ignominious defeat in the election, but some observers thought the ballot campaign was far from a fair test of no-fault. Patrick Johnston, a Democratic assembly member, was among them. During the campaign, Johnston had bought time on Sacramento television stations, which reached his more rural district, to run commercials urging voters to reject all five initiatives. Johnston considered 103 "unbalanced" because, while it imposed some much needed regulation on insurers, it had done nothing about the other part of the problem, the personal injury system. He thought that Proposition 103, with its rollbacks and discounts, was likely to fail, because it didn't address all the underlying causes of rising insurance costs.[41] In 1986 Johnston had been appointed chair of the assembly Finance and Insurance Committee by Willie Brown. Johnston was familiar with no-fault through his work as aide to state senator John Garamendi, who had introduced a no-fault bill in the 1979–80 session. The experience left him less than enthusiastic about the prospects for no-fault. Johnston told his staff that no-fault was the one insurance issue he didn't want to become involved in; he called it a "morass."[42]

But soon after the initiative battle, Johnston ran across an article on no-fault that piqued his interest. The article was by Judith Bell, a lobbyist with Consumers Union, a group perhaps best known for publishing *Consumer Reports*. Consumers Union had supported Proposition 103, but Bell argued that while 103 would "provide lower rates in the short term . . . the automobile insurance market still needs a change to control costs in the long term." Bell urged legislators to ignore both the trial lawyers and the insurers and "craft a good no-fault system."[43] Johnston decided to call Bell up for a meeting about no-fault. He knew Bell and Harry Snyder, Bell's boss, because they had been frequent witnesses before Johnston's insurance committee. The two were zealous advocates of deeper regulation of the insurance industry. Like Johnston, they had opposed Proposition 104 because of its non-no-fault provisions. Together the three discussed what a better no-fault proposal would look like. Consumers Union had traditionally supported the high-verbal-threshold no-fault system enacted in New York. Johnston sent one of his legislative staff to New York to study that system.[44]

Consumers Union was an attractive partner in any no-fault venture. Unlike the insurance industry, it could not easily be tarred as supporting no-fault for self-interested reasons. Indeed, Consumers Union had credibility precisely because it had been one of the insurers' worst enemies in the legislature and had campaigned for Proposition 103. But the organization had also strongly supported no-fault for years. It had even distributed a book written by Jeffrey O'Connell, the academic who had long before inspired the first wave of no-fault.

Just one month after the defeat of 104, Johnston and Consumers Union announced that they would introduce a no-fault bill closely modeled after the New York system. The Johnston bill required drivers to carry first-party insurance providing $50,000 in medical benefits, $3,000 for funeral costs, and up to $2,000 per month in lost-wage compensation for three years. Lawsuits would be allowed only when total losses exceeded $50,000 (by far the highest monetary threshold in the nation) or in the case of a "serious injury." Proponents of the Johnston plan sold it as a way to stabilize insurance rates. They pointed to the experience of New York, where rates had increased only 4 percent a year since no-fault was instituted, and they contended that the plan would remove about 80 percent of auto accident cases from the courts.[45] Johnston's bill was introduced into the legislature in January 1989 as assembly bill 354.

While Johnston and Consumers Union were promoting their version of no-fault, another group was moving in the same direction, though by a quite different path. A coalition of minority groups began to develop their own version of no-fault. These groups were drawn to the issue of auto insurance by the same concerns about cost as Consumers Union, but for a different reason. State law required automobile insurance for all drivers in California. Yet even the most stripped-down policies in urban areas were extremely expensive. A national study in 1995 found that the poorest fifth of Americans spent 16.3 percent of total household income on auto insurance, but for poor Californians in the late 1980s the burden was undoubtedly much higher.[46] Auto insurance was a luxury that low-income drivers could not afford, yet to go without auto insurance was a crime. According to some estimates, this made between four million and six million low- and middle-income Californians, many of them Hispanic or black, criminals.[47] It also raised costs for other drivers, who were forced to carry uninsured motorist coverage to protect themselves.

The minority coalition was led by Latino Issues Forum, a small advocacy group created in 1988 to promote the concerns of low-income minorities on public policy issues. Latino Issues Forum avoided traditional civil rights or bilingualism issues typically of interest to minority groups. Instead, the group's goal was to inject minority voices into areas where they had been left out, such as health care and urban growth restrictions—or in this case, automobile insurance.[48]

Latino Issues Forum was joined by Public Advocates, a general public-interest law firm that specialized in consumer issues. Established in 1971, the group spent much of its time over the next two decades in court against insurers, bringing twenty-nine lawsuits over issues such as redlining, the practice by which businesses avoid selling services in poor and minority neighborhoods. Public Advocates had become involved in auto insurance issues through its legal challenge to the state law requiring drivers to be insured. The group had argued that the law was unfair to low-income drivers because of the lack of affordable insurance. After several years in the California court system and a favorable preliminary ruling by the state supreme court, the group's challenge was eventually dismissed. The experience had sensitized the group to the problems in the California auto insurance system.[49]

Latino Issues Forum and Public Advocates had been approached by Harvey Rosenfield to join the coalition of groups supporting Proposition 103 and to bring other minority groups along. But after studying 103, Latino Issues Forum and Public Advocates concluded that the bill addressed only middle-class concerns, with no provision for a low-cost policy. Rosenfield's attitude typified that of middle-class reformers, according to the executive director of Latino Issues Forum, John Gamboa: "They always say, 'we'll take care of your constituency last. Let us take care of the main problem first.' Last never happens for us." Gamboa was concerned that, if the current version of 103 passed, all pressure to change the insurance system would dissolve. Gamboa's group urged Rosenfield to enlarge the proposition to deal with the problems of low-income drivers. When Rosenfield refused, Gamboa and the head of Public Advocates, Robert Gnaizda, wrote an article denouncing all five insurance initiatives.

After the election, LIF and Public Advocates approached the state insurance commissioner, Roxanni Gillespie, to discuss their concerns about the lack of low-cost insurance policies. Gillespie invited insurers and trial lawyers to meetings with minority groups to work on the problem. The trial lawyers ignored the invitations.[50] But some of the insurers came. They told the minority groups that only a no-fault policy could bring costs down to a level that low-income drivers could afford.

Supporting no-fault was a turning point for the minority groups. They were concerned about weakening the tort system but came to believe that removing minor auto accidents would actually improve the system. They also believed that the ability to sue was not as powerful an issue for their poor and minority constituents as it was for the rest of society.[51] Gnaizda believed that the traditional personal injury system was nearly worthless for low-income drivers. Few victims, he argued, collected from the system: half were at fault and so ineligible; others were involved in single-car accidents with no one to collect from. Even those who had a good case against another driver had a tough time because insurance companies could play hardball in litigation against the poor. Moreover, the system made buying insurance a foolish move for low-income drivers; their insurance protected them only from claims by other drivers, and they had few assets to protect anyway. It was no wonder that so many drivers went "bare."[52]

Working together, the insurers and a coalition led by Public Advocates and Latino Issues Forum developed an outline of a program that would create a no-frills no-fault policy priced at $160. As in all no-fault systems, the policies would pay benefits directly to the driver, regardless of fault. The minority groups believed that this feature of no-fault made auto insurance both affordable and desirable for low-income drivers. Moreover, the policy would cost the same across the state, a major boost for urbanites, who under the territorial ratings system paid much higher premiums than suburban and rural Californians.† The policy would provide

---

†Proposition 103 had included a provision eliminating territorial ratings, but like many of its provisions, this one had not been implemented.

the minimum coverage under California law, $15,000 per person and $30,000 per accident. In exchange for the low price, those who chose the policy would give up the right to sue for pain-and-suffering damages except in cases of serious and permanent injuries. Gillespie announced that actuaries in the state insurance department had determined the policies would break even without a state subsidy.[53]

The proposal put forward by Latino Issues Forum and the other minority groups shared with Johnston's bill the no-fault concept. The motivation behind the proposal, however, was entirely different. By stripping down the coverage, their plan created a cheap policy for low-income drivers. Johnston's proposal was aimed at the bulk of middle-class drivers who already had insurance and were concerned about rising rates.

Johnston and the forum seemed headed in different directions, but a quirk of geography helped bring them together. The offices of Latino Issues Forum, Public Advocates, and Consumers Union all happened to be in the same building. In fact, the three groups were located so close together that to a visitor it was hard to tell where one office ended and the other began. Although the three groups had split over the Rosenfield 103 ballot initiative, with Consumers Union supportive and Latino Issues Forum and Public Advocates in opposition, they maintained a good relationship. Consumers Union had attended some of the meetings between minority groups and insurers that had resulted in their no-fault proposal. Consumers Union decided to invite Johnston to a meeting with the two other groups to discuss merging their efforts.

Gamboa and Gnaizda told Johnston that the New York–style plan in his bill would leave insurance policies far too expensive for their low-income constituencies. Johnston saw their point. In addition to helping solve the problem of rate stabilization, the no-frills plan would address the equally troublesome problem of uninsured motorists. Moreover, Johnston saw an opportunity. By joining forces with the no-frills no-fault program advanced by the minority groups, Johnston could gain much broader support for the no-fault concept. This enlarged coalition would help to politically isolate the plaintiff lawyers, sure to be the main source of opposition to the Johnston bill. Hence Johnston decided to drop the $50,000 coverage of his original bill to $15,000, creating a plan much like the one the minority groups had outlined.[54]

The new bill was endorsed by a wide range of groups, including the NAACP's Western Region, the American G.I. Forum, the California Council of Urban Leagues, the Mexican American Political Association, the Rainbow Coalition, the Black Business Association of Los Angeles,

Chinese for Affirmative Action, and the Filipino-American Political Association.[55] Gradually some insurance groups, with varying degrees of enthusiasm, also came to endorse the hybrid proposal. Thus the no-fault plan created an unusual coalition of insurers, minorities, Republicans, and Consumers Union—groups often aligned against each other on other issues.

As the no-fault bill was coming together, Speaker Brown was beginning to develop his own auto insurance bill. Brown and CTLA had opposed the Johnston bill from the outset, calling it "a fraud without a mandated reduction in rates" and arguing that it was "ludicrous" to embrace a no-fault bill when no-fault had been so resoundingly defeated in an election held less than six months before.[56] Brown's bill was an attempt to address the problems of rising rates and uninsured motorists without resorting to no-fault. In late May Brown called a press conference to outline his bill. The bill tightened safety rules, created a fast-track arbitration system for some auto insurance claims, and offered a minimum-coverage "lifeline" plan that would cost $350 for very-low-income drivers. The same plan would cost $500 for lower-class and middle-class drivers. The lifeline plan would be subsidized by other drivers through their insurance, but the details of the subsidy system had not been developed. Brown said that his bill was still evolving and was not in final form.[57]

At Brown's side at the press conference was Ralph Nader, who along with Harvey Rosenfield had helped beat Proposition 104 and bring 103 to victory. Nader declined to endorse the Brown bill, but he criticized Johnston's sharply. Rosenfield was similarly critical. He argued that insurers had revived no-fault in an attempt to distract the public from the implementation of his Proposition 103, which the insurers were contesting in court.[58] The resurrection of no-fault put Nader and Harvey Rosenfield in the uncomfortable position of opposing minority groups and a respected consumer organization, Consumers Union. In a meeting in late May with members of the coalition for the Johnston bill, Nader and Rosenfield were criticized by coalition members for sticking too faithfully to the plaintiff lawyers. Nader, in turn, argued that the coalition was being used by the insurance industry. He said that, by giving up rights to file lawsuits and get pain-and-suffering damages, people insured under no-fault would become victims of a "two-class insurance system" in which those who could afford more insurance would have more ability to be compensated for accidents. Nader said that the minority groups had compromised too easily with the insurers and had "accepted crumbs." Rosenfield said that he opposed "proposals which would deny the poor their legal rights and dehumanize them." Representatives of minority groups supporting the Johnston plan argued with Nader that poor people got little under the current system and that few were able to afford the insurance the law required. Although the meeting was reported to be respectful, it dramatized the split within the consumer movement.[59]

For the minority and consumer groups behind the Johnston proposal, the split was extremely painful. They considered Nader a valuable ally and had worked with him and his organizations on other issues. Aligning themselves with insurers in opposition to Nader was a bizarre position. Gnaizda had approached Nader in an attempt at compromise but found Nader unwilling to consider anything involving no-fault. He and Gamboa believed that Nader's position was a product of an ideological opposition to any limitation on personal injury litigation, no matter the rationale. Nader, they believed, had what Gnaizda called a "Vietnam strategy": stop any attempt to change the tort system, because it might weaken the system against other incursions.[60] Harry Snyder, of Consumers Union, argued that Nader's attachment to the tort system was religious in character and that his "theology makes each accident a meal ticket for the trial lawyer."[61] Nader, for his part, thought Gnaizda and Consumers Union had a naive view of no-fault. No-fault, like workers' compensation, could never provide victims the same benefits as the traditional tort system. Moreover, Nader believed that any system that eliminated pain-and-suffering damages was "dehumanizing."[62]

As the conflict within the consumer movement simmered, Brown's bill continued to evolve. He claimed that savings from various safety measures and regulations aimed at keeping uninsured motorists off the road would help insurers save enough to offer a $220 low-cost policy, rather than the $350 to $500 he had mentioned at the press conference with Nader and Rosenfield. Brown also added a provision creating a no-fault system for property damage to cars. Motorists could choose whether to have collision coverage for their own car, but they would not be liable for damage to another car.

On June 21 both the Brown and Johnson bills advanced out of Johnston's Insurance and Finance Committee despite their contradictory approaches to the automobile insurance problem. Johnston attributed this to the desire on the part of some Democrats to support both him and Brown.[63] The climax of the conflict between Brown and Johnston came June 28 in the assembly Ways and Means Committee. Both bills were again thought to be ready for passage to the floor until Brown began a heavy lobbying campaign culminating in a caucus with Democratic committee members just before the committee meeting. The meeting itself was chaotic. Brown, who was not a member of the committee, appeared before it to announce that he was willing to amend Johnston's bill into his own so that he could fuse the best features of both bills. But Brown left the details of how he would do that for later. Supporters of the Johnston bill argued that it made no sense to haphazardly meld the bills together, because they were fundamentally different. But Brown was able to collect enough votes from his Democratic allies on the committee. The Brown bill was amended and then passed on a 13 to 6 vote.

Pushed by Brown, the melded bill passed through the assembly. When the bill reached the senate, CTLA lobbied hard to remove the no-fault provisions from the bill. They were removed, with no objection from Brown. Thus what remained of Johnston's bill was excised.

The Brown bill was criticized on several grounds. An editorial in the *Sacramento Bee* labeled it the "Anything-But-No-Fault Bill" and suggested that Brown had brought it forward only to kill Johnston's bill. The *Bee* argued that the resulting bill would not cover all low-income drivers or poor drivers and said the actuarial assumptions underlying the subsidy system were "completely untested."[64] The *Los Angeles Times*, like the *Bee* a proponent of the Johnston bill, claimed that the Brown bill was written by plaintiff lawyers and that the arbitration system included in the bill "could create a new insurance mess."[65] Brown argued that the money saved by bringing uninsured motorists into the insurance system would subsidize the low-cost policy. Insurers claimed that those savings would not be enough and would have to be supplemented by higher premiums paid by the rest of their customers. Republican governor George Deukmajian cited these concerns when he vetoed the Brown bill in October.

Brown's deft maneuvering had gotten the Johnston bill killed, but Deukmajian's veto left the issue of auto insurance costs unresolved. It was yet another example of deadlock between two of the most powerful interests in California politics, plaintiff lawyers and the insurance industry. As in the initiative campaign, each side was able to veto the proposals of the other, and no compromise was forthcoming. Pressure remained on the legislature to do something about the problems of rising rates and uninsured motorists. Thus 1990 began where 1989 had started, with Johnston and Brown again squaring off. Governor Deukmajian's veto message had suggested that Brown and the governor work out a compromise measure on auto insurance. Brown's point man on auto insurance, Billy Rutland, spent several months negotiating with the governor's staff, with no success.[66]

Meanwhile Johnston's bill again advanced to the Ways and Means Committee. This time Brown took no public position on the Johnston bill, but his work behind the scenes was evident. Brown asked Johnston to drop the bill before a committee vote, but Johnston refused.[67] When the committee met to discuss the bill on January 18, allies of Brown tried to kill it with various procedural maneuvers and amendments. The meeting featured several angry exchanges, with supporters of the Johnston bill arguing that the Brown allies were attempting to avoid a vote on the merits.[‡] Strange enough, among those leading the charge to amend the Johnston bill were two of its coauthors, assembly members Steve Peace and Richard Polanco. When those attempts were defeated, the two abstained on the final vote. The abstentions insured the bill's defeat: it fell one vote short of the twelve needed for passage. As one Republican supporter of Johnston noted, the bill was widely thought to have been "Speakerized"—killed by Brown from afar.[68] Thus once again Brown and CTLA had managed to keep the Johnston bill bottled up in committee. Despite the unusual coalition of minority, consumer, and insurance groups behind it, no-fault had again failed to reach the floor.

No-Fault in the California Senate

Patrick Johnston moved from his assembly seat to an open seat in the state senate in 1990. In the senate Johnston no longer had to contend directly with Willie Brown, but he did have another formidable opponent in Bill Lockyer, the chairman of the senate Judiciary Committee. Powerful and sharp tempered, Lockyer had a reputation as a legislator who could be painful to cross.[69] Lockyer had worked with Brown and CTLA on the famous Napkin Deal and on a series of bills in the Judiciary Committee. Like all the members of the Judiciary Committee and like most Democrats in the legislature (including, until 1989, Patrick Johnston), Lockyer received generous campaign contributions from CTLA. But Lockyer had a much more direct relationship with the trial lawyers: he

---

[‡]One part of the meeting was transcribed by the *Sacramento Bee:*

JOHNSTON: "If you have misgivings about my proposal, then you should vote no. Cleanly vote no rather than hiding behind (procedural) moves."

PEACE: "The problem Mr. Johnston has is that his sponsors will not allow him to take any amendments. I don't want to see this bill killed. This bill will get the votes to get out of this committee today with the amendments."

NOLAN: "Et tu, Steve? As you stick your dagger into the people's one hope of lowering their auto insurance rates, do it consciously. What you're deathly afraid of is being recorded on this vote as a no."

(Rick Kushman, "Plenty of Blame as No-Fault Bill Dies in Capitol," *Sacramento Bee,* January 18, 1990, A3)

was one of them. During his years in the legislature, Lockyer had attended law school. In 1990, after a new California term-limits law brought the end of his senate career in sight, Lockyer became an apprentice part-time lawyer in a personal injury law firm.[70]

Lockyer opposed no-fault on principle. He argued that it was a violation of the principle of personal responsibility, rewarding careless and negligent drivers for their actions. He claimed that Republicans, who talked a lot about personal responsibility, were hypocritical to support a proposal that eroded the principle. Moreover, Lockyer was not convinced that no-fault saved money or distributed it any better than the traditional system.[71]

If Lockyer presented an obstacle for Johnston, the new Republican governor of California, Pete Wilson, was an asset. Soon after taking office, Wilson announced at a news conference that he would fight for the Johnston bill. Appearing with minority and consumer group leaders, Wilson argued that there had been "a frenzy of litigation that has sent rates skyrocketing, and Californians are fed up."[72] Wilson's predecessor, George Deukmajian, had been lukewarm on no-fault and had never endorsed the Johnston bill. Deukmajian had taken a relaxed stance in the skirmish between Brown and Johnston, announcing after vetoing Brown's bill that he would work on a compromise with the speaker. But Wilson clearly wanted to take the fight straight to Brown and the trial lawyers. At a second news conference a month later, Wilson blamed CTLA for no-fault's past defeats. "It is no secret why we have not been able to get [no-fault]. It is because we have a system of tort liability in which the trial lawyers have persisted in making automobile insurance unaffordable."[73]

Brown, in turn, argued that voters had already rejected no-fault, and advocated the newest version of his own low-cost, subsidized insurance plan. The governor vowed to veto Brown's bill, which he said would force middle-class Californians to subsidize low-income auto insurance buyers. The Brown bill, coauthored by Lockyer, passed the assembly early in the spring and awaited senate action. Under Brown's bill, families of four with incomes of $25,000 or less would have their insurance policies subsidized by other drivers, but 80 percent of the subsidy was claimed to come from savings made by reducing the number of uninsured motorists. The Brown alternative was criticized by Johnston's supporters as being skimpy on details and poorly researched. Brown had promised a $300 policy, but a letter from Consumers Union to Lockyer pointed out that the amount in the bill had never been filled in and no actuarial analysis had been performed to demonstrate whether the subsidy system would be sound.[74]

The no-fault coalition, perhaps cheered by Wilson's endorsement, planned to step up its efforts. Insurers decided to fund a major advertising campaign to whip up public support for no-fault and put pressure on the legislature. This represented a much greater commitment than the insurers had made before, when Johnston's bill had stalled in the assembly. Partly by design, the insurers had been the less visible part of the no-fault coalition, with Consumers Union and the Latino Issues Forum taking the lead. Although the insurance industry had generally supported Johnston's bill, many individual companies had stayed away from the effort. Two of the biggest auto insurers in the state, State Farm and Farmer's, had chosen not to lobby on the issue. Consumers Union had even suspected that State Farm was trying to kill the bill behind the scenes, and was reassured only when it received a letter of support from the company.[75] But when Johnston moved to the senate, State Farm and Farmer's, along with most of the industry, again became actively involved in pushing no-fault.[76]

There were many reasons for the insurers to be less than fully enthusiastic—or unified—in their support of the no-fault bill. First, the fallout from the disastrous initiative campaign had made insurers leery about another no-fault effort. Although talk of another initiative based on the Johnston plan occasionally surfaced, insurance lobbyists joked about a new rule of industry etiquette—"Don't use the 'i' word around here."[77] Second, the insurers were in the midst of a major regulatory and legal fight over the implementation of the victorious Proposition 103, which had tightened regulation of the industry and mandated immediate rollbacks in premiums. The California Supreme Court had ruled that the across-the-board 20 percent rollback in 103 was unconstitutional but allowed the insurance commissioner to implement individualized rollbacks as long as they provided insurers with a reasonable rate of return. Third, even if insurers had been focused on no-fault, the Johnston bill was not nearly as attractive to insurers as 104 had been. The stripped-down policy in the Johnston plan meant less profit for insurers than a more expensive benefit package because fewer dollars would flow through the insurance system. Moreover, the Johnston bill had none of the other goodies for insurers that 104 had included.

Finally, support for the no-fault concept itself was not uniform among the insurers. Those companies who had experience in no-fault states tended to be more enthusiastic; those who were California-only compa-

nies worried that the system would not work in their state. State Farm worried that in a litigious state like California the Johnston bill's verbal threshold was not tough enough to stop ingenious lawyers from bringing lawsuits. Small, niche companies worried that their competitive advantages would be erased in a no-fault system and they would be crushed by the giants.

Yet despite all these concerns, insurer support for no-fault had actually strengthened by the time Johnston's bill reached the senate. The insurers contributed more than a million dollars to a public campaign for the no-fault bill, with each insurer paying in proportion to its market share.[78] The insurers, working with the minority groups, hired a campaign consultant, Sal Russo, to direct an advertising and lobbying effort.

The primary obstacle for the no-fault bill was Lockyer's Judiciary Committee. The three Republicans on the committee were solid votes for the Johnston bill. Presley and Keene, two Democrats, were also supporters. To get the necessary six votes on the eleven-member committee, however, the Johnston bill had to pick up one of the remaining six Democrats. Lockyer and Nicholas Petris were firmly opposed to no-fault.[79] Thus the coalition concentrated on three prime targets: Diane Watson, Art Torres, and David Roberti, all from Los Angeles districts with heavy minority populations.[80]

The goal of the campaign was to rouse constituents in the Los Angeles districts and convince them to put pressure on their representatives. Russo ran full-page ads in the *Los Angeles Times* and *San Francisco Chronicle* and sent out two mailings to voters in the three Los Angeles districts. He also created a petition drive for the Johnston bill in the districts. Both the ads and mailings urged readers to call their senators. As a follow-up, Russo phoned constituents of the three senators and asked them if they supported the no-fault plan. Those constituents who were positive about the bill were connected automatically to their senator's office.[81] While Russo's organization received the lion's share of insurer money, Latino Issues Forum was given about $75,000. Working with a Latino advertising firm, the group placed ads in Latino and black newspapers and radio stations in the Los Angeles districts.[82] The campaign succeeded in generating a heavy response. By early May, Roberti had received more than a thousand phone calls and letters on the bill. Roberti said he had never recalled so expensive a campaign directed to a specific hearing in his twenty-five years in the legislature.[83]

The campaign was itself the subject of attack, however. Roberti claimed that the money poured in by insurers undermined the efforts of

the other groups: "The strongest thing this bill has going for it is its intense backing from the Consumers Union," he said.[84] Brown argued that it was "unseemly" for "grass-roots, nonprofit, do-good organizations" to take money from insurers for advertising. "The word ought to go forward that it's not a consumers bill," the speaker added. "It is . . . an insurance carriers bill—otherwise they wouldn't spend that kind of money on (its) behalf."[85] As before, the minority and consumer groups aligned with the Johnston bill were vulnerable to the charge that they were being used as fronts by insurers. Ralph Nader came to California to campaign against the bill, arguing that it was an "anti-consumer power play by insurance companies."[86] In addition, an ad suggesting that, without no-fault, uninsured Latino immigrant motorists might face deportation was criticized as sensationalistic. The ad produced panicked calls to senator's offices, which was not appreciated. Although CTLA said it could not match the insurers' efforts, it did spend an estimated $60,000 counterattacking in the black and Hispanic media.[87] As the showdown in the senate neared, Governor Wilson and Speaker Brown personally lobbied the key senators. The governor, the attorney general, and the state's major newspapers all endorsed the Johnston bill. The coalition had succeeded in putting intense pressure on the Democrats in the Judiciary Committee.

On May 28 the committee considered the Johnston bill. After hours of testimony and deliberation, the vote showed how close the coalition had come: 5 to 5 with one abstention, just one vote away from passage. Petris, Lockyer, Marks, and two of the targeted senators, Watson and Roberti, voted against the bill. The third target, Torres, abstained. Roberti said that Proposition 103 should be given time to be implemented and that Johnston's bill would not help the middle class. Torres and Watson said they resented the mass media campaign and said that many who contacted them were ill informed.[88] Marks claimed that he had walked into the committee meeting still unsure about how he would vote, but the testimony of a CTLA lobbyist, Will Glennon, had moved him to vote no.[89]

What truly swung the balance was unclear. But once again, no-fault had been stopped in committee by one vote.

Redux

Since 1990, several unsuccessful attempts have been made to bring no-fault to California. The most serious effort was yet another initiative campaign, this one in 1996. In several respects the 1996 no-fault campaign was significantly different from the 1988 election. The 1996 initia-

tive, Proposition 200, was a "pure" no-fault scheme that barred nearly all lawsuits, unlike 104, which allowed them in cases of "serious and permanent" injuries. Prop. 200 also was untainted by all the non-no-fault measures that Prop. 104 had contained. Moreover, Prop. 200, along with two other antilitigation measures, was supported financially by Silicon Valley high-tech companies; the insurance industry, so central to the 104 campaign, stayed out, still daunted by its experiences in 1988.

In other respects, though, the 1996 battle was a repeat of 1988. As in the battle over the Johnston bill, the struggle over Prop. 200 created a nasty split among consumer activists. On the anti-no-fault side in this round was Consumers Union, which opposed the "pure" no-fault approach of 200. Consumers Union was joined, unsurprisingly, by anti-no-fault stalwarts Ralph Nader and Harvey Rosenfield. But Rosenfield's old organization, Voter Revolt, which had sponsored Prop. 103, had by 1996 made a remarkable flip over to the pro-no-fault side, a maneuver that put the group at the center of the 200 campaign. Rosenfield and other consumer activists claimed that Voter Revolt had become a shell organization used by the Silicon Valley business interests behind 200 and the other antilitigation initiatives to provide a proconsumer gloss to their campaign.[90] For their part, two prominent long-time consumer activists allied with the 200 campaign, Bill Zimmerman and Michael Johnston, argued that Rosenfield himself had been bought by plaintiff lawyers, who had provided the bulk of funding for his organizations.[91]

As these charges and countercharges flew, the plaintiff lawyer lobby—renamed the Consumer Attorneys of California—mounted an expensive television ad campaign against the initiatives. This time, instead of targeting the insurance industry, their ads portrayed the corporate sponsors of the initiatives literally as wolves who would prey on consumers if given the chance. One ad morphed a Silicon Valley executive's face into that of convicted savings-and-loan felon Charles Keating.[92] The ads claimed that insurance rates would skyrocket and health care choices would be restricted if 200 were enacted into law. The campaign in favor of the package, meanwhile, employed the familiar technique of lawyer bashing, portraying lawyers as greedy, bumbling, and litigious. One ad featured actor Charlton Heston, who urged voters to rein in "those ambulance chasers."[93] As in 1988, each side of the no-fault battle attempted to villainize the other.

The 1996 effort also resembled the 1988 campaign in its outcome. Proposition 200 was defeated easily, garnering only 35 percent support. (The two other antilitigation initiatives on the ballot failed as well, but by narrower margins.) Voters, faced by claims and counterclaims about a complex public policy proposal, appeared to follow what many observers consider the standard rule in initiative elections: when in doubt, vote no.[94] Backers of Prop. 200 cited the difficulty of explaining the benefits of no-fault to voters and the troubles they had raising money for television advertising. Lacking the insurer money that had fueled the Prop. 104 effort, the 1996 no-fault campaign was outfinanced by opponents, a result supporters attributed to the "strange-bedfellows nature of the coalition."[95] The 1996 campaign took a somewhat different tack from the 1988 effort, but it too confronted the fundamental problems involved in creating a pro-no-fault coalition.

ANATOMY OF A FAILURE

The failure of no-fault in California had several causes. The various coalitions that supported it were shaky and easily divided. The main financial backers—insurers in the first round, big business in the second—aroused distrust. The policy itself was complex and hard to explain to the public, which was skeptical of any proposal that seemed to slight individual responsibility for auto accidents. These weaknesses were eagerly seized upon by plaintiff lawyers and their allies in consumer groups, who conducted a vigorous campaign against no-fault.

One of the most interesting features of the antilitigation effort in this case was the strange coalition it created. Proponents of the Johnston bill were able to build an alliance that included insurers, the defendants in most auto tort cases, and minority and consumer groups, which represented plaintiffs' interests. The basis of the coalition was that both sides could benefit by "cutting out the middlemen," the lawyers, who were arguably draining resources from both. The alliance was a brilliant political stratagem, but the case also demonstrates just how difficult it is to make it work. Groups that represent plaintiffs and groups that represent defendants tend to be far apart in ideology and to harbor great distrust of each other. Plaintiff groups that do choose to align with defendant groups find themselves in a difficult position. Organizations such as Latino Issues Forum were never very comfortable being allied with insurers and Republicans against the Nader wing of the consumer movement and the mainstream of the California Democratic party. Both consumer and minority groups knew that on many other issues—redlining, for example—the insurers would be their next opponents. Moreover, minority and consumer groups risked being labeled as fronts for the insurance industry and losing support from their membership or their allies. The post-Rosenfield leaders of Voter Revolt suffered this fate when they were excoriated for joining with Silicon Valley business interests in the ill-fated 1996 campaign.

Another problem for those seeking to "cut out the middleman" is that the plaintiff groups' allegiances to the middlemen—the plaintiff lawyers—are often very strong. No-fault proponents in the legislature were able to muster support among consumer and minority groups, but they were unable to bring Ralph Nader or Harvey Rosenfield to their side. After successfully opposing the insurance companies' version of no-fault in Proposition 104, this pair then went on to help defeat the consumer-minority-insurer alliance on the Johnston bill and, several years later, crush Prop. 200. Ralph Nader's commitment to traditional tort law has made it difficult to unify the consumer movement in any antilitigation effort.

Prolitigation forces used clever tactics to split the plaintiff-defendant coalition behind no-fault. They developed alternatives to no-fault that did not involve restrictions on lawsuits. In the first ballot election, Proposition 103 offered the enticing alternative of lowering rates by slicing the allegedly excessive profits of insurers. It is not surprising that, in trying to find a solution to the problem of rising rates, voters eschewed the one offered by the group most identified with the problem—insurers—and instead chose one created by apparently disinterested consumer activists. In the legislature, Brown and Lockyer deflected support away from no-fault by creating several alternatives aimed at rate stabilization and aid to uninsured motorists. Whatever the merits of these plans, they gave legislators pressed by the public to "do something" about insurance rates a way to vote for change without voting against CTLA. While the Johnston bill's supporters were able to put pressure on the legislature to deal with the various problems of auto insurance, they could not get the public to insist on no-fault. Even in the senate campaign, when legislators received thousands of phone calls in support of the Johnston bill, legislators who voted against no-fault could with some justice contend that the public knew little about it and were calling only to voice frustration over the current system. While the details of no-fault can be of great interest to insiders such as journalists and policy makers, public knowledge of no-fault is limited, and thus, so is public support. Faced with a mandate only to "do something" about the problems of rising rates and uninsured motorists, legislators could choose routes other than no-fault.

All three no-fault campaigns were vulnerable to attack because of the way the auto insurance issue was framed. John Kingdon, in his seminal book on public policy making, suggests that, for a proposal to be enacted, it must be connected to a problem that is considered pressing.[96] In this case, the problem of escalating auto insurance rates was clearly considered pressing by many Californians and by backers of Proposition 104, and the Johnston bill framed no-fault as a way to solve it, as did proponents of Prop. 200 several years later. But this created serious difficulties for the pro-no-fault side. Nearly all the debate over no-fault concerned whether it really would reduce or stabilize rates or whether it really could support a cheap policy for low-income drivers. As a step toward rate reduction, no-fault takes a somewhat circuitous route. On one hand, no-fault reduces costs by chopping fees paid to lawyers and reducing the payout of pain-and-suffering costs. On the other hand, no-fault *increases* costs by compensating at-fault drivers. Thus, depending on which version of no-fault is implemented, it can result in either rising policy premiums or lowered ones. The versions offered by the insurers in the 1988 ballot campaign and by Johnston in the legislature were fairly conservative verbal-threshold systems, and similar policies in other states had resulted at least in slowing the growth of auto insurance costs. The 1996 measure, Prop. 200, was a "pure" no-fault proposal that was even more likely to keep rates down. But California, renowned for its litigiousness, is not necessarily like other states, and so the actuarial consequences of a no-fault plan could be endlessly debated. The proponents of Prop. 200 claimed, based on a Rand Institute for Civil Justice study, that it would decrease insurance rates 25 to 34 percent; opponents, using figures from no-fault states, argued that the initiative would zoom rates as much as 40 percent.[97] It was easy for opponents to argue that California would end up like New Jersey, where no-fault had turned into an actuarial disaster, rather than New York, usually acknowledged a success.

The framing of no-fault as a solution to rising rates meant that many of the strongest arguments for the policy played little or no role in the debate. For example, the fact that no-fault would compensate all those injured in an accident, not just those injured by an at-fault driver, was almost never raised, except as a criticism. The uncertainty critique of the traditional liability system, which holds that accident victims are compensated unevenly based on factors having little to do with the accident itself, also played no role in the debate. The backers of both 104 and the Johnston bill tried to highlight the possible benefits of no-fault in speeding payments to victims and limiting fraud, but they failed to attract much notice. Instead, attention focused on actuarial predictions about the effects of a no-fault system on premium rates. Thus the way the problem of auto insurance was defined in California handicapped the move for no-fault from the beginning.

Another vulnerability went to the heart of the no-fault idea. No-fault implicitly rests on the view that auto accidents are best understood as a predictable social hazard rather than a product of the bad deeds of individual drivers. This was not a view shared by Californians, as the anti-104 campaign's polling showed. Voters bristled at the thought that, as one of the anti-104 commercials put it, under no-fault "a bad driver is no longer responsible" for his or her transgressions. A vote for no-fault was portrayed as a vote against individual responsibility, an almost unimpeachable principle in American political discourse.

The vulnerabilities of no-fault, however, would not have mattered without an opposition ready to exploit them.[98] No-fault in California had two major, unyielding sources of opposition: plaintiff lawyers and consumer advocates Harvey Rosenfield and Ralph Nader. Nader and Rosenfield were clearly instrumental in the defeat of Proposition 104. Plaintiff lawyers helped organize the Prop. 100 campaign and funded the greatest chunk of the drive against 104, but Voter Revolt's Prop. 103 was the initiative that beat both 100 and 104. The insurer's initiative was an easy target for the consumer activists, and the "David and Goliath" theme in the ballot campaign clearly resonated. The polling data available suggests that 104 was unpopular from the start, despite the early advertising by the industry campaign. The insurers, for all their money, had a tough task trying to convince skeptical voters that an industry-backed initiative would help consumers more than a measure created by consumer activists. The campaign for Prop. 200 suffered as well from a David and Goliath image, this time with Silicon Valley business interests playing the role of the giant.

As powerful as Nader and Rosenfield proved to be in the ballot campaigns, however, it seems unlikely that they would have beaten the Johnston bill without CTLA's efforts. Nader and Rosenfield were, after all, isolated in their stand on the Johnston bill: a coalition of minority and consumer groups opposed them. Democrats inclined to vote for no-fault could plausibly argue, given this lineup, that they were acting in the interests of consumers, despite Nader's rhetoric. It is hard to believe that the one-vote margins that blocked no-fault would have stood up in the absence of the plaintiff lawyers' lobbying campaign.

The conclusion that plaintiff lawyers played a major role in the defeat of no-fault has something of a "dog bites man" flavor. No one should be surprised by this finding. Plaintiff lawyers are widely reputed to be major obstacles to litigation-reducing reforms such as no-fault. Still, the case of no-fault in California illustrates just how significant the efforts of the plaintiff lawyers can be. As Sal Russo, the insurance industry consultant who worked on the Johnston bill, put it: "You had the universe lined up on one side and the trial lawyers on the other side. Now we know who's more powerful."[99] Russo was indulging in some hyperbole, of course, but the plaintiff lawyers did battle an array of interests with only Nader and Rosenfield as steady allies. The influence of the plaintiff lawyers on legislators in the no-fault battle stems from several sources. Most important, CTLA had key allies in both the assembly and senate. In the assembly, Willie Brown exerted great effort on no-fault auto insurance, proposing alternatives and pushing his party members to line up against the bill. In the senate, Bill Lockyer also advanced alternatives.

What makes CTLA such an important ally to the Democratic leadership? As all of my interviewees stressed, CTLA is an important source of campaign finance for the Democratic party. In the years covered by the no-fault controversy, CTLA regularly showed up in the top five of all nonparty political action committee (PAC) contributors. During this period the group gave 86 percent of its contributions to the Democrats.[100] In the 1988 primary, for example, CTLA donated $873,246, $775,557 of which went to Democrat candidates, CTLA's total donations in this period put it just behind the first-place insurers' PAC on the list of interest group contributors.[101] Measured as a percentage of all PAC financing, CTLA's contribution is not very large: in the 1988 primary, California Democrats collected more than $25 million in PAC money. But the contribution numbers include only money given through CTLA's PAC. They do not take into account plaintiff lawyer money given through other means. For example, in 1991 Brown and Lockyer both benefited from fund-raisers thrown for them by CTLA.[102] In addition, CTLA has also been willing to concentrate large sums on candidates in tough elections or on ballot measures the Democratic leadership opposes. When Brown wanted to punish a rebelling assembly Democrat, for example, CTLA contributed more than $100,000 to a primary opponent Brown supported.[103] Thus CTLA's contribution cannot be measured by annual PAC totals alone. CTLA, along with teachers groups and unions, is one of a few dependable sources of contributions for Democrats in California.

But if money were the only source of CTLA's influence, the insurers, with vastly larger resources, could easily defeat them. Indeed, insurers gave sizable contributions to Democrats during the no-fault wars; after being cut off by CTLA, Johnston received heavy contributions from insurers. If campaign finance were simply an auction for the favors of legislators, insurers could easily dominate plaintiff lawyers. Moreover, individual legislators like Johnston know that they can find money no matter how they line up in the insurer-versus–plaintiff lawyer battle.

Thus, while financing is one basis of the relationship between plaintiff lawyers and Democrats, there is also a shared worldview. Lockyer explained the alliance between the Democrats and the plaintiff lawyers simply: "When the rich and powerful want to be immunized for their bad behavior, we (Democrats) just have a natural reaction: 'Hey, we're with the little guy.'"[104] He argued that Democrats and plaintiff lawyers share a "philosophical and emotional commitment to the underdog. I'm glad there's a group of lawyers who aren't just trying to bill rich people by the hour. They'll take a chance and represent people who otherwise don't have access to justice."[105] Plaintiff lawyers share with Democrats a concern for victims and a suspicion of big businesses such as the insurance industry. "CTLA's self-interest is congruent with the underdogs in our society, the victims of negligence," Lockyer has said. "Democrats tend to have a sympathy for the underdog."[106] A CTLA lobbyist put it in much the same way, arguing that plaintiff lawyers protect victims from those who try to evade responsibility for causing injury. "That's a very Democratic concept, protecting the little guy against the institutions."[107] Brown and Lockyer are closely tied to the plaintiff lawyers by financial contributions. But they also share a political outlook and a history of working together. In case studies, as in voting research, it is difficult to sort out these strands of a political relationship. Whatever the relative contributions of these strands, the relationship between plaintiff lawyers and the Democrats is a strong one that is very hard to disrupt. Even on an issue like no-fault, when minority and consumer groups argued that plaintiff lawyers had pitted themselves against the interests of the underdogs, the alliance of Democratic leaders and the CTLA largely held firm.

Besides this relationship, CTLA has several advantages unique among the participants in the tort reform debate. CTLA is concerned with a narrow range of issues, but within that range the membership is unusually unified and active, willing to contribute time and large sums of money. In addition, CTLA's members are, after all, trial lawyers and thus particularly skilled at advocacy. The paid lobbyists that CTLA hires are also viewed as among the best in Sacramento. When CTLA's interests are threatened, it can mount an unusually intense campaign.

The triumph of the plaintiff lawyers is yet another example of one of the oldest stories in American political science: concentrated interest beats diffuse interests. CTLA, a group of about five thousand members, took on almost single-handedly an army of insurers, minority groups, and Consumers Union whose numbers and resources together easily overwhelm those of the plaintiff lawyers. For the lawyers, maintaining tort litigation in auto accident cases is a major concern. The Rand Corporation estimates that, nationally, auto accident cases represent three-quarters of all fees collected in personal injury lawsuits.[108] Plaintiff lawyers knew that under Prop. 200 this source of income would have dried up almost entirely, while under Prop. 104 and the Johnston bill it would have been significantly curtailed.[109] Insurers, by contrast, knew that they could still be profitable without no-fault, and because of differences in both philosophy and economic structure within the industry, insurers had varying levels of enthusiasm for no-fault efforts. Insurers were able to mount an extremely intense ballot campaign for 104, but only because it was highly favorable to them, with provisions that had nothing to do with no-fault tucked into the initiative to guarantee support. The Johnston bill was not nearly so favorable, and so insurer support never reached the phenomenal levels of the ballot campaign. On Prop. 200, insurers, having once been burned, stayed out of the fight. Insurers can make profits in non-no-fault systems; minorities and consumers can benefit from insurance reforms other than no-fault. Only for the plaintiff lawyers was no-fault crucial to their livelihood.

It is impossible to prove that CTLA tipped the balance in this case. Still, the story of no-fault in California provides strong support for the view that some litigious policies are maintained by lawyer interest groups.

Other Explanations

Commentators have linked the proliferation of litigious policies in the United States to a rights consciousness among Americans, suggesting that Americans naturally frame issues in terms of rights and so resist efforts to limit legal rights. No-fault involves a serious restriction on the right to sue, but this was not the focus of the debate, either during the ballot campaigns or in the legislature. Instead, the debate turned on criticisms of the insurers and on the purely utilitarian question of whether no-fault would indeed lower rates. So the rights consciousness of Americans played little or no role in this case.

Another explanation for litigious policy making rests on the high number of lawyer policy makers in the United States. Unfortunately, the

Table 3.2. Support for No-Fault in Three Committee Votes

	Democrats	Republicans
Lawyers	23% (3/13)	100% (2/2)
Nonlawyers	29% (6/21)	89% (16/18)

NOTE: These figures cumulate the April 18, 1989, vote of the California assembly Finance and Insurance Committee, the January 17, 1990, vote of the assembly Ways and Means Committee, and the May 28, 1991, vote of the senate Judiciary Committee. All legislators with JD degrees were coded as lawyers. Because a bill must receive more than half the votes of the full committee in order to pass, abstaining and absent legislators were counted as "no" votes.

case provides no clear test of this explanation. One test is to see whether lawyers and nonlawyers in the legislature differ in their voting patterns on bills that reduce litigation. In three committee roll-call votes on the Johnston bill, lawyers were in fact more likely than nonlawyers to take an anti-no-fault position: 67 percent of the lawyers voted against the Johnston bill, compared to 44 percent of the nonlawyers. The problem with this finding is that, when partisanship is introduced as a control, the differences are all but erased. Among Democrats, 78 percent of the lawyers opposed the Johnston bill, but 71 percent of the nonlawyers opposed it, as well. (See Table 3.2.) The heavy partisanship in voting on no-fault, combined with the low number of Republican lawyers in the sample, makes the lawyer–policy maker theory impossible to confirm or disconfirm through these roll-call votes.

Observers suggest that judiciary committees are graveyards for tort reform, partly because of their high lawyer composition, and in this respect individual votes are suggestive. In the crucial senate Judiciary Committee vote, for example, five of six lawyers on the committee opposed the Johnston bill, whereas four out of five nonlawyers supported it. Of the eight Democrats on the committee, all but two were lawyers. The two Democratic nonlawyers split their vote, and the three Republicans on the committee, all nonlawyers, voted for the Johnston plan. Thus Democratic lawyers provided nearly all of the votes against the bill, but it is not clear if their stance was influenced more by their partisanship or their profession. The two are hard to separate even in the legislature as a whole: of the twenty-eight lawyers in the California legislature during this period twenty-two were Democrats.[110]

When we move beyond the voting patterns to the details of the case, this ambiguity remains. The two most ardent opponents of no-fault in the legislature, Bill Lockyer and Willie Brown, were both lawyers. Lockyer was actually working in a personal injury law firm at the time, and Brown, while not himself a personal injury lawyer, had worked as a trial lawyer in criminal defense, an area within the bar that is often associated with plaintiff tort practice. Again, however, Lockyer and Brown's actions may reflect more their positions as leaders of the Democratic party and the need to respond to an important constituency than their experiences as lawyers.

The Dogs That Didn't Bark

As suggested at the outset of this chapter, the Constitutional Theory, for all its merits, can't help us understand the fate of no-fault auto insurance proposals. That is because the Constitutional Theory concerns the choice between litigation and welfare-regulatory programs, not the decision between litigation and private insurance that was made in this case. Yet the Constitutional Theory is still relevant to this story. It can help us understand why, to return to the old social science cliché, some dogs didn't bark: why other alternatives to solving the auto liability issue in California were never considered.

First, no one in this case considered the possibility of using government as a first-party insurer. In some other nations where no-fault systems have been developed, such as New Zealand and three provinces of Canada, the programs have been administered by governmental bureaucracies. In the United States, by contrast, no-fault programs, beginning with workers' compensation and continuing with auto insurance, are usually administered by private insurers.[111]

Second, though Speaker Brown did propose a state-run arbitration program, other kinds of governmental intervention into auto accident disputes were not seriously considered. A management approach to auto accident compensation, exemplified by Japan, involves the development of state-funded mediation and advice centers, which encourage potential litigants to resolve their claims without the use of lawyers or litigation. No one in the California no-fault case considered such a method of handling auto tort claims.[112]

Finally and most basically, no one advanced government-guaranteed health care insurance or an expanded government-run disability insurance program as possible solutions to California's auto insurance problems. Even within the United States, the tort liability system provides only a fraction of the compensation given to those involved in auto accidents. A study of accident compensation by the Rand Institute for Civil Justice suggests that only one-third of all auto accident compensation comes from tort; for other types of accidents tort is even less significant, amounting to 11 percent of compensation overall.[113] Mostly, those who suffer from accidents recoup their losses from private and public insurance. In most economically advanced nations, more generous government provision of health and disability benefits takes much of the pressure of compensating accidents off the tort liability system. In the United States, the welfare state is smaller, and so there is greater pressure for compensation through tort.[114] The propensity for litigating auto accident claims among Californians, for example, is undoubtedly stimulated in part by the fact that many of them lack health insurance. Moreover, exponentially increasing medical costs were a major source of premium increases during this period. Yet no one connected the problem of tort liability to the issue of adequate health and disability insurance coverage.

Thus several bureaucratic modes of handling auto accident injuries—governmental no-fault, state-funded mediation and advice centers, and government-funded health and disability programs—were ignored while a private insurance solution was advanced. As the example of no-fault auto insurance suggests, the American constitutional tradition sharply restricts the repertoire of antilitigation reformers in the United States.

CHAPTER 4

A SHOT OF ANTILITIGATION REFORM

The Vaccine Injury Compensation Program

On the morning of July 3, 1981, Julie Schwartz, then a four-month-old, was vaccinated for diphtheria, pertussis (commonly known as "whooping cough"), and tetanus. The so-called "DPT" vaccine that Julie received had all but wiped out diseases that in the past were a major cause of death among American children. DPT vaccination was required by law in most states and was routinely administered to young infants. Julie had gotten two previous injections of DPT without any noticeable reaction. But several hours after the third injection Julie went into a seizure; her whole body shook for more than a half-hour. She was taken to an emergency room with what her pediatrician noted as a reaction to the vaccine.

The seizure Julie suffered that day turned out to be just the first of many, some of them lasting as long as an hour, that she would have for the rest of her life. By her first birthday the seizures had bruised Julie's brain so severely that she lost all function on the right side of her body. She was diagnosed as learning disabled and required physical therapy and speech therapy. She was hyperactive, with a low attention span, and frequently irritable. From time to time she would have long, terrifying full-body seizures requiring her to be rushed to the hospital. Julie's father, Jeffrey Schwartz, testified to the Maryland legislature in 1983 about the impact of Julie's injuries on his family:

> I can't find any way to express adequately the emotional costs Donna and I have had to endure without respite over the past 2 years—the fear, the pain, the sorrow, the confusion, the anxiety, the helplessness, the rage, the hopelessness, the stress, the unrelieved exhaustion and the depression.
>
> These are the right labels for the feelings, but they cannot convey what the experience has been like. It has felt like a nightmare—with no waking, no escape. This is not to mention the direct financial costs and the other indirect costs that we have had to pay.

> Nor does this tally up what is perhaps most important—the pain and loss that Julie has suffered, continues to suffer, and may well suffer for the rest of her life. Other families have suffered far worse even than we.[1]

A year after this testimony, Julie lapsed into a long seizure, stopped breathing, and died.

Julie's parents believed that their daughter's injuries and eventual death were caused by the vaccine she had been given. Further, they believed that the DPT vaccine was poorly made and that the medical establishment had not done enough to warn parents of its dangers.

They were not alone. Of the millions of children vaccinated safely each year, a tiny percentage suffered severe reactions. Estimates of injury rates were heavily disputed. A 1985 study by the American Medical Association (AMA) suggested that each year about sixty-three American children suffered severe brain injury or death from reactions to vaccines, though others put the numbers much higher.[2] DPT by all accounts caused the most reactions, but vaccines for polio, measles, mumps, and rubella also injured a few children (and a few adults). Like the Schwartzes, some families of these children blamed vaccine manufacturers and doctors for what they believed was the promotion of dangerous vaccines.

Faced with the heavy burden of raising a severely injured infant or the pain of a child's death, a few of these families opted to sue the vaccines' manufacturers in court. But winning a verdict in a vaccine case was no easy task. The law of vaccines was unclear and varied from state to state; in many states there were no recorded cases and thus no law at all. Just getting into court usually required identifying the manufacturer of the vaccine that had been administered, a hurdle that by itself could prove insurmountable.[3] Many courts followed the rule that vaccines were "unavoidably unsafe products," so that vaccine makers could not be blamed if a few children suffered severe reactions.[4] In a few instances negligence had been demonstrated because a "bad batch" had been delivered.[5] Another small group of cases involved claims that doctors had administered vaccines negligently, either because of the child's age or because of previous reactions. And some plaintiffs, beginning in the late 1960s, successfully argued that the vaccine makers had failed to directly warn consumers of the dangers of a vaccine.[6] But those cases were the exceptions. By the early 1980s, when Julie Schwartz suffered her first seizure, most families received nothing at all from the tort system.[7]

Yet while the legal system seemed uninviting to parents, developments in the 1980s made it seem dangerously unpredictable to the vaccine industry.

Courts began to accept new theories of liability, and large verdicts and settlements multiplied. When the federal government, in the mid-1970s, accepted liability for reactions to the swine flu vaccine, more than 4,000 damage claims were filed and the United States paid out more than $72 million on more than 750 claims.[8] This particular explosion of litigation can be attributed to the government's liberal approach to compensating for purported swine flu vaccine reactions. But by the mid-1980s makers of all vaccines were feeling increasingly threatened by litigation.

Two cases in particular rattled the manufacturers. In 1984 a jury returned a verdict of $1,131,200 based on a new legal theory: that Lederle, a maker of DPT, could have marketed a safer vaccine but chose not to develop it.[9] In another case the same year a jury awarded $2 million in compensatory damages and $8 million in punitive damages after the plaintiff argued that the company should have informed parents that the Salk polio vaccine was safer than the Sabin vaccine that was administered.[10] Although the $10 million verdict was later overturned, outcomes such as this led manufacturers, anticipating huge liabilities, to raise the prices of their products.

By far the most common target of litigation was the DPT vaccine. Within five years a trickle of DPT lawsuits became a flood. The price of DPT zoomed from 11 cents in 1980 to $11.40 by 1986, an increase of more than 10,000 percent. Even with these increases, some manufacturers, claiming they could not find liability insurance at any price, left the vaccine business altogether. In 1985 the Centers for Disease Control advised physicians to delay booster shots to children in order to avert a shortage of DPT.

A SUCCESSFUL ANTILITIGATION REFORM

The problem of vaccine injuries, though obscure, is consequential because it threatened the practice of vaccination, one of the major sources of improvement in public health in the twentieth century. By the mid-1980s, critics of litigiousness such as Peter Huber cited vaccine litigation as a particularly disastrous example of tort law in action.[11]

For this study, the case of vaccine injury compensation is important in another respect: it is a rare instance in which Congress adopted a replacement antilitigation policy. Indeed Congress's response to the vaccine injury problem represents one of very few successful antilitigation efforts of any kind at the federal level—and potentially one of the strongest challenges to the Constitutional Theory. Reform proponents in this case faced many of the same obstacles that plagued no-fault supporters in California. They had to cobble together an alliance of plaintiffs and defendants, groups who had little in common and much enmity and distrust between them. They had to assuage doubts that a no-fault system would be fairer and more efficient than the system it replaced. Further, they had to convince all concerned that vaccine injuries should be handled as a social problem, an unavoidable cost of vaccination for which all should pay, rather than a product of the sins of pharmaceutical companies.

But proponents of vaccine compensation reform had an even tougher task than no-fault supporters in California, because the compensation program they proposed was to be administered not by private insurance companies but through a government program. This put their proposal at odds with the incentives that I've suggested arise out of the American constitutional tradition. Under the traditional tort litigation system that governed vaccine compensation, decisions were made by a variety of state and federal courts, and payments came from vaccine companies. In replacing this system with a government program, policy makers had to (1) designate a single national-level decision maker for vaccine cases and (2) create a new governmental compensation fund. As the Constitutional Theory suggests, both these moves go against the normal inclinations of activists in the United States. According to the Constitutional Theory, activists seek litigious policies because court-based implementation (1) insulates policies from enemies (the insulation incentive) and (2) requires little or no budgetary spending (the cost-shifting incentive). Vaccine reform proponents had to overcome both of these incentives.

Many factors made vaccine litigation particularly ripe for reform. All the interest groups involved—parents, doctors, manufacturers—had strong reasons for seeking a change. Moreover, even those who would typically reject a replacement reform for litigation recognized vaccine injuries as a unique case, one in which litigation had some particularly pernicious effects. Yet it still took an extremely skillful politician and some adept legislative maneuvering to get the reform enacted. Thus this case offers a sense of the possibilities—and limits—of antilitigation reform efforts.

THE DEVELOPMENT OF A NO-FAULT PLAN

The first important moment in the history of vaccine injury politics was the creation in 1982 of Dissatisfied Parents Together (DPT). In April 1982 WRC Television, an NBC affiliate in Washington, D.C., ran a news report claiming that 272 American children each year were left severely disabled and retarded by the vaccine for pertussis.[12] The pertussis vaccine is administered along with vaccines for diphtheria and tetanus in the DPT shot. The news report argued that the pertussis vaccine had not been adequately tested for safety and that many cases of vaccine injury were going undiagnosed and unreported. The report received wider publicity when it was later shown on the NBC program *Today*.[13] In the aftermath of the reports, many parents of vaccine-injured children called WRC to get more information. Through the television station, four parents of vaccine-damaged children, including Jeffrey Schwartz, the father of Julie Schwartz, met and formed DPT.

The parent group would eventually expand to include families of those injured by a range of vaccines, but at the outset the group's focus was on the pertussis vaccine. DPT's primary goals were to further research and expose the dangers of the DPT vaccine. But the parents also sought alternatives to costly lawsuits to get compensation for their children's injuries.[14] Soon after DPT's formation, the group began working with the American Academy of Pediatrics (AAP) on ways to restructure the tort litigation method of compensating families of vaccine-injured children. Pediatricians had been concerned with the problem of vaccine injuries for several years. In 1977 the AAP had concluded that vaccine-injured children should be compensated for their injuries without having to go to court and without having to prove that vaccine makers were at fault.[15] This "no-fault" approach to compensating vaccine injuries has been established in six European nations and, to a limited extent, in the state of California.[16]

No-fault systems, remember, aim to improve on the traditional tort method of compensation by replacing the disputing process with a first-party insurance scheme. As the name implies, the issue of fault is eliminated. One is paid simply because an injury is sustained. Medical costs and wage losses are compensated, but the injured person generally agrees to limit or give up claims for punitive or pain-and-suffering damages, which can be quite high. In exchange the injured person receives compensation that is more prompt and more sure. No-fault systems are classic antilitigation devices because they attempt to take disputes out of the courtroom and bureaucratize them. But while all no-fault systems share this basic aim, they range widely in the way they are administered and funded. They vary, for example, in the degree to which they socialize the costs of injury. As the California no-fault auto case study suggests, no-fault in the United States is usually run by private insurers. Many systems outside the United States are like New Zealand's, in which compensation comes out of a taxpayer-financed government program.

No-fault systems also vary in the degree to which they move away from the judicial model of decision making. In the New Zealand system one applies to a government bureau for compensation, and the ability to appeal the agency's decision is limited. In the U.S. workers' compensation system, by contrast, administrative hearings take on a quasi-judicial tone, with lawyers for both sides arguing about the severity of an employee's injury and the amount of compensation deemed adequate.[17] In some no-fault systems, such as New Zealand's, traditional tort recovery is almost completely barred; in others, such as the "add-on" no-fault automobile insurance programs in some states, the injured can choose between no-fault and tort recovery. Thus no-fault systems vary tremendously in the degree to which they move away from traditional tort litigation.[18]

DPT was receptive to a no-fault system because it promised more adequate compensation for vaccine-injured children. The parents and the pediatricians, though, had quite different notions about what a good no-fault system would look like. For more than a year the two groups traded comments on proposals. The most basic sticking point between DPT and the pediatricians was on who would administer the compensation scheme. This was an important point, because while a no-fault system would eliminate the issue of whether vaccine makers were negligent, it still left the troublesome matter of causation. In each case, the decision maker would still have to judge whether the child's symptoms were actually caused by a vaccine reaction. If the child's injuries were not the result of the vaccine, they would not be compensable. The pediatrician group wanted the compensation system to be administered by experts within the Department of Health and Human Services.[19] For the parents this was anathema. They told the pediatricians that they would never accept a plan that lodged control over compensation in the hands of health officials or medical experts.[20]

The parents' aversion to a bureaucratic remedy stemmed from their perspective on the DPT vaccine. Health officials and pharmaceutical manufacturers believed that vaccine injuries were the inevitable—and rare—consequence of a nationwide vaccination program. The few cases of vaccine injury, they believed, were far outweighed by the dangers of unchecked disease. Many parents, however, believed that the pertussis vaccine was far more dangerous than the medical establishment would admit. Barbara Loe Fisher, a founding member of DPT, argued that the trials of DPT in Britain that had been cited to prove the safety and effectiveness of the vaccine used a less reactive formulation, were flawed in the manner in which adverse reactions were monitored, involved children older than those given the shot in the United States, and employed British doctors more willing than their American colleagues to discontinue a child's vaccinations after a reaction. A widely quoted British study had concluded that DPT caused permanent neurological damage in 1 out of 310,000 vaccinations. Fisher's analysis of American research led her to a much higher estimate: of the roughly 3.3 million children vaccinated each year, 11,000 were suffering lasting neurological damage, and nearly 1,000 were dying. Fisher believed that about 13 percent of all sudden infant deaths in the United States were caused by DPT.[21]

The parents maintained that evidence of the pertussis vaccine's hazards had been hushed up in a misguided effort to promote vaccination. Moreover, the system for reporting vaccine injuries was woefully inadequate, seemingly designed to minimize the vaccine's dangers. Thus many of the parents in DPT harbored a deep mistrust of the medical establishment. Fisher expressed this view of the scientists, drug manufacturers, doctors, and government health officials who had guided vaccine policy: "If they stubbornly refused to see the problem because of their eagerness to believe the vaccine was less dangerous than the disease, then they are guilty of engaging in bad science. If, on the other hand, they deliberately covered it up, they are guilty of systematically sacrificing a certain portion of our children without our knowledge."[22] DPT saw the Department of Health and Human Services as part of the vaccine problem rather than part of the solution. The Department's provaccine stance gave it an incentive to minimize the dangers of the pertussis vaccine. Thus DPT ardently opposed giving the department control over compensation.

Schwartz testified before the Senate Labor and Human Resources Committee while his organization was negotiating with the pediatricians. He stressed that the body deciding claims should be "completely independent of any governmental or private agency responsible for promoting vaccines or controlling health care costs."[23] An attorney who had represented several parents in lawsuits echoed Schwartz's argument, contending that putting Health and Human Services in control would be "somewhat analogous to putting Al Capone in charge of alcohol tax enforcement."[24]

There were other differences between the parents and the pediatricians. Whatever the shape of the compensation program, the parents wanted to preserve the ability to sue in a traditional tort claim. DPT was nervous about whether a no-fault system would work as promised and consequently wanted to be able to bypass it if necessary. Further, the parents wanted to preserve the tort system as a way of attracting public attention about the need for safer vaccines and as a deterrent to negligent manufacturers and doctors.[25]

The pediatrician group preferred an exclusive remedy but recognized that without the parents' support no change in the vaccine litigation system was likely.[26] After months of haggling, AAP and DPT released a draft of a bill establishing a no-fault vaccine system financed through a surtax on vaccines. Parents would apply to the U.S. federal district court in Washington, D.C., which would appoint a special master to decide whether an injury was compensable based on a table of vaccine reactions. To win an award, parents would have only to demonstrate that their children had developed the reactions outlined in the table after a vaccination. If dissatisfied with the special master's ruling, parents could appeal it to the D.C. Circuit Court. The no-fault program would compensate for all unreimbursed medical and custodial costs and lost earnings, plus up to $100,000 for pain and suffering. Parents of children who died as a result of vaccine reactions were eligible to receive between $300,000 and $700,000. In addition, the plan provided for "reasonable attorney's fees," 20 to 25 percent of the total award. Most importantly, the bill allowed parents to choose between the new system and the tort system.

The draft agreement between DPT and AAP became Senate resolution 2117 (S. 2117), which was introduced into Congress by Senator Paula Hawkins, a Republican from Florida, in November of 1983.[27] In June 1984 Henry Waxman, a Democrat from California, introduced a companion measure in the House.

A "Precarious" Supply

Both Waxman and Hawkins had become interested in alternative compensation schemes because of their concerns about rising vaccine costs. By the fall of 1984 cost was not the only issue; some feared that the supply of vaccines, especially the DPT vaccine, was endangered. In that year Wyeth Pharmaceutical dropped out of distributing the DPT vaccine, leaving Lederle and Connaught as the only commercial suppliers.[28] Connaught, meanwhile, was reporting difficulty in finding liability insurance and was considering leaving the U.S. market. When two lots of Lederle's DPT vaccine failed to pass company standards, the Centers for Disease Control advised physicians to delay booster shots to children in order to avert a vaccine shortage.[29]

Representative Waxman called a hearing of the Subcommittee on Health and the Environment, which he chaired, to explore the causes and consequences of a possible shortage. The companies primarily blamed the uncertain and escalating costs of liability, saying that the spiraling level of claims made it hard to get insurance. Lederle president Robert Johnson had estimated that DPT lawsuits against his company asked for compensation that was two hundred times greater than 1983 sales of the vaccine, and that the amount demanded for polio lawsuits was twelve times 1983 sales.[30] Vaccines represented just 2 percent of the gross revenues of Lederle's parent company, American Cyanamid, yet total claims amounted to several times its total revenue.[31]

The growth in litigation rates was well documented, but the dimensions of the supposed shortage proved difficult to specify. Wyeth at one point had told government officials that it planned to quit manufacturing DPT, but then changed plans and continued producing the vaccine. Wyeth's vaccine was sent to Lederle to distribute under its own name. Thus Waxman learned that Wyeth had not gotten out of the business after all.[32] Wyeth's maneuver led to charges that vaccine manufacturers were pursuing a "Chicken Little" strategy in order to get relief from vaccine liability. Jeffrey Schwartz charged that the "so-called 'shortage'" was "primarily a public relations ruse intended to stampede the Congress into cutting off the rights of injured children to sue negligent drug companies."[33] Yet no one could dispute that the number of companies producing vaccines of all types had declined, creating fears about the nation's vaccine supply. Lederle was by 1984 the only maker of the polio vaccine. Merck made the only measles, mumps, and rubella vaccine. In 1985 a panel of experts commissioned to study the vaccine problem by the National Academy of Sciences' Institute of Medicine concluded that "precarious" supplies of vaccines posed a "threat to the public's health."[34]

The DPT shortage, if there was a shortage, was eased in 1985 by the announcement that Connaught Laboratories had worked out an insurance arrangement and would continue to manufacture and distribute DPT. Wyeth meanwhile dropped out of the market entirely, leaving Lederle as the only other supplier. Connaught's occasional technical problems and both companies' problems in securing insurance coverage led to continued fears of a shortage and pronouncements of crisis.[35] As already noted, Lederle's price for DPT reached $11.40 by 1986; it had been just 11 cents six years earlier. Of the increase, $8 was said to cover liability expenses.[36]

The Hawkins Bill and Its Critics

In April 1985 a revised version of the Hawkins-Waxman bill was introduced into the Senate by Paula Hawkins.[37] S. 827 tightened the original bill's compensation scheme by restricting recovery to cases of injuries lasting at least one year or resulting in death. The original bill had allowed claimants to reject the special master's award and commence a lawsuit; in the revised version the claimant was locked into either a lawsuit or the compensation system once it was chosen. The bill narrowed the table of injuries that were deemed compensable under the no-fault program but also allowed claimants to argue that "off-table" injuries had been caused by vaccines. Compensation for the death of a child was limited to $250,000; pain-and-suffering damages were expanded to $250,000.

For manufacturers the bill offered two new benefits. It authorized federal backup insurance in case they could not get liability coverage, and it foreclosed tort lawsuits based on the "duty to directly warn" theory of liability, a major line of litigation against the vaccine makers. Hawkins was trying to attract support for the compensation program from the manufacturers and from other health groups.

The vaccine makers, however, were unimpressed by both S. 827 and S. 2117. Wyeth, Lederle, Connaught, and Merck all criticized the bills for maintaining the tort option. From their perspective, the bills created a system of "double jeopardy": they would be paying a surtax to support the compensation program, but they would still be faced with the threat of unpredictable tort verdicts as well. Lederle, the only maker of polio vaccine and one of the DPT manufacturers, was particularly critical of the bills, arguing that they covered conditions that could not be linked to vaccines.[38]

The Reagan administration was even more critical. It opposed the basic concept of a no-fault program. The administration found "no compelling evidence that the existing method of compensating victims through the tort system is inadequate."[39] It criticized the program as overly generous to claimants, both in the kinds of conditions compensated and in the amount of compensation allowed.[40] The administration also criticized the special master process, arguing that any determination of compensation should be made by a judge, with the government acting as respondent in order to make sure weak claims were not compensated.[41] The administration had its own solution to the vaccine litigation problem, one more in keeping with its approach to product liability issues generally. The cause of the tort litigation problem, the administration argued, was the unpredictability of jury verdicts. By far the greatest share of this unpredictability came from punitive and pain-and-suffering awards. Thus the administration proposed a discouragement reform that would eliminate punitive damages and restrict pain-and-suffering damages to $100,000.[42]

The administration proposal was just one of several being floated in the mid-1980s. The American Medical Association and the Pharmaceutical Manufacturers Association endorsed a plan created by a commission of representatives from medical and pharmaceutical groups. Under the plan, officials within the Department of Health and Human Services would administer a no-fault compensation program based on standards developed by medical experts. Claimants could appeal the department's decision in federal courts but only on restricted grounds. The AMA plan made the no-fault system an exclusive remedy; vaccine manufacturers could be sued only by the federal government to recover for claims resulting from negligent conduct.[43] The AMA criticized the Hawkins bill because it lodged the compensation program in the courts and created a nonexclusive remedy.

Illinois representative Edward Madigan, the ranking Republican on the House subcommittee, also worried that the bill gave claimants "two bites of the apple."[44] Early in 1985 Madigan introduced House resolution 1780 (H.R. 1780), a bill written by Lederle and supported by Wyeth. The Madigan plan created a system in which eleven regional panels of medical experts would arbitrate claims. The panels could award up to $1 million in damages paid directly by the manufacturer. If the parents rejected the panel's finding they could choose to bring a traditional tort claim, but total recovery would be capped at $1 million. Those choosing to avoid the panels entirely would not be limited by the cap.[45] The American Academy of Pediatrics and several of the vaccine manufacturers also created alternative vaccine compensation reforms, none of which reached Congress.[46] Many ideas were floated, but none advanced very far in the legislative process.

ENACTING A VACCINE PROGRAM

Representative Waxman believed that the only way to pass legislation was to get all the groups most involved—the parents, manufacturers, and doctors—together on one package. Waxman's strategy was, as one congressional aide put it, to come up with "everybody's second choice." It was not an easy undertaking. The groups seemed far apart on the major issues. None of the three major manufacturers of childhood vaccines—Lederle, Connaught, and Merck—supported S. 827. Lederle had consistently and stridently opposed the no-fault concept; Connaught had criticized the no-fault plan in S. 827 for being nonexclusive. Merck had been the most restrained of the three. It strongly supported a no-fault compensation system but wanted only limited tort recovery alongside it.[47] Waxman found it easiest to negotiate with Merck.

In July of 1986 Waxman held a press conference to announce his newest proposal, H.R. 5184. The bill differed significantly from its predecessors, with the biggest changes tilting toward the demands of the manufacturers. One major shift was that the bill required parents to file first with the no-fault compensation system; in previous bills parents could choose between no-fault and traditional tort. With H.R. 5184 the parents could commence a tort lawsuit only after receiving a final judgment in the no-fault system.

A second change was that the bill extended much stronger protection to vaccine makers in tort litigation. Like S. 827, it closed down any litigation based on the "failure to directly warn" theory, but it went beyond this to shield manufacturers from "unavoidable" injuries where the vaccine was duly prepared and accompanied by proper warnings. Even more important, the bill eliminated any litigation based on "a theory of strict liability, absolute liability, or any other theory in which the wrongful conduct of the defendant is not the basis of liability." Manufacturers were also made immune from punitive damages if their vaccines complied with Federal Drug Administration (FDA) standards. Finally, the bill included a provision allowing the secretary of health and human services to respond to claims for compensation and to contest those he or she considered lacking in merit. Waxman made this change in response to criticisms from the Justice Department that without a respondent the claiming process was unconstitutional, since there would be no actual "case or controversy" in the district court, as required under Article III of the U.S. Constitution.

With H.R. 5184 Waxman reached his goal of gaining manufacturer support: Merck, the maker of the measles, mumps, and rubella vaccine and the largest of all the pharmaceutical companies in the vaccine business, endorsed the bill.[48] But while Merck was coming on board, DPT was jumping ship. The parents strongly opposed the strengthening of manufacturer's defenses in tort litigation and several other aspects of H.R. 5184. At a hearing of Waxman's subcommittee in July, the parents found themselves in the strange position of aligning with Lederle against the bill.[49]

With time running out in the 99th Congress, Waxman began "shuttle diplomacy" among the vaccine makers, pediatricians, and parents. Waxman particularly needed the support of DPT. To persuade the parents to sign onto the bill, Waxman made several concessions, among them a weakening of the tort restrictions. He included a provision allowing plaintiffs to prevail if they could show that the manufacturer "failed to exercise due care," even if it had complied with federal regulations. Moreover, the tort restrictions remaining in the bill were applied only to injuries suffered after the enactment of the law. With the resulting bill, Waxman was able to keep his delicate coalition of DPT, Merck, and various medical groups together. On September 18 Waxman got his bill out of the House Energy and Commerce Committee on a unanimous vote.

Another obstacle, however, was emerging. The vaccine program was to be funded by a startup appropriation from the federal government, followed by a surtax on vaccines. The surtax had to be approved by the House Ways and Means Committee. But with H.R. 5184 taking shape so late in the year, there was little time to consider a new and complex tax proposal. The Ways and Means Committee chair, Illinois Democrat Dan Rostenkowski, insisted that Waxman wait until the next year to fund the program.[50] In the interest of getting something passed in the 99th Congress, Waxman agreed to strip out the financing for the program. Without financing, the compensation program could not go into operation, but passage of the stripped-down bill would build momentum for a budget provision and establish a framework for the program. On October 14 the stripped-down bill passed the House on a unanimous vote.

The Final Showdown

Yet H.R. 5184 was still in great danger. The Reagan administration's strong opposition to the no-fault scheme jeopardized the bill in the Republican-controlled Senate. The vaccine bill was one of several health-related measures that had been passed out of one house or the other but faced serious obstacles on the way to passage. The ranking leaders of the health-related committees in both houses—Waxman and Madigan in the House, Orrin Hatch and Ted Kennedy in the Senate—met together to decide what to do with these orphan provisions. The four decided that they would package them together, so that all would either be voted up or down.[51]

The four took S. 1744, a bill to improve community health programs that had been passed by the Senate, and added an array of provisions, including the vaccine program. The final package had something for everyone. It included a bill by Hatch to allow the domestic pharmaceutical manufacturers to sell drugs abroad that were not yet approved by the FDA if the importing nations approved the drugs. The export bill was strongly supported by the Reagan administration, which considered it a major boost for the pharmaceutical industry. Because Ohio senator Howard Metzenbaum vehemently opposed the drug exporting measure, the bill also included a new Alzheimer's disease initiative that Metzenbaum had sponsored. A bill supported by the AMA that eased obstacles to reporting a doctor's record of medical malpractice lawsuits was also added. To top it all off, Hatch and Madigan included a repeal of a federal health planning law, a target of the Reagan administration and congressional Republicans.

The omnibus measure passed the House on a voice vote and reached the Republican-controlled Senate on the last day of the 99th Congress. Because of the Reagan administration's strong opposition to the compensation program, a series of senators put "holds" on the bill, thus blocking consideration. Hatch worked throughout the day to get the holds lifted, keeping the Senate in session while he lobbied the administration to support the bill. At one point Hatch became so frustrated he nearly gave up. The turning point came when he reached Attorney General Edwin Meese, who happened to be at a wedding, by telephone. After Hatch's conversation with Meese, the administration agreed to instruct Senate Republicans to unfreeze the bill.[52] It passed on a voice vote.

Although the Reagan administration had allowed the omnibus health bill to pass, it retained the option of vetoing the bill. Opposition to the vaccine plan was centered in the Justice Department, where Meese argued against creating a tax-funded program for which "no legitimate national need has been demonstrated."[53] A wide variety of groups campaigned to urge President Reagan to sign the bill. Hatch appeared at a news conference with Waxman and the AMA, the American Academy of Pediatrics, the Pharmaceutical Manufacturers Association, the Industrial Biotechnology Association, and parent and mental health groups in support of the measure. The National Parent Teacher Association conducted a grassroots campaign. Parent groups held a candlelight vigil in Lafayette Park, across from the White House, and in four cities besides Washington, D.C. Pharmaceutical companies, including Connaught, a late convert to the compensation bill, lobbied the White House. The *Chicago Tribune, Washington Post,* and *New York Times* all editorialized in favor of the bill.

Within the Reagan administration, opinion on the omnibus health bill was divided. Several cabinet departments—Treasury, State, Commerce, and Agriculture—urged approval, in large part because of the drug export provision.[54] Most within the administration, however, took a dim view of the vaccine injury provision, concerned that it would become a new out-of-control entitlement program funded by general tax revenues.[55] Within the White House, the offices of Policy Development, Communications, and Intergovernmental Affairs all advised Reagan to veto the package.[56]

The strongest opposition to the bill came from the Justice Department. In a memo to James Miller, director of the Office of Management and Budget (OMB), Assistant Attorney General John Bolton laid out the case against the vaccine program. First, Bolton argued that placing the program in the judicial branch undermined presidential powers: "Unlike an agency-administered entitlement program, there would be no centralized authority to control and oversee the scope and functioning of the program," Bolton noted. Indeed, he wrote, congressional staff "frankly conceded" that the whole point of locating the program in the courts was to prevent the president and his officers from controlling it. This was particularly worrisome, Bolton claimed, because the program could easily expand beyond victims of vaccine reactions, becoming "one of the largest and most expensive entitlement programs in the United States." Second, Bolton thought judges would be under "extraordinary pressure" to provide compensation to hundreds of thousands of children suffering from serious medical problems such as epilepsy or cerebral palsy, even if their condition was only tenuously linked to a vaccine. Bolton noted the examples of the swine flu program, in which the federal government had agreed to pay for flu vaccine–related injuries, and the black lung program, which compensates coal miners for mining-related respiratory illnesses: both had cost far more than originally estimated. The vaccine compensation program, Bolton argued, was even more likely than those actuarial disasters to spiral out of control. Third, Bolton argued that the compensation program, far from resolving the vaccine supply crisis, might actually worsen it. Parents with strong claims, he wrote, were likely to continue suing in court; those with weak claims would take advantage of the program, and the manufacturers could end up paying both bills. The tort law reforms built into the bill, Bolton argued, would fail to effectively protect vaccine makers if parents chose to sue in court. Finally, Bolton worried that the compensation program would serve as a precedent, undermining the administration's campaign for tort reform and inviting the passage of other injury compensation measures. Bolton concluded that the vaccine provisions in the Omnibus Health Act were so "fundamentally unacceptable" that Reagan should not sign the legislation.[57]

The strongest defense of the vaccine program came from White House counsel Peter Wallison. Wallison argued that, while no-fault compensation was generally a bad idea, vaccine injuries were a special case: "[T]he children who suffer these losses are not voluntary users; they are compelled by state and local jurisdictions to be vaccinated." Wallison noted that under the normal tort system, the children would be uncompensated, since their injuries did not result from anyone's negligence. But leaving severely injured children and the parents uncompensated seemed "unacceptable," not least to the courts, which had disregarded traditional tort doctrine and awarded multimillion dollar judgments, driving vaccine makers out of the business. The vaccine compensation program was a solution to this problem. Moreover, Wallison argued, the vaccine proposal was fundamentally different from the black lung program, to which it had been compared. Unlike black lung, the vaccine program was to be funded through a tax on vaccines, so that the cost would fall on users. Further, the class of claimants was "inherently limited"—Wallison cited a Centers for Disease Control estimate of ninety-two hundred. The vaccine program, he concluded, was consistent with the administration's tort reform goals. The administration favored tort reform because it protected manufacturers from unjust claims, Wallison wrote, and that was precisely what the vaccine program would do.[58]

Health and Human Services secretary Otis R. Bowen was more ambivalent—critical of the design of the vaccine program but worried about a vaccine shortage. According to a report by a White House staff member, Bowen was "very concerned about the incidence of disease that will reappear" without some commitment to resolving the vaccine litigation problem.[59] A memo from Bowen to OMB director Miller called the vaccine program design "flawed at best," combining "the worst aspects of a quasi-administrative mechanism for resolving claims with the existing tort system." Nonetheless, Bowen concluded that "these provisions—while clearly not the proposals the Administration wanted—could have a beneficial effect on both the supply and price of vaccines" and urged the president to sign the bill.[60]

A memo to President Reagan summarizing the cabinet's views on the bill reflected the administration's ambivalence. The memo, written by OMB deputy director Joseph Wright, told Reagan he faced "the most difficult of choices":

> On the one hand, the bill contains provisions which could lead to the implementation of a new Federal vaccine compensation program which is not warranted, would create a new bureaucracy, could well expand into a much larger and more pervasive entitlement program than now anticipated, and is believed by some to be inconsistent with the Administration's tort reform

proposals. On the other hand, the victims entitled to the compensation program are children required by law to be vaccinated and will have an adverse reaction to the procedures through no fault of their own or the manufacturers of the products. In addition, Title I [of the bill] contains drug export provisions long sought by this Administration—provisions which would improve our trade balance, create new jobs, stimulate greater research and development in this country, and strengthen our industrial base.[61]

Indeed, the decision about what to do with the Omnibus Health Act proved so difficult that Wright's advice to the president was revised. The November 10 draft of the memo, which urged a veto, was redrafted; the new version, dated November 13, told the president to sign.[62]

If the compensation plan had stood alone, President Reagan almost certainly would have vetoed it. As it was, he signed the omnibus bill on November 14 "with mixed feelings." In his signing message, Reagan criticized the compensation plan's retention of the tort remedy so that "there continues to be the opportunity for very substantial and inequitable differences in liability judgments awarded similarly situated plaintiffs." Reagan also objected to lodging the program in the federal judiciary rather than the executive branch, saying that administering an entitlement program in this manner raised concerns about separation of powers.[63] Reagan claimed that the bill's lack of funding was a major factor in his decision to sign. The program, after all, would not begin until a funding mechanism was devised—and Reagan would have another chance to veto that. Reagan advised Congress that any financing bill should address the administration's concerns and should be structured so that no funding came out of the U.S. treasury.[64]

Getting a Budget

Waxman had left perhaps the toughest part of his task ahead of him. Financing the vaccine program was difficult because estimates of the total cost of the program were uncertain. Injuries sustained as far back as the 1920s could theoretically be advanced for compensation; no one could know for sure how many claims would be brought. Lederle president Robert B. Johnson, still highly critical of the compensation program, warned of a "flood of claims both old and new."[65] The Reagan administration also argued that the compensation program's cost might spiral out of control. At one point the administration suggested scrapping the whole compensation fund idea in favor of a private no-fault insurance scheme.[66]

The House Subcommittee on Select Revenue Measures recommended at a meeting in the summer of 1987 that a surtax should not be used to pay for injuries suffered before the program went into effect. Instead general revenues of $315 million should be appropriated to set up a trust fund. Yet even with this provision, the Congressional Budget Office concluded that a per-dose tax on the DPT vaccine would have to be set at $8, which would nearly double the vaccine's price.[67] Because the program would not shut down tort filings, Lederle said it would not reduce its prices when the program went into effect.[68] Since the compensation program was aimed in part at keeping vaccine prices low, Waxman and other members of Congress balked at adding such a high surcharge. Waxman and his staff tried to find a way to keep the surtax on DPT under $5.[69]

Waxman decided to fundamentally restructure the compensation program. He split it into two parts, one for compensating for injuries suffered before the program went into effect, the other for new injuries. The preprogram injuries were to be compensated out of general tax revenues, with $80 million authorized for each of the program's first four years. Claimants would be compensated for future unreimbursed medical and custodial expenses but could recover only a total of $30,000 for attorney's fees, lost earnings, and pain-and-suffering combined. Claimants with preprogram injuries were still eligible to choose tort litigation instead, and the new manufacturer defenses in the legislation would not apply to them. Waxman set a ceiling of 3,500 on claims that could be paid for preprogram cases.

Postprogram claims were to be paid out of a surtax on vaccines. The tax was set at $4.56 for the DPT vaccine, $4.44 for the measles, mumps, and rubella vaccine, and 29 cents for the polio vaccine. The only cap on postprogram damages in the compensation system was a limitation of $250,000 on pain and suffering and $250,000 for the death of a child. "Reasonable" attorneys fees were to be provided, even when claimants lost. Postprogram claimants would be required to apply to the compensation program first and could commence tort litigation only after rejecting a final judgment. The program would temporarily shut down if it reached a ceiling of 150 total paid claims in any twelve-month period.

To meet objections about locating the program in the federal court system, Waxman found a new venue. The United States Claims Court, established in 1982, is a legislative-branch court created by Congress under the Constitution's Article I to handle claims against the federal government. Judges in Article I courts, unlike their colleagues in the more familiar Article III (judicial branch) courts, are not appointed for life. Further,

Article I courts are not bound by the Seventh Amendment to the Constitution, which guarantees the right to a jury in cases where more than $20 is in dispute. The move to the Claims Court was designed to address concerns about the constitutionality of lodging a quasi-administrative, quasi-judicial program in an Article III court. Claimants would apply to special masters in the Claims Court; the Department of Health and Human Services would act as respondent and contest claims it considered questionable.

With all these changes, Waxman was able to get his coalition of medical groups, manufacturers, and parents together, but the Reagan administration still opposed the plan. In a letter to Michigan Democrat John Dingell, the chair of the Energy and Commerce Committee, Health and Human Services Secretary Otis R. Bowen wrote that the administration believed the no-fault plan to be "so flawed that action should not be taken to activate the program."[70] But when the compensation funding became part of the massive 1988 budget reconciliation bill, the Reagan administration once again ended up signing on.

THE PROGRAM IN ACTION

The Vaccine Injury Compensation Program went into operation in October 1988. As of February 2002 the program had paid out more than $1.3 billion to 1,705 claimants.[71] To apply for compensation, a claimant sends a petition, complete with medical records, to the Claims Court. The Claims Court turns a copy of the file over to the Public Health Service, a division of the Department of Health and Human Services (HHS). Medical experts within the Health Service make a recommendation on whether to compensate. A group of lawyers within the Justice Department who specialize in vaccine cases read the report and decide whether to contest the petition.

Contested cases are heard by special masters, attorneys who work only on vaccine cases. Cases can be disposed of without a hearing, and when they are held the hearings usually last only a day or two.[72] Claimants are represented in the hearings by lawyers, who present cases with testimony and expert witnesses. The program pays the attorney's fees and other costs of all claimants, even those who are unsuccessful, though fees are limited to $30,000 for preprogram cases. If the claimant prevails, negotiations commence over the size of the award. Either the claimant or the Justice Department can appeal to a Claims Court judge; further appeal is to the U.S. Court of Appeals for the Federal Circuit. Of

4,409 cases adjudicated by June of 1997, only 52 (1.1 percent) had been appealed to the Circuit Court.[73]

If claimants can show they suffered an injury listed on the program's vaccine injury table, Justice Department lawyers have the burden of proving that something other than a vaccine caused the problem. If claimants have injuries that are not on the table, they must show by a preponderance of evidence that the injuries were caused, or significantly worsened, by a vaccine covered by the program.[74] Because the rules favor claimants with "on-table" injuries, cases often hinge on whether claimants actually suffered the symptoms listed in the table or on how the table should be interpreted.

By February 2002, 1,705 of the 5,453 claims adjudicated had been granted compensation. Preprogram claimants have been successful in 28 percent of cases; postprogram claimants have fared better, winning around 43 percent of claims.[75] The largest award was for $7.9 million; the average is $824,463.[76] A study of the program after a little more than a year of operation estimated transactions costs as only 9.2 percent of the total budget, an extraordinarily low level compared to traditional litigation.[77] But as in other replacement schemes, such as workers' compensation, over time the amount of lawyering and adversarialism in the compensation program has grown. A 1999 General Accounting Office report criticized the program for adjudicating claims slowly: only 14 percent of claims were decided within a year, 39 percent took between two and five years, and 18 percent dragged on over five years. The GAO report attributed the delays not only to a deluge of preprogram claims in the early 1990s but also to the growth in the staff of the Justice Department, which has allowed lawyers there to use more aggressive tactics in defending the fund.[78] Myriad complaints about the adversarialism of the vaccine compensation process have been aired both in Congress and the media.[79]

Underlying the contentiousness is a continuing debate about the safety of vaccines. The compensation act transformed the way disputes over vaccine injuries were processed, but it could not end the bitter struggle over the extent to which vaccine reactions cause childhood maladies. That battle rages in the vaccine program, where medical experts and HHS officials regularly square off against parents, their lawyers, and opposing medical researchers. HHS officials who review compensation claims simply reject many of the theories that link vaccines to injuries, according to program observer Derry Ridgway. In this they are backed up by medical researchers, who, for example, "disbelieve nearly all claims of serious pertussis vaccine-related injuries."[80] Just as the parents' group feared, health officials have been able to modify the compensation program to reflect their view of vaccine injuries. In 1995 and 1997 HHS, basing its decision partly on reports by the Institute of Medicine, used its powers under the compensation act to modify the vaccine injury table, removing three injuries listed in it and adding seven more. Two legal challenges to the table modifications, contending that they exceeded the agency's powers under the Constitution, were rejected by the Federal Circuit Court of Appeals.[81] The contents of the table are crucial because claimants have a much easier task in on-table cases: once a claimant shows that an injury is on the table, the burden of proof shifts to the Justice Department, which must demonstrate that the injury had some other cause. Claimants with on-table injuries prevailed in 35 percent of cases through 1999; those with off-table injuries won only 13 percent of the time.[82] HHS table modifications would seem to have had the net effect of worsening the chances of claimants, because one of the injuries removed from the table—residual seizure disorder—was the source of 40 percent of all compensated claims.[83] Indeed, it's not at all clear that the family of Julie Schwartz, the girl whose story began this chapter, could win a claim for compensation under the new rules. Yet the changes do not seem to have lowered the success rate of claimants. In fact, program statistics suggest a higher percentage of successful claims in recent years.[84]

Nonetheless, critics argue that the program no longer lives up to Congress's goal of settling claims "quickly, easily and with certainty and generosity."[85] The changes in the table have likely increased the contentiousness in the program, since claims for residual seizure disorder are now hard fought.[86] The legal fees provided to complainants by the program, critics say, are inadequate, making it difficult to find good lawyers.[87] Some argue that the program has become too miserly, drifting away from Congress's wish that claimants be given the benefit of the doubt. They note that though the vaccine surtax has been reduced to 75 cents per dose, the compensation trust fund has continued to build up, reaching $1.4 billion in 2000.[88] Legislation to address these issues has been introduced in Congress, and program officials continue efforts to streamline the compensation system. Despite all the criticisms made about the compensation program, however, it is hard to find anyone who argues that the traditional tort system would better handle the complex issues involved. Critics seek changes in the program, not repeal.

Manufacturers' fears that claimants would reject compensation awards and file a traditional tort lawsuit appear misplaced. Of 3,142 vaccine injury claims adjudicated through 1995, only 70 claimants have filed motions rejecting the judgment. Of 421 postprogram claimants, only 12 have rejected judgments. It is likely that fewer still have actually filed a lawsuit.[89] There are, though, indications that more litigation may be coming, fueled by concerns over the effects of thimerosal, a substance containing mercury that has been used as a preservative in vaccines.[90]

Nonetheless, the liability climate for the manufacturers appears to have been transformed by the compensation law. The number of lawsuits filed against makers of DPT, by far the largest category of vaccine litigation, has declined precipitously. (See Figure 4.1.) Thanks in part to this change in the liability climate, research and development of vaccines has exploded. The "whole cell" version of DPT has been replaced by the less troublesome acellular version, a change for which the parents group had long campaigned. Several new vaccines—for chicken pox, hepatitis B, HIB (a type of influenza), and rotavirus—have gone into wide use and are now covered by the program. The head of Merck's vaccine unit has called this the "best time" for vaccine research in decades, with vaccines being developed for more than twenty diseases, including such scourges as childhood ear infections, malaria, gastric ulcers, and AIDS. The vaccine law, according to one pharmaceutical company official, has "turned the industry around," encouraging biotech companies to enter what had been a dead-end field.[91]

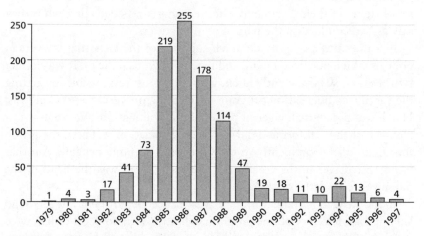

Figure 4.1. Lawsuits against DPT Vaccine Manufacturers, 1979–1997.
SOURCE: U.S. Department of Health and Human Services.

ANATOMY OF A SUCCESSFUL REPLACEMENT REFORM

The vaccine injury compensation bill is a rare instance in which Congress passed a replacement antilitigation reform. Though the replacement mechanism is quasi-judicial, it clearly differs significantly from traditional tort litigation. Individual vaccine makers are no longer on trial, negligence is no longer an issue, specialized decision makers preside rather than jurors, and payments are made from a government trust fund. Vaccine injury compensation has been moved from an adversarial legal model, where decision making rested in the hands of juries and judges across the nation interpreting vague, varied, and evolving rules, to something closer to the bureaucratic model, where centralized, specialized "special masters" apply a comparatively clear set of standards. Moreover, though the program has some unusual features, particularly the use of an Article I court, it socializes the risk of vaccine injuries in a manner typical of no-fault replacements. Thus this is an important case for understanding the politics of litigation in the United States. How do we account for the success of this antilitigation campaign?

Once again, some common explanations for the place of litigious policies in the United States find no support in the case. For instance, "rights talk"—a supposed cause of litigious policy making—was nowhere in evidence. There was little rights rhetoric and almost no discussion about impairing the "right to sue." Of course the Waxman bill did not eliminate the right to sue, but it did put significant obstacles in the way. The parents sought to preserve the tort option, but they did not use the rhetoric of rights in their argument. Their emphasis was deterring what they saw as bad conduct on the part of manufacturers.

Nor does this case provide much support for the view that lawyers in policy-making positions create and defend litigious policies. It was in fact two lawyers, Waxman and Hatch, who were most responsible for getting the vaccine compensation program enacted. Before he came to Congress, Hatch was a defense lawyer in personal injury litigation; Waxman was a member of the California Trial Lawyers Association (CTLA), the group that figured so prominently in the California no-fault struggle. Another important player in the creation of the vaccine bill was the head of the parents' group, Jeffrey Schwartz, also a lawyer.

In the Reagan administration, it was Justice Department lawyers who led opposition to the vaccine program, while those in nonlegal offices were divided in their views, with the director of Health and Human Services,

Otis Bowen, tepidly supportive. The strongest defense of the compensation act, however, was made by a lawyer, White House counsel Peter
Wallison. Moreover, the Justice Department, though opposing the vaccine
bill, proposed its own set of discouragement reforms, designed to limit the
rewards plaintiffs could receive in tort litigation. Even the Justice Department lawyers, then, were far from pure in their defense of litigation.

Because this bill passed unanimously or by voice at each step in Congress, there is no appropriate roll-call vote, either at the committee or the
floor level, that could be used to compare the position of lawyers and
nonlawyers. Thus the only support for the lawyer policy-maker theory in
this case is the differences within the Reagan administration between Justice and the other departments.

There is also little evidence that lawyer interest groups had much of a
role in this case. Indeed, with some minor exceptions, they stayed out
entirely. The Association of Trial Lawyers of America (ATLA), the plaintiff lawyer group, studied the vaccine bill to see if it might become a
precedent for other no-fault systems but decided that vaccine injuries
were a unique problem and the vaccine compensation program a unique
solution. Convinced that the bill would have only limited impact, the
group decided that it would defer to the judgment of the parents' group.
ATLA's political strategists reasoned that, if DPT signed on to a no-fault
proposal, there was no room for ATLA to oppose it. The plaintiff
lawyers would simply look as if they were trying to protect their fees and
opposing their clients in the process. So ATLA avoided taking a position.[92] ATLA may have been influenced by the Waxman's involvement in
the issue. Waxman was a devoted ally of ATLA and, as noted above, a
former member of CTLA. His dedication to the bill was another indication that ATLA had little to gain and much to lose by becoming involved
in the issue.

The American Bar Association became involved in only one aspect of
the vaccine litigation debate, the issue of where to locate decision making
in the no-fault program. The ABA urged that the program be moved to
the Claims Court, reasoning that it was a more appropriate venue for
such a quasi-judicial process. Other than this, the ABA never took a
stand on the wisdom of the Waxman bill.[93]

Finally, a small group of vaccine lawyers who called themselves
"Advocates for a Safe Vaccine" did testify at one hearing on vaccine
compensation issues. This seems, however, to have been the limit of the
group's activity on the Waxman bill. Advocates for a Safe Vaccine was

primarily concerned with publicizing the dangers of the DPT vaccine and was not involved in negotiating the bill.[94] Thus lawyer interest groups played almost no role in the outcome of this case.

The Constitutional Theory

The case presents a challenge to my main explanation for the distinctively litigious policy style of the United States, the Constitutional Theory. In this case, seemingly contrary to the theory, litigation was replaced by a quasi-bureaucratic system for compensating injuries. Yet on closer examination the story of vaccine compensation in many respects fits with the Constitutional Theory.

THE CONTROL INCENTIVE   The control incentive arises, remember, because of an activist's desire to gain power over the activities of states and localities. No group involved in the vaccine bill needed to do this to meet its objectives. While vaccinations are often administered by state and local agencies, the issue at hand was compensation for vaccine injuries, a matter on which none of the states except California has been active. The vaccine case differs in this respect from the story of the Americans with Disability Act (ADA). There, activists were seeking to make major changes in the operation of state and local government services. Here there was no such need and thus no corresponding incentive for activists to resist an antilitigation reform.

THE INSULATION INCENTIVE   As the Constitutional Theory predicts, many of the parties involved in the vaccine bill were wary of lodging decision making in a bureaucratic agency, and their wariness shaped the outcome, though it did not forestall a replacement reform. Medical groups and the manufacturers wanted a purely bureaucratic system, in which officials in Health and Human Services would decide claims, but the parents were unwilling to accept anything that placed final decision making in the hands of the HHS bureaucracy. As the Constitutional Theory suggests, they feared that the agency's implementation of the compensation program would be shaped by its political environment, particularly the medical establishment's influence. The parents valued the relative independence of the judiciary and so sought to preserve recourse to the courts. The Reagan administration and the manufacturers, meanwhile, worried that the program would be too generous, and so added a feature that made the program look more like traditional litigation. Citing constitutional concerns, they insisted that Justice Department lawyers represent the government in all disputed vaccine claims, thus moving the program further away from a bureaucratic model toward a hybrid of bureaucratic and adversarial legal models.

Because of the concerns of parents and the Reagan administration, the vaccine compensation program, for all its innovations, retains many features of traditional litigation. Decision making still takes place in a kind of court, with both sides represented by lawyers and a kind of judge (the special master) presiding. The Court of Federal Claims is less independent than Article III courts, because its judges are not lifetime appointees. All the same, the court is much more insulated from executive or congressional control than an agency. It is hard to imagine, for example, that the court could be pressured into changing its decisions by the threat of budget cuts, as has often happened with agencies.

Yet this level of insulation was still not enough for the parents. They feared that the program would become controlled by forces that did not share their view of vaccines, and so take a direction they disliked (a fear that subsequent events may have borne out). The parents insisted on retaining the ability to bring a traditional tort lawsuit in a regular court. The retention of a tort remedy, albeit in diminished form, was a crucial aspect of Waxman's compromise. Thus even in this case, the insulation incentive was at work.

THE COST-SHIFTING INCENTIVE   Litigious policies allow policy makers to do good things for constituents without paying for them. Replacing litigious policies with a government-administered fund, as in this case, means coming up with a budget for the fund. As this story of the vaccine program suggests, this is one of the most vexing aspects of government replacement reforms. Waxman struggled mightily to put together a budget for his program.

In replacing litigation with a social insurance fund, the government shoulders all the uncertainties previously borne by defendants. A social insurance fund is far more difficult to budget than most government programs because costs depend on the number of people who happen to file claims, a number difficult to project. Critics, especially the Reagan administration, warned that the vaccine program would be flooded by claims, much like its precursors, the black lung and swine flu programs. To meet these concerns, Waxman had to fundamentally reshape his program, dividing pre- and postprogram claims, funding them from separate sources, and severely limiting payouts. The preprogram limits were particularly stringent. Claimants were compensated only for future expenses, plus a maximum of $30,000 for attorney's fees, lost earnings, and pain and suffering combined. Waxman was able to find the money to fund the program, but the difficulties he encountered—and the stringent payout limits he imposed—suggest why policy makers would ordinarily be loath to replace litigation with an administrative system.

Causes of Success
Strong forces were necessary to drive all the actors in this case to pursue reform despite major obstacles. The crisis in vaccine supply provided the main stimulus. The fact that vaccine makers were leaving the market, together with the Center for Disease Control's recommendation to delay booster shots to avert a shortage, drove Representative Waxman and Senator Hawkins to get involved in the issue. Fear of vaccine shortages also helped to gain support for restructuring the tort system from medical groups and from the media. It is not at all obvious that there really was an actual shortage, but reports of a possible shortage created a crisis atmosphere.

A second factor in the successful antilitigation effort was the alliance of plaintiffs (represented by DPT) and defendants (represented by Merck and, at the end, Connaught), along with medical and public health groups, in support of the compensation bill. The alliance was partial in that one defendant, Lederle, opposed the bill, and another, Connaught, supported it only after it had passed the House. By contrast, the plaintiff side in this case was represented about as fully as one could imagine. Unlike the no-fault case, in which consumer and minority groups claimed to speak for the interests of plaintiffs, DPT was actually composed of (and led by) potential or actual plaintiffs. While some parents did defect when DPT endorsed the Waxman bill, DPT could credibly speak for the interests of plaintiffs as a group.

It is difficult to think of two more unlikely partners than parents of vaccine-injured children and vaccine manufacturing companies. Such an odd alliance, however, required particularly strong incentives on both sides and a skillful political entrepreneur like Henry Waxman to build it.

The vaccine program promised to solve the problems of each group in the alliance. For the parents the problem was compensation. For the doctors the problem was vaccine supply. For the manufacturers the problem was financial viability. All three groups could see these as issues of uncertainty created by the tort system. The uncertainty of the tort system was thus a consistent theme in the vaccine litigation debate and another factor in the antilitigation effort's success. On the parents' side uncertainty mattered because it meant that, while a few families collected large verdicts or settlements, many more got nothing at all. The outcome depended on such variables as the state in which the case was brought, the legal theories accepted by the court, the ability to locate the manufacturer of the vaccine, the manufacturer's willingness to settle, and the sentiment of the jury. A no-fault system promised much more reliable compensation.

On the manufacturer's side the uncertainty of outcomes in tort litigation was the key problem. High liability costs, while unpleasant, can be passed on to consumers. Uncertain costs are much worse. They mean that the manufacturer is constantly gambling on the future, particularly if insurance cannot be obtained. Since insurers thrive on predictability, the uncertainties of tort liability make them hesitant about staying in the market. Robert Johnson, the president of Lederle, identified unpredictability as the chief fault of the tort law system: "Under the present tort law remedy it is simply impossible to predict costs of the vaccine business, and a manufacturer is constantly faced with the possibility of court and jury awards which may wipe out the entire income of one or more years of vaccine sales. This is not only an unreasonable burden for a manufacturer, but must ultimately affect the nation's entire vaccine resource."[95]

Lederle's chief objection to the Waxman bill was that it did not go far enough in eliminating uncertainty, because it retained the tort option. Merck and Connaught, by contrast, were willing to settle for the Waxman bill, perhaps hoping that the vast majority of parents would choose the no-fault system, as it appears they have done.

The other groups involved in the vaccine bill—doctors, public health organizations, and officials—simply wanted to stabilize the vaccine supply. The proponents of the no-fault system were able to convince them that the Waxman bill would do this by minimizing the vaccine manufacturers' risks. Thus the problem of uncertainty played a major role in cementing the alliance for a replacement antilitigation reform.

Comparisons

The broader significance of the vaccine litigation debate can best be understood in a comparative context. In Japan and the European nations that have addressed the problem of vaccine injuries, the dominant solution has been a compensation system that lodges decision-making power in health and welfare agencies funded through general revenues. This pattern reflects these nations' more bureaucratized and socialized approach to public policy as compared to the United States. Faced with the issue of vaccine injuries, these nations extended their more highly developed social insurance systems to meet yet another need.[96]

In the United States such a bureaucratized and socialized solution was resisted. The parents fought to keep the program out of the health bureaucracies and to retain the ability to sue manufacturers in court. Waxman, confronted by concerns that the vaccine program would drain the treasury, found it necessary to fund the bulk of the program through a surtax on vaccines. These features of the compensation act suggest the extent to which participants continued to frame vaccine injuries as a responsibility of vaccine makers rather than as a social hazard for which everyone in society should be obligated to pay. As in the no-fault auto case, the move from an individualized definition of a problem to a socialized definition was contested.

And yet vaccine injuries seem a uniquely social problem. Vaccines eliminate disease only if everyone gets them. That is why states require parents to vaccinate their children. Children who are injured by vaccines are in a sense bearing the cost for the rest of society.

Most of those involved in the vaccine debate recognized that vaccine injuries are a unique case that demanded a special response. But even with these considerations in mind and even with the serious attention that vaccine supply problems created by tort litigation attracted, American policy makers chose an approach that retains many of the features of court-based compensation. A pure social insurance approach was rejected out of hand as overly bureaucratic and dangerously generous (or dangerously ungenerous!) to claimants. As with the development of the ADA, the vaccine injury case suggests that the American preference for litigation lies in a deeply rooted distrust of the bureaucratic welfare state. Once again, the antistatism of the American constitutional tradition deeply shaped the policy chosen.

CHAPTER 5

UNDERSTANDING THE LITIGATION DEBATE

When George H. Bush proclaimed in a 1992 presidential debate that Americans were "suing each other too much and caring for each other too little" he was echoing a common theme.[1] For many commentators, litigation signifies a rupture in the moral fabric of American society. Selfishness and greed, it is said, are eroding the norms of responsibility and caring on which healthy community life is based. Stories of litigiousness run amok, in this view, are parables about the decline of community values. When lawsuits are filed over playground squabbles among children, or injuries suffered in a weekend basketball game, or against ministers who offer pastoral counsel, something basic has gone wrong.[2] Litigation, according to this account, is a reflection of social decay.

The three case studies in this book tell a different story. They suggest that the prominence of litigation in American life results not from the litigiousness of individual Americans but from the structures created by American public policy. While litigation horror stories are often deployed to suggest that Americans are sue crazy, the evidence to support this view is scarce. There is, however, plenty of evidence for the proposition that American public policy is distinctively court centered. And this may help account for the perception of a litigation-crazed society. Litigious policies produce an atmosphere in which lawyers, legal rights, and the threat of litigation loom, even when Americans settle their differences without going to court, as they usually do.

The familiar morality tale about America's supposed litigation explosion is wrong on another count as well. As the case studies suggest, litigious policies are not some novel development but rather the consequence of fundamental and enduring aspects of American politics.

Litigious policies, according to this book's account, result from a collision of two forces: a demand for public action on social issues—in this book auto accidents, vaccine injuries, and the plight of people with disabilities—and a constitutional tradition premised on curbing this demand. Litigious policies offer activists a way around the obstacles to public action built into American politics.

The constitutional tradition creates three specific incentives for activists to pursue litigious policies. By lodging implementation in courts, activists can (1) insulate implementation of policy from political enemies (the insulation incentive), (2) do good things for constituents without spending governmental dollars (the cost-shifting incentive), and (3) gain power over the actions of states and localities (the control incentive). To succeed, attempts to restrict litigation must overcome these incentives. The cases illustrated each of the incentives at work. The next section draws on the cases to probe the mechanisms of the Constitutional Theory and suggest how future research into litigious policy making might proceed.

THE INSULATION INCENTIVE

In both the vaccine and disability cases, the major actors favored a role for the judiciary because they feared what an unchecked bureaucracy would do to their favored policies. Disability activists and parents of vaccine-injured children believed that agency enforcement of their favored policies could easily be derailed, through "capture" or simply inertia. They saw courts as a friendly forum. This calculation illustrates the way in which American constitutional structures reinforce a cultural suspicion of government bureaucracies: separation of powers makes American agencies particularly permeable and unstable, and the structure of the American judicial system makes courts a particularly attractive venue for activists.

In the case of the Americans with Disabilities Act (ADA), activists never even considered the possibility of implementing their goals without a judicial mechanism. There is no direct evidence on why this was so, but the background of the disability rights movement makes a strong circumstantial case that antibureaucratic impulses were involved. Previous experiences with bureaucratic administration of rights laws had disappointed disability activists. Moreover, many of these activists had a lifetime of bad experiences with bureaucracies, as clients of disability services and welfare programs. They saw the turn to disability rights as a turn away from a paternalistic, dependency-inducing therapeutic welfare state. In this belief they were joined by seemingly unlikely allies, Reagan and Bush administration officials. Whatever their disagreements, both sides could come together to support a rights-oriented, court-enforced approach to the problem of disability.

A similar pattern occurred in the vaccine case. Parents of vaccine-injured children continually voiced their distrust of medical groups, the Reagan administration, and the Health and Human Services Department. The parents were not convinced that a compensation system run by an agency would be administered fairly. They feared that, whatever the design of the program, unsympathetic medical groups would take it over and that the Reagan administration's management of the program would prove anything but generous. After much wrangling among the interest groups involved, the law that emerged lodges decision making in a court, albeit a streamlined, quasi-bureaucratic court, and retains the parents' ability to sue.

The cases suggest the significance of two constitutional structures that make the insulation incentive distinctively strong in the United States: separation of powers and judicial independence. As Terry Moe has argued, the strategy of insulation is both more necessary and more attractive in a system of separation of powers.[3] It is more necessary to policy designers because differences in policy goals between Congress and the president in such a system can make agency implementation especially problematic. Although the two sides may cooperate enough to enact legislation, each may rightly fear that the other will derail what it has sought to achieve by taking control over the agency. This fear is particularly strong, of course, in an era in which divided government, with the two parties splitting control of the branches, has become the norm. In both the vaccine and disability cases, conflict over implementation was sure to erupt. Without court-based implementation, control over the policy would pass to whichever side gained control over the agency, a thought bound to inspire fear in all those involved in the legislation.[4]

The insulation strategy is also more attractive in a separation-of-powers system because it is likely to be more effective. In a parliamentary system, a new government has little difficulty repealing the formal structures created by a previous government, so there is much less incentive to create such structures in the first place. With a single vote, all the work that goes into creating a detailed statute like the Vaccine Injury Compensation Act or the Americans with Disabilities Act can be undone. In a system of separation of powers, by contrast, legislating change is always difficult, so formal structures tend to endure. Thus activists in a separation-of-powers system have a greater incentive to build in provisions for judicial implementation because they know that future policy makers will have great difficulty removing them.[5] Though Congress has tinkered around the edges of both the disability and vaccine laws, it is highly unlikely that it would significantly restrict, much less eliminate, the provisions for judicial implementation built into both laws.

Another feature of the Constitution, the structure of the American judiciary, also strengthens the insulation incentive. The American judicial system has what Mirjan Damaska has labeled a coordinate structure, as opposed to the hierarchical arrangement of European legal systems.[6] In the legal systems of most advanced economies, judges are career civil servants who join the judiciary directly after law school and spend their careers rising up the ranks. These judges are socialized into legal systems in which there is a clear, unitary hierarchy, a chain of command. In the United States, by contrast, judges are appointed through a political process; most reach the bench at midcareer by coming to the attention of a politician, often through their political activities.[7] Moreover, in the American judicial system a horizontal organization of authority predominates. Judges from different circuits and districts often come to different conclusions on the same legal issues, and even judges within a district may differ. Adding to the independence of American courts is the use of juries staffed by "laypeople," whose presence is justified in part as a means by which to inject community values into the legal process. In the U.S. legal system, substantive justice is valued along with rule following, and decision makers disagree markedly in their notions of justice. The Supreme Court is nominally at the head of the federal judicial system, but it can review only a fraction of lower-court rulings and so cannot impose uniformity.

This structure makes American courts friendly forums for activists for several reasons.* First, the *decentralization* of courts means they are less subject than federal agencies to swings of political fortune. The composition of the federal judiciary gradually changes with each presidential administration, but the change is always far from complete—and far less immediate than the turnover in agencies. Parents of vaccine-injured children, and disability activists knew that whatever the views of future

---

*Many of the following characterizations, which describe aspects of the federal court system, also apply to many state court systems. The diversity of state judicial systems, however, makes some generalizations inapplicable. For example, in many states judges are elected or must win retention elections, making them more accountable and less independent than judges in the federal system. Nonetheless, many of the mechanisms that make the insulation strategy so attractive at the national level clearly operate as well at the state level.

administrations, there would always be some judges (or a jury) sympathetic to their claims. The decentralization of American courts makes them a reassuring venue for activists.

Because U.S. courts are decentralized, they are relatively *unaccountable* for their decisions, and this too makes them attractive to activists.[8] In a separation-of-powers system, an agency that makes a controversial decision is subject to both executive and congressional pressure—and budget cutbacks.[9] If the Equal Employment Opportunity Commission (EEOC), in enforcing the ADA, angers members of Congress or the administration, it can be punished for its transgressions. But there is little that can be done to a judge who makes a controversial decision, except perhaps impeachment, a rather unlikely threat. When, for example, the Supreme Court held that the ADA required the Professional Golfers' Association to provide disabled pro golfer Casey Martin a cart, there was little recourse for golfing traditionalists enraged by the decision.[10] The only way to overturn such a ruling, even for future cases, is to pass new legislation, an endeavor that can be quite difficult in a system of separation of powers.[11] Thus a decision enforced by courts is far more insulated from political opposition than one made by agencies. Further, court-based policies, even more than agency-based policies, weaken what Douglas North has called the "traceability chain." Voters unhappy with a particular court decision cannot easily trace responsibility for it back to choices made by legislators and thus are in a poor position to demand policy change.[12] As a result, when activists favor policies that will be costly to implement or otherwise controversial, they will be drawn to court-based enforcement.

American courts are also less *responsible* than agencies for policy outcomes, and this too can make them desirable for activists.[13] Because issues come to courts in piecemeal form, judges are less likely than agency officials to consider the impact of their decisions on a governmental program or policy arena. A judge's overriding impulse is his or her own sense of legality, not governmental effectiveness. Moreover, judges in different districts do not coordinate their decisions, so they are not provided an overall view of policy implementation. This presents both dangers and opportunities for activists. On occasion, it can make activists less inclined to lodge decision making in courts, because they fear the incoherence that may result. Congressional supporters of the food stamp program, for example, added to the law limits on judicial intervention because they feared expansionary rulings that would bankrupt the program.[14] But under other conditions, activists can take advantage of the fact that courts will take their demands much further than an agency would. For example, welfare rights activists in the 1970s successfully asked courts to expand eligibility for welfare programs beyond the boundaries set by welfare officials. Indeed, the activists tried to expand eligibility rapidly enough that the program would become overrun with claims, prompting radical change.[15] From an activist's perspective, the bureaucrat's narrow focus on implementing programs smoothly can be an impediment; the judge's independence from these concerns is a potential boon.

Finally and perhaps most importantly, the judicial system is *accessible,* always open to anyone who has the minimal resources necessary to file suit. With courts, activists need not worry, as they would with agencies, that a budget crunch or political opposition might at some point imperil implementation. The EEOC, one of the agencies charged with implementing the ADA, was backlogged with discrimination cases for years and today can fully investigate only a fraction of the claims that come to it. No surprise, then, that disability activists wanted the opportunity to bring their discrimination claims to court.

Thus the distinctive aspects of the structure of American government, particularly judicial independence and separation of powers, create a strong incentive for activists of all stripes to favor litigious policies. And this in turn helps to explain the distinctively litigious policy style of the United States.

That said, it is important to note that the insulation incentive is not ever-present. When activists see no danger that a bureaucratic agency will deviate from their wishes, they have no reason to favor court-based implementation. Indeed they may even seek to limit any role for courts, including judicial review of agency decisions.[16] This is the case wherever interest groups have formed a tight subgovernment of mutually reinforcing interests, an "iron triangle" or "policy monopoly" in the terminology of Frank Baumgartner and Bryan Jones.[17] Baumgartner and Jones point to some familiar examples of policy monopoly: the nuclear power industry for years dominated nuclear regulatory policy, agricultural interests dominated agricultural policy, and those who benefited from the building of dams dominated waterway policy, all with minimal input from "outsiders." The purpose of government policy in these areas was uncontested: promotion of industry through government support. Thus the coordinate, divided structure of American government had minimal effect in these realms; the affected interests created an island in which outside actors deferred to their expertise. When their favored policies are uncontroversial, activists need not worry about conflicts over implementation, so they needn't write detailed instructions for agencies or use courts to enforce these instructions. Hence many of the regulatory laws that arose out of the New Deal—those that governed transportation, communication, and natural resources, for example—involved minimal use of courts and broad agency discretion. Even today, courts play a comparatively small role in policy realms such as agriculture and defense.

The insulation incentive can grow or lessen in strength over time, depending on the vigor of policy monopolies. As Baumgartner and Jones demonstrate, policy monopolies are not static: they are born, they age, and they die. The nuclear energy policy monopoly was destroyed by environmentalists, who brought concerns about the dangers of the nuclear industry to public attention. Natural resources policy also has been transformed by the rise of environmentalism, which has inspired a much more critical attitude toward activities such as dam building. When a policy monopoly is eroding, new activists arrive on the scene, and these new activists will seek ways to bypass, or control, agencies "captured" by older, rival interests, often by creating new rights to sue. When the nuclear energy policy monopoly broke down, antinuclear groups sought to control the Atomic Energy Commission by contesting nuclear license applications in court.[18] Similarly, the National Environmental Protection Act, enacted in 1969, allowed environmental activists to challenge the waterway policy monopoly, by forcing would-be dam builders to defend the environmental impact of their projects in court.[19] What causes policy monopolies like that of the dam builders to erode, or to form in the first place, is far beyond the scope of this book. The significance of policy monopolies for this study is, however, clear: when policy monopolies fade, the insulation incentive is stimulated, and when policy monopolies are robust, this incentive does not operate.

The three cases in this book involved policy realms where no policy monopoly existed. In disability policy the old monopoly built around rehabilitation and welfare programs has eroded, and there are continuing conflicts among business, local government, and disability groups over what accommodations should be provided to disabled people. Auto insurance, similarly, is a highly controversial policy arena in which various interests—chiefly industry, lawyer, and consumer groups—collide. And while vaccine policy traditionally has been an uncontroversial area dominated by physician and public health groups, when the issue of vaccine injuries arose it clearly broke up their monopoly.

In the absence of policy monopolies, activists were wary of leaving implementation in the hands of government bureaucrats.[†] As these cases suggest, where there is no policy monopoly, activists fear that agency implementation will be derailed, and so they are attracted to litigious policies.

Thus the insulation incentive not only helps explain the distinctively litigious American policy style but might also help to explain variations in that style over time and across policy realms. Further research on the insulation incentive could measure these variations. If this aspect of the Constitutional Theory is valid, litigious policies will vary inversely with the strength of policy monopolies, withering when policy monopolies are robust, proliferating when and where they have broken down.[20]

THE COST-SHIFTING INCENTIVE

Litigious policies offer policy makers the tantalizing possibility of something for nothing—benefits for their constituents at little cost to them. Litigation is mainly funded by the parties who do the litigating, with only minor costs for the government. No wonder, then, that litigation-promoting policies multiply and attempts to replace litigation falter.

The Americans with Disabilities Act promised to protect the civil rights of disabled people, get them onto the job market, and generally bring them into the mainstream of American life—all at a relatively low cost to the federal government. Indeed, some proponents of the ADA argued that the law would *save* money for the federal government, because it would reduce welfare payments to disabled people. The Vaccine Injury Compensation Act reversed this equation. It was a clear fiscal loser—the government was taking on a new budgetary responsibility. Proponents of the vaccine act had the daunting task of devising a funding mechanism to compensate vaccine-injured children. Only under exceptional conditions—a looming vaccine shortage in this case—would one imagine policy makers voluntarily taking on this job.

In the no-fault auto insurance case, no policy maker did. As is typical of debates over the tort system, no one proposed that California's auto insurance crisis be resolved by an expansion of government, either in the form of health care reform or an accident insurance fund. This reflects a

---

[†]In the no-fault case, voters apparently feared putting implementation in the hands of *insurance company* bureaucrats: they feared insurers in much the same way that the Constitutional Theory posits that American activists fear government bureaucracies.

basic fact of tort politics: for all the discontent that surrounds it, tort law does have the great attraction for policy makers of being a method of compensating injury that does not drain the government treasury. Efforts to replace tort litigation with some governmental program run up directly against the cost-shifting incentive. That's why the replacement reforms that have been adopted in the United States generally employ private insurance—not governmentally funded programs—as an alternative to litigation.

The cost-shifting incentive is strengthened in the United States by a decentralized political structure and an antistatist constitutional tradition, both of which make revenue raising particularly difficult for American policy makers. Sven Steinmo, in his comparative study of taxation, emphasizes the structural side of this equation. The United States has a comparatively small welfare state, he argues, "not simply because of the prominence of individualistic values, but rather because of the tax policy biases inherent in the fragmentation of its political institutions."[21] Specifically, Steinmo concludes that the decentralization of political authority in the United States has stifled reformers in their efforts to broaden the tax base and required them to create a vast number of tax "expenditures," write-offs for particular constituencies. While Steinmo downgrades purely attitudinal explanations for the shape of the American state, the structures he emphasizes both reflect and reinforce a constitutional tradition built on antistatism. Americans are, according to some cross-national studies, more reluctant than citizens of other nations to make the government responsible for taking care of social needs and more fearful that the expansion of government will weaken their independence and undermine their liberties.[22] The mutually reinforcing combination of antistate attitudes and a decentralized political structure makes the cost-shifting incentive particularly robust in the United States.

That said, the cost-shifting incentive for litigious policies would seem to operate to some degree in all democracies. The prospect of pleasing constituents without spending budget dollars should be alluring to any elected politician. The appeal of litigious policies, though, is likely to vary across nations and over time. It should be strongest in nations like the United States that have the tightest budgetary constraints. In addition, it should be particularly strong in tough fiscal periods, when budgetary resources are scarce, so that policy makers need off-budget mechanisms to reach their goals. Further research on the cost-shifting incentive could employ historical and cross-national data to test these hypotheses.

THE CONTROL INCENTIVE

Litigious policies are in part a product of federalism, as the ADA case study suggests. Disability activists sought to control a myriad of state and local agencies yet did not want to rely on federal agencies to do this. By winning the right to contest local policies in court, disability activists gained power over thousands of local units of government. Moreover, they developed a means of control that dodges the political and legal difficulties that accompany federal agency actions against local governments.

Disability rights laws were modeled after civil rights laws, which were developed in large part to assert control over the racist policies of local governments. In both instances, federalism led activists who wanted to control local policy to do so through courts. This is a pattern repeated across policy realms. Many of the pioneering environmental statutes, for example, gave individuals the right to sue states and localities when they were responsible for pollution. The expansion of Fourth, Fifth, and Sixth Amendment litigation in the criminal process gave reformers the ability to gain power over the thousands of local units that make up the criminal justice system in the United States. Litigious policies create a route by which activists can triumph over federalist barriers.

Indeed, the proliferation of litigious policies aimed at state governments, along with other forms of "unfunded mandates," stimulated a backlash in the 1990s. In Congress this backlash resulted in the passage of the 1995 Unfunded Mandates Reform Act, which requires the Congressional Budget Office to estimate the costs to state and local governments of any legislation passed by a congressional committee. The unfunded mandates law also creates a point of order by which any member of Congress can object to provisions costing states and localities more than $50 million a year.[23] A more significant site of backlash, though, has been the federal courts, which in a string of cases have struck down litigious policies aimed at states. In *City of Boerne v. Flores,* the Supreme Court ruled that Congress had exceeded its powers when it gave individuals the right to sue states and localities under the Religious Freedom Restoration Act (RFRA).[24] Since *Boerne,* the Court has struck down lawsuits against states based on the False Claims Act, the Fair Labor Standards Act, and the Age Discrimination in Employment Act.[25] The Court's latest decision in this genre, *University of Alabama v. Garrett,* ruled that provisions in the Americans with Disabilities Act granting individuals the right to sue states for money damages were unconstitutional.[26] The Court's ruling in *Garrett* and the other cases after *Boerne* is limited in two respects. First, it covers only suits for money damages; citizens can still sue to enjoin discriminatory conduct or policies. Second, *Garrett* covers only the actions of states. It does not reach city, county, and other local units of government, even though these localities receive their power only through delegation from states. Whether the Court will extend the logic of *Garrett* further, to cover injunctive relief and suits against localities, remains to be seen. In any event, *Garrett* and its siblings represent a major counterattack against the use of litigious policies to gain power over the actions of states. The control strategy has thus become a target in the continuing battle between states and the federal government.

There are, however, many policy realms in which the control incentive does not operate. These are areas in which national activists need not gain power over local and state governments to achieve their goals. This was the situation in two of the cases in this book, vaccine compensation and no-fault auto insurance. No-fault was a state case, so the control incentive—governing relations between national-level activists and state and local governments—did not really apply. As for vaccine compensation, it was not an area in which states and localities presented a barrier.

Further research on the control incentive could test two of its implications. First, if the control incentive is an important cause of litigious policies, areas of joint responsibility between the national government and the states should be particularly litigious. The least litigious realms should be areas such as defense and foreign policy where the national government dominates.

Second, if the control incentive operates beyond the United States, federalist nations such as Canada and Germany should have more litigious policies than unitary nations such as France and New Zealand. Moreover, because the growth of international legal structures, such as the European Union, has created a kind of federalism in several regions, there should be a corresponding growth of litigious policies in these areas, as activists at the center attempt to use courts to gain power over the policies of member states. Indeed processes like this may help to account for what looks like, as one recent book has put it, "The Global Expansion of Judicial Power."[27] Thus this aspect of the Constitutional Theory may help explain the judicialization of public policy outside the United States.

ALTERNATIVE EXPLANATIONS FOR LITIGIOUS POLICIES

In each of this book's three case studies, we considered some alternative explanations for the growth and retention of litigious policies in American government. The cases provided a mixed verdict on these explanations.

Rights and American Individualism

The idea that Americans think of issues in terms of rights and thus resist attempts to limit litigation seems plausible on its face. But when this theory was applied to the cases in this book, its weaknesses became apparent. In two of the cases, no-fault auto insurance and vaccine injury compensation, rights talk played a surprisingly marginal role. The invocation of the "right to sue" or the "right to compensation for injury" was infrequent. Perhaps the right to sue has been discredited by all the publicity in the last twenty years about the purported litigation explosion. Certainly both these cases show that opponents of antilitigation reforms can rely on other, more promising arguments. In the ADA case, however, rights talk was central. The reformulation of disability as a civil rights issue was pivotal, mobilizing a wide range of interests behind the ADA and neutralizing most of the business groups that might have been expected to oppose it.

What made "rights" so powerful in one case and so marginal in the others? More broadly, why do some rights claims win acceptance in the United States, while others—rights to social assistance, for example—languish? These questions suggest the difficulty of thinking about rights discourse as a general cause of litigious policies. It may be more helpful to consider why particular forms of rights talk flourish while others fail to catch on. In the ADA case, the redefinition of disability as a rights issue served both the interests and ideology of disability activists. It gave disability activists the inspiring example of the civil rights movement to follow and a handy way to explain their struggle to potential allies, first civil rights leaders and Democrats, then conservative Republicans. Republicans who would have opposed other kinds of rights—rights to new social welfare programs for disabled people, for example—supported disability rights because they saw them as reinforcing the independence of disabled people. Rights talk, then, functioned effectively in the ADA case not because of some generalized power of "rights" but because of the particular features of disability rights.

The best studies of rights in American politics have helped us to understand not rights in general but the ways in which particular kinds of rights function in American political discourse. Michael McCann's *Rights at Work?* shows how the attempt to establish rights to "comparable worth" pay equity failed to gain general acceptance yet still provided benefits to its proponents.[28] Gerald Rosenberg's *Hollow Hope* suggests the conditions under which newly enunciated constitutional rights can effectively change society.[29]

Even Mary Ann Glendon's *Rights Talk,* a book whose title seems to promise an examination of all rights, is really an investigation into the prominence of one brand of rights, so-called "negative rights"—rights of freedom from outside interference.[30] Glendon attributes this prominence to the strength of liberal individualism in American political thought. Americans, she says, have been steeped in the Lockean notion that there's a sphere of autonomy that no one should be able to invade.[31] Thus it seems natural for them to think about matters like abortion or the regulation of guns in terms of rights, because each of these can easily be seen as an instance of interference with autonomy. Glendon's genealogy of rights talk is persuasive within its own sphere, but it doesn't apply very well to rights to social equality, which include disability rights. Equality rights have a different genealogy and a different rhetorical structure. Where negative rights protect citizens from government, rights to equality create a duty on the part of government to protect the individual from discrimination. In practice this means that federal agencies and courts can investigate the practices of private companies accused of discrimination and punish them if they are found guilty. "Keep off my property" or "it's my body" or "I can say what I wish" are a long way from "treat me equally by enforcing the law so as to provide me with the accommodations I need." Glendon's book shows how a certain brand of rights functions in American discourse, but contrary to her title, her analysis can't be applied to all forms of rights.

This is most obvious in the case of rights to social assistance. In fact there is a relative *dearth* of rights discourse in the United States when it comes to campaigns for universal health care or a minimum level of welfare benefits.[32] Ironically, in her own discussion of rights to social assistance, Glendon has ascribed the lack of rights talk in this area to the same factors that she believes promotes "negative rights talk."[33]

As this suggests, the appeal of rights talk varies tremendously with the type of rights invoked. Further study of the place of rights in American politics should focus on these variations and their causes. The cases in this book demonstrate at least that rights consciousness is not invariably a factor in the politics of litigation.

Indeed, much more consistently voiced than rights talk in the cases presented here is what might be called "punishment talk," an underrated aspect of American public policy discourse. Participants in each of the cases called for litigious policies because they considered it necessary to punish malefactors in order to achieve their goals. This desire for punitive sanctions is a characteristic that Steve Kelman, in his comparison of workplace safety regulation in Sweden and the United States, found typical of American regulators. Kelman argues that the American belief is rooted in the individualistic idea (which he traces to the English political theorists John Locke and Thomas Hobbes) that people will normally pursue their own interests without regard for the community's needs and that people are likely to have widely varying ideas about what is right. For those who share this vision, society is extremely limited in its ability to reshape norms informally and must instead rely on legal coercion to control behavior.[34] The desire for punishment is hard to miss in criminal justice politics, which has been dominated in recent years by "get tough" measures such as "three strikes" sentencing laws and a renewed emphasis on capital punishment. Research indicates that, among affluent democracies, the United States metes out some of the toughest punishments for nonviolent property and drug crimes, a policy that is at least partly responsible for the incarceration of nearly two million people in American jails and prisons as of 2001.[35]

The desire to punish individuals shaped all three of the cases. Thus the campaign consultant who successfully beat back Proposition 104 in California found that voters responded less to a rights argument than to a punishment argument—that bad drivers should pay the price for their mistakes. Similarly, parents of vaccine-injured children demanded—and received—the continued ability to punish vaccine manufacturers by suing them. And disability activists wanted the full panoply of remedies, including punitive damages, in order to enforce the dictates of the ADA. Litigation seemed in each of these cases a wonderful way of emphasizing the individual's responsibility for wrong.[‡] Replacements for litigation— no-fault auto insurance and the vaccine injury program—were resisted because they seemed to weaken the principle of individual responsibility.

Another consistent theme in each case, also related to American individualism, is a distrust of large institutions and the professionals who guide them. Ralph Nader was effective in his campaign against no-fault because he presented himself as the disinterested common person speaking

---

[‡]Though of course in some of these cases the "individual" was in fact a corporation.

against a powerful and distrusted interest, the insurance companies. Disability activists grew to distrust the bureaucrats and medical specialists designated to care for them, believing that these well-intentioned professionals were all part of a system that manipulated them. Parents of vaccine-injured children, naturally enough, distrusted the manufacturers of the vaccines, but their distrust also extended to medical groups and to the federal bureaucracies, particularly Health and Human Services. In each case individuals questioned the judgments of experts and the motives of those representing powerful interests. And in the vaccine and ADA cases, litigation seemed to offer a way for the powerless to challenge the powerful.[§] As Ralph Nader says, where else but in court can a lone person beat General Motors? The logic here is that the power differential between the haves and the have-nots is much narrower in court than in other venues. Whether true or not,[36] it is a powerful idea, one that antilitigation reformers often must overcome. Those who sought to curb litigation found themselves hard-pressed to defend approaches to solving social problems that relied on bureaucratic institutions, either private or public. Litigation was considered attractive because it seemed to offer people a more individualistic, more responsive mechanism for achieving social justice. Thus rights talk, and a concern for the vindication of rights, was one source of the appeal of litigious policies, but it was not by any means the dominant one.

Lawyer Interest Groups

This study provides a mixed verdict on the role of lawyer interest groups in sustaining litigious policies. In the one case in which lawyer interest groups were highly mobilized, no-fault auto insurance, the antilitigation effort failed. In the two cases in which lawyer interest groups were generally uninvolved, however, the outcomes were mixed. Taken together, the cases suggest that lawyer interest groups can in some instances be very influential but that the scope of their influence is limited.

Several other tentative conclusions can be drawn from this study about lawyer groups. First, levels of mobilization among lawyer groups vary enormously. In the no-fault auto insurance debate in California, plaintiff lawyers were far more mobilized and active in litigation politics than all the other parts of the bar combined. The bar association played

---

[§]The no-fault case concerns the ability of accident victims to sue bumbling drivers, but since the drivers are usually represented by their insurance companies, this is an ambiguous example.

little or no role, and other lawyer organizations were relatively unmobilized. This appears to be the pattern in many replacement and discouragement antilitigation efforts, though more extensive research is needed.[37] In the arena of management efforts—alternative dispute resolution, for example—there appears to be much more broad participation in policy making, with the heterogenous bar associations at the forefront. But the strong incentives in replacement and discouragement struggles mean that plaintiff groups are likely to be much more aggressive in mobilizing their members and developing ties to legislators than are bar associations.

The connections between plaintiff groups and the Democratic party have gone relatively unexplored in the academic literature, which concentrates on the politics of the bar associations.[38] That might have been an appropriate choice thirty years ago, when the bar associations were nearly the only lawyer interest groups. But in the legal world, as in the rest of the world, interest groups have since multiplied and diversified. Much more attention should be paid in general to the full range of lawyer interest groups and in particular to the Association of Trial Lawyers of America (ATLA) and its state affiliates.

A second finding from the cases is that lawyers are more aggressive in protecting what they have than in seeking new opportunities. Thus lawyer groups are more likely to be active in replacement efforts like no-fault, where they fight to protect old forms of litigation, than in resistance cases like the ADA, where new forms of litigation are being created. ATLA's policy for many years of serving only as legislative goaltender rather than goal scorer underlines this pattern.

Third, the power of plaintiff lawyer groups stems in part from the fact that plaintiffs themselves usually are not well organized. In the vaccine case, where plaintiffs had formed a very active group, ATLA found itself on the sidelines. While ATLA's passivity was partly attributable to specific aspects of the case—the relative infrequency of vaccine litigation and Representative Henry Waxman's background as a supporter of plaintiff lawyers—the group was also deterred by the unseemly prospect of differing publicly with the people it was supposedly dedicated to helping, parents of vaccine-injured children. Plaintiff lawyers gain much of their legitimacy in politics by claiming to speak for the victims, but if plaintiffs have a separate organization, they can speak for themselves. This facilitates cooperation between plaintiffs and defendants, thus allowing the two sides to cut out the lawyers, a major premise behind replacement efforts. The most significant of all replacement reforms, workers' compensation laws, were made possible in part because the plaintiffs in workplace litigation, workers, were represented by labor unions. The unions and business groups could align themselves in a classic plaintiff-defendant alliance.[39] Where plaintiffs are represented only loosely, by consumer groups, such alliances are far less likely. Moreover, as long as Ralph Nader is an important part of the consumer movement, we can expect that at least some consumer groups will stick with the plaintiff lawyers in any replacement or discouragement struggle, Nader's break with ATLA notwithstanding.

The main finding here is that, where they are mobilized, plaintiff lawyer interest groups provide a significant barrier to replacement reforms. Plaintiff lawyer groups, though, mobilize in a limited number of policy domains. The influence of lawyer groups in issue areas besides tort and technical matters such as civil procedure seems limited.

Lawyer Policy Makers

With one exception, no major differences could be found between lawyer and nonlawyer policy makers in their approach to attacks on litigious public policies. The exception was the no-fault auto case, in which the lawyer legislators also happened to be Democrats. In that instance there was no way to tell whether the lawyers acted as they did because of their profession or their party.

Unfortunately the measures used in this study to test the impact of lawyer policy makers were fairly crude. In the jargon of methodologists, the tests lacked "power." For the most part, judgments were made based on impressionistic study of the cases, a method prone to measurement error. In two instances roll-call studies were employed, but in one of those cases, no-fault, the results were inconclusive.

To gauge the impact of lawyer policy makers more precisely, it is necessary to analyze voting on a wider range of issues. To do this, I analyzed House roll-call votes on litigious policies in the 104th Congress in 1995–96. This Congress, the first controlled by Republicans in forty years, had an unusual number of votes on litigious policies. Newt Gingrich's "Contract With America" had promised a package of tort reform measures designed to reduce litigation and a set of proposals to reduce opportunities for appeal in the criminal justice system.[40] Mostly, then, these were classic discouragement policies, designed to limit or even eliminate various forms of litigation. But the ascendant House Republicans had also promised to *create* new forms of litigation, most importantly a right for property owners to sue to recover losses suffered because of environmental regulations.

I analyzed House votes in which a litigious policy was the main matter
of dispute and in which at least twenty members of a party voted against
the party majority.[41] (I excluded party-line votes because I was interested
in variation between lawyers and nonlawyers *within* parties.) I cumu-
lated twenty such votes into an index of propensity to support litigious
policies. The votes covered policy realms such as death penalty appeals,
Clean Water Act enforcement, and racial discrimination lawsuits, as well
as tort litigation involving faulty products, stock market fraud, and medical malpractice.

Even with pure party-line votes excluded, party affiliation had an
enormous impact on voting. Democrats voted for the prolitigation side
on an average of 67 percent of the votes, Republicans 17 percent. Of the
twenty votes that were analyzed, in only two did a majority of Republicans take the prolitigation side. Those two votes involved the creation of
a new property rights law and a new right to sue regulatory agencies. On
the other votes, the litigious policy under review served Democratic
objectives and so received the vast majority of Democratic votes. Litigious policies, then, were supported or opposed based mainly on the ends
they served, and the battle over them in the 104th Congress was overwhelmingly a partisan struggle.

It was also an ideological struggle, in which liberals typically favored
litigious policies and conservatives opposed them. In order to see how
conservatives and liberals compared in their propensity to favor litigious
policies, I used a summary measure of a representative's voting record
that places it on an ideological scale relative to the voting pattern of his
or her colleagues.[42] The 20 percent of members with the most liberal voting records favored litigious policies 82 percent of the time; the 20 percent of House members with the most conservative records averaged
only 15 percent support.

In this context, being a lawyer had a comparatively small, though sta-
tistically significant, impact on a House member's support for litigious
policies. In a regression equation that takes into account party, voting
record, and characteristics of each House member's constituents, lawyers
average roughly 4 percent more support for litigious policies than their
comparable nonlawyer colleagues.[43] These results suggest limited support
for the lawyer–policy maker theory. The votes were mainly along ideological and party lines, but lawyers were slightly more likely than nonlawyers
from the same party and with otherwise similar voting records to favor
litigious policies. Attending law school and practicing law, it seems,
makes legislators more supportive of litigation as a problem-solving

mechanism. The magnitude of this effect, however, appears too small to be a primary explanation for the distinctively litigious shape of American public policy. The regression equation, for example, suggests that, even if the lawyers in Congress had instead chosen other occupations, none of the outcomes of the twenty votes analyzed would have changed.

Of course, voting is only one measure—and since dichotomous, a fairly crude one—of a legislator's position. For this reason, roll-call studies may understate the effect of lawyers on the policy-making process. We might instead seek to measure the level of other kinds of legislative prolitigation activity. For example, we might examine who offers or negotiates amendments or who attends and speaks in committee meetings, as Richard Hall and Frank Wayman have done in other contexts.[44] Further, we might extend our scrutiny beyond legislators to include members of policy communities, whether inside or outside of government. The case of the ADA shows how such communities can, by defining a problem in a particular way, nearly predetermine the outcome of a legislative battle. My impressionistic conclusion is that in this case the litigious mechanisms of the ADA were not the result of lawyer influence. Moreover, in the no-fault and vaccine cases, it was law professors and lawyers who first developed the antilitigation reform. But conclusions like this would be much stronger if we found a more systematic way to study the impact of lawyers in policy communities. Thus while this study, in line with the literature on lawyer legislators, casts doubt on the notion that lawyers are a major contributor to the distinctively litigious policy style of American government, the impact of lawyer policy makers is a topic that merits further study.[45]

EXPLAINING ANTILITIGATION SUCCESSES

A major goal of this book is to understand why antilitigation efforts, despite the obstacles arrayed against them, sometimes succeed, and the factors that contribute to this success. Three themes stand out from the cases: the centrality of plaintiff-defendant alliances, the stimulus of a crisis in production, and the significance of unpredictability as a rallying point for antilitigation reformers. My analysis of these themes suggests how they might apply to other types of antilitigation efforts. Remember that the cases in this book were drawn from just two of the categories of antilitigation efforts, resistance and replacement. We may, however, be able to gain some insight from the cases into the other two categories, management and discouragement. (See Table 1.1, page 28.)

Plaintiff-Defendant Alliances

The development of an alliance between groups representing plaintiffs and those representing defendants is a crucial factor in replacement efforts. The vaccine case included a fairly inclusive alliance, with a parents' group representing plaintiffs and two of four vaccine manufacturers in support of the replacement reform. In the no-fault case, the alliance was somewhat less strong because the consumer and minority groups who supported the reform only symbolically represented plaintiffs and the Naderite wing of the consumer movement actively criticized the alliance. In the ADA case, there was no plaintiff-defendant alliance and no success in the antilitigation effort.

Thus plaintiff-defendant alliances seem a necessary though insufficient prerequisite for success. Further, the prospects for success increase as the alliance becomes more inclusive: the greater the participation in the alliance by actual litigants, the less likely that some other plaintiff or defendant group, or a lawyer interest group, will effectively oppose the replacement scheme. We can measure inclusiveness by the proportion of those engaged in ongoing litigation who are parties to the alliance.

The example of the proposed national tobacco bill fits this line of analysis. The objective of the bill was to settle all the major lawsuits against the tobacco industry. Though in many respects this bill was more a lawsuit settlement than a replacement reform, the politics it created had many of the features associated with replacement schemes. As in the no-fault and vaccine cases, the bill came about because of a plaintiff-defendant alliance: antitobacco groups worked out the plan through negotiations with tobacco companies. For the companies, the settlement was astoundingly expensive: $368.5 billion to be paid out over twenty-five years, along with many other concessions to smoking foes. But the settlement was well worth the price to tobacco makers because, like the manufacturers in the vaccine case, they would gain certainty over their liabilities. Class action lawsuits and punitive damage awards would be banned; smokers would be encouraged to apply to an industry fund for compensation instead of bringing suits.[46] For the antitobacco groups, the compromise also brought the benefit of certainty. Few plaintiffs had prevailed in tobacco litigation, and no one knew whether a future bonanza was in the offing. But the plaintiff-defendant alliance was far from inclusive; many antitobacco groups refused to endorse the plan. In Congress, they denounced the plan as a sell-out and urged strengthening its provisions. When the plan's congressional backers acceded to these demands, they lost the support of the tobacco companies and their allies in the

Republican party, which doomed the legislation.[47] As in the no-fault case, the lack of an organization that could credibly speak for all plaintiffs, together with the inability of proponents of the original settlement to bring all groups associated with plaintiffs together, killed the measure. (The state attorneys general who settled their lawsuits with tobacco manufacturers had a much easier time of it, since the plaintiffs in those cases were comparably few in number.)

A similar pattern can be seen in the recurring efforts to settle hundreds of thousands of lawsuits against asbestos manufacturers and their insurers. Some of these have involved proposals to enact a legislative replacement reform. A host of asbestos bills were introduced into Congress in 1997, after the Supreme Court struck down a settlement of asbestos lawsuits. One bill would have established an Asbestos Resolution Corporation to fund claims and an administrative panel, staffed by doctors, to settle them. This replacement scheme was endorsed by a bipartisan group in Congress but was attacked by groups associated with plaintiffs, in particular unions, Naderite consumer groups, and plaintiff lawyers.[48] As in the no-fault and tobacco cases, asbestos reformers have so far failed to build a fully inclusive plaintiff alliance and so have been unable to advance a replacement scheme.

The conditions under which inclusive alliances form remains an open question. Alliances may be easier to construct when litigation causes a crisis in the production of some good or service, as discussed in the next section. Another key variable, though, seems to be the degree to which plaintiffs and defendants are already organized into groups. Plaintiff organizations such as the parents' group (DPT) in the vaccine case or labor unions in the effort to enact workers' compensation laws greatly facilitate cooperation. In cases such as no-fault auto or tobacco there is no group that can claim to speak for all plaintiffs, making it impossible for replacement proponents to form a truly inclusive alliance. Limited plaintiff organization may help explain why in many cases replacement reforms, or even class action settlements, have failed to be adopted.

The case of the September 11th Victim Compensation Fund appears to complicate this analysis, since that replacement reform was enacted so rapidly that potential plaintiffs never had the chance to organize. It seems no stretch, however, to conclude that the *latent* political power of the victims shaped the outcome. Congress, heavily lobbied by the airline industry, first considered a plan that would have simply limited the liability of the airlines involved in the incident, but Democrats, joined by their consumer and plaintiff lawyer allies, insisted on a compensation fund for victims as a trade-off, the classic pattern of replacement politics.[49] It is easy to imagine what would have happened if Republicans had rejected this deal—or if plaintiff lawyers had gone out on their own to oppose the compensation fund in favor of traditional tort law, as they often do in replacement politics. The September 11 victims are a relatively well defined group, unlike, say, smokers or those injured in auto accidents. It would be comparatively easy for them to organize effectively—and rather painful, one suspects, for any politician or interest group to oppose their pleas for compensation, given the great public sympathy for September 11 victims. Politicians and interest group leaders have good imaginations on matters like this, so it is not hard to believe that, in deciding what to do about September 11 liability, they considered the consequences of opposing victims. Thus while technically the September 11 fund was not backed by a fully inclusive plaintiff-defendant alliance, the only group missing, the victims themselves, likely had great influence over the outcome.

In summary, the creation of plaintiff-defendant alliances seems an important theme in replacement efforts. Moving beyond the replacement category to other types of antilitigation reforms, we can speculate that in management efforts plaintiff-defendant alliances are likely to be crucial as well. The entire basis of management schemes, after all, is to smooth conflict between the parties by changing the ways in which disputes are handled. By contrast, plaintiff-defendant alliances cannot occur in discouragement cases, since by definition this category involves an attempt by defendants to restrict the opportunities of plaintiffs.

Production Crises

The pronouncement of a crisis in production of some good or service seems an important theme in each of the cases. In the vaccine case, there clearly was a crisis in production, with rising product costs and at least the threat (and perhaps the actuality) of a shortage. In the ADA case, opponents could warn of an eventual crisis but obviously could not proclaim an immediate one. In the no-fault case, it is not nearly as easy to judge whether there was a crisis. If we consider auto insurance as a commodity that can be analogized to vaccines, then the price of the good was rising, but there was no immediate threat of a shortage—producers were not leaving the market in droves. Of course, in a market economy the price of some goods and services will always be rising rapidly. We may want to reserve the term *crisis* for instances where policy makers perceive that a product may soon disappear from the market. If we restrict the term in this way, then the vaccine case is both the only case in which there was a crisis in production and the only one in which the antilitigation effort was successful. Crises as severe as the one in the vaccine case may be uncommon, but the pattern here suggests that where they occur, replacement efforts are more likely to be successful.

If we create a lower standard of "crisis" and define it as a rapid rise in price that is perceived as being due to litigation costs—a definition that includes the no-fault case—another conclusion suggests itself. Crises of this type may simply create the possibility, not a guarantee, of success for antilitigation efforts. As in the no-fault case, policy makers can respond to such crises in a variety of ways, only one of which involves replacement reforms. Thus a price crisis would be of much less benefit than a shortage crisis to antilitigation reformers.

This might help explain the failure of reform in areas such as tobacco, asbestos, and breast implants. Litigation in these areas has threatened, and even destroyed, the financial viability of whole industries, but it has not really created either a price or shortage crisis. Asbestos is no longer sold, and breast implants are made out of a variety of materials. No matter how bad cigarette litigation gets for the tobacco companies, no shortage of tobacco is likely to result, and price increases are not likely to provide a rallying point for reform. Litigious policies seem most likely to be effectively attacked when they cause breakdowns in products, services, or institutions deemed important to society.

Here again, the example of the September 11th Victim Compensation Fund fits the pattern. The fund was created during a major crisis in the airline industry: the airlines claimed that without liability relief, they would cease operating within a week. Indeed, the compensation fund was enacted into law as part of a larger measure bailing out the airline industry, the Air Transportation Safety and System Stabilization Act. The immediacy of the airline crisis drove legislators to devise the compensation fund in record time, just eleven days after the attack.

For either version of the crisis hypothesis we would expect the findings here to apply not only to replacement politics generally but also to discouragement efforts, which are an even more direct response to the claim that expanding litigation is causing chaos. In fact the first two waves of discouragement tort reform coincided with two waves of insurance cost increases, first for malpractice insurance in the 1970s, then for general liability policies in the 1980s. Crisis seems to be a major theme at least in battles over tort litigation.

Uncertainty

The unpredictability created by litigation was a rallying point for anti-litigation efforts in all three of the cases. In the vaccine case, it was the central problem for both manufacturers and parents, defendants and plaintiffs. Creating stability for the manufacturers and reliable compensation to parents was the main goal of the Waxman bill. Uncertainty was also the main complaint of business opponents of the ADA. They were, however, in the unenviable position of making predictions about the future rather than verifiable statements about the past. In the no-fault case the proponents of Prop. 104 tried to develop the uncertainty theme, but it ended up getting lost in all the discussion about car insurance rates.

Thus we can conclude that replacement and resistance antilitigation reforms are more likely to be successful where policy makers see uncertainty as a major problem. Uncertainty may also be a factor in some discouragement reforms, particularly caps on damages, since these also can be promoted as reducing variability in awards.

Uncertainty seemed to be a much more significant stimulus to antilitigation efforts than another frequently voiced concern, transaction costs. While transaction costs are usually of great concern to public policy experts who study litigation, it may be difficult to make them the fulcrum of antilitigation efforts. Plaintiffs and defendants worry most about total costs, not transaction costs. A replacement reform like the vaccine program may create losses for either side that swamp transaction losses. Moreover, it is hard to measure transaction costs and even harder to prove in advance that a replacement reform will lower them. Transaction costs of around 50 percent are common in studies of tort litigation, an astonishing figure.[50] Many replacement reforms are designed specifically to lower these costs, and some of those that have been adopted (like the vaccine law) have proven to do so. Yet transaction costs have not provided a rallying point for antilitigation reformers.

WHAT'S WRONG WITH THE LITIGATION DEBATE

What do the findings of this study have to say for those involved in the litigation debate? There may be strategic insights for those engaged in antilitigation struggles. The study may help antilitigation reformers choose their battles more carefully and promote their policies more effectively. It may, conversely, help defenders of litigation understand where they are most vulnerable. But helping the various interests conduct their struggles more wisely was not the goal of this book. Instead I want to draw on the findings to suggest how we might be able to improve the quality of the litigation debate.

Sociolegal scholars routinely decry the civil litigation debate because it relies so much on horror stories and poor data. Thus Marc Galanter criticizes the "debased debate" on civil litigation, and Stephen Daniels and Joanne Martin condemn the "tactical use of passion" in public relations campaigns by tort reform interests.[51] A typical position of sociolegal researchers is that we don't really know much about the civil litigation system or the impact of particular reforms, but we do at least know that claims made by antilitigation reformers about the need for their proposals are highly exaggerated.[52]

These commentators' criticisms of the litigation debate are undeniably accurate. Popular discourse and legislative debate about civil litigation frequently bog down in unrepresentative and even fictional horror stories. The statistics that have been most widely quoted—for example, that the United States has 70 percent of the world's lawyers or that tort litigation costs $300 billion a year—are often misleading, of questionable validity, or just plain made up. Moreover the debate generally focuses on tort litigation, which in fact is only a small slice of all legal conflict.

Sociolegal scholars have made a real contribution to raising the level of the litigation debate by helping to develop our knowledge of the civil litigation system. Nonetheless, their reaction to the litigation debate seems somewhat innocent. Anyone familiar with the struggle over regulation in American politics will find much that is familiar in the litigation debate. It is common in politics that good data are lacking, that discussion centers on dramatic anecdotes and questionable statistics, and that powerful interests are able to frame issues in dubious ways. Moreover, as this book's introduction suggests, claims of a litigation explosion, while exaggerated, do reflect an underlying reality that few sociolegal scholars would deny: Americans use litigation to resolve a wider range of social issues than they did in the past and than citizens of other nations do today.

The problem with the litigation debate, I believe, is far more fundamental than sloppy use of data or the calculated manipulation of anecdotes. Missing from the debate is an understanding of the role of litigation in American policy making generally. In their arguments about whether the United States has too many (or too few) lawsuits, participants in the litigation debate often ignore the larger connections between litigation and American public policy. But as the cases presented here suggest, American attitudes toward alternative methods of resolving social problems—particularly distrust of bureaucratic regulation and the

welfare state—shape the litigation debate in profound and often unex-
amined ways.

Litigation and Its Alternatives

Let me illustrate the connection between litigation and public policy with
a story from my own family history. My grandmother, who grew up in
rural Kansas in the early 1920s, spent the first decade of her adult life
employed as a maid. Frugal and hardworking, she was able to put away
some money in a bank account. But when the Depression hit, the bank in
which she had deposited her money failed, wiping out her life savings.

In theory my grandmother could have sued the bank and perhaps its
officers to recover her money. Of course such a lawsuit probably would
have been useless, since the bank was an "empty pocket," like many
financial institutions in the Depression. But even if litigation would have
offered potential rewards, I am confident that my grandmother would
have resisted going to court. Steeped in western Kansas individualism,
my grandmother was bound, in the lexicon of sociolegal scholars, to
"lump it."[53] Like many during the Depression, she accepted a devastat-
ing loss as a fact of life. Fortunately the bonds of community and family
sheltered her from the worst consequences of this loss. If the bank's failure had left my grandmother destitute, she could have turned to her family, who doubtless would have taken her in.

What would my grandmother do today, in a much less self-reliant,
more litigious climate? Would she sue? Thanks to the savings-and-loan
debacle of the 1980s, we have an answer to this question. When the
S&Ls collapsed, thousands of grandmothers just like mine lost their life
savings. Yet there was no civil "litigation explosion," though there were
many criminal cases filed against those involved in the S&L industry.
Instead of suing, the grandmothers, and everyone else, waited for the
government to pay them back for their losses.

The bailout of the S&Ls was hardly an unmixed good. The enormous
bill for the bailout was passed on to taxpayers and helped to further swell
the budget deficit. Some say that the scheme of insuring deposits helped
create the S&L mess by encouraging consumers to deposit their money
recklessly in shaky financial institutions. Yet it is social insurance
schemes of this kind that have made debt collection litigation propor-
tionally less common today than it was in the early twentieth century. In
this area, at least, there has been a kind of litigation implosion.[54]

As the example of debt collection suggests, demands for justice—or at
least compensation for injury—can be satisfied in many ways, only one

of which is litigation. Lawrence Friedman has written of a seemingly inexorable march among all economically advanced nations toward "total justice," which he defines as the expectation of fair treatment and recompense for injury. As society becomes more prosperous and technologically proficient, Friedman argues, people come to expect to be treated fairly and to have the bumpy stretches of their lives straightened out by the government.[55] It becomes unacceptable to say that, when a child becomes severely brain injured because of a reaction to a vaccine, that's just a family's tough luck, or that people who have a disability should accept a lesser position in society, or that Grandmother can be taken in by her family when the bank loses all her money—or that the victims of a terrorist attack should bear the cost of their injuries entirely on their own. If a society can make life more fair and just, the sentiment grows, it should.

Friedman portrays total justice as a phenomenon common to all economically advanced countries. But as Robert Kagan points out, the *mechanisms* of total justice vary from nation to nation.[56] In western Europe demands by activists are mainly satisfied through the welfare-regulatory state. The United States has a large welfare-regulatory state as well, but it leans more heavily than other advanced economies on courts and litigation. These mechanisms—the welfare regulatory state on one hand, courts and litigation on the other—reflect alternative models of social decision making. The welfare-regulatory state is organized on the model of bureaucratic rationality, in which apolitical civil servants make decisions on the basis of rules and procedures handed down by a higher authority. Courts and litigation in the United States, by contrast, are organized according to the model of adversarial legalism. In adversarial legalism, social issues are organized as disputes between parties. The parties have the burden of invoking (and enforcing) the rules, the decision makers (judges and juries) are not tightly bound to a higher authority, and the rules themselves are constantly in dispute and evolving.[57]

Adversarial legalism and bureaucratic rationality are just two of several models that nations use for social decision making. Jerry Mashaw and Robert Kagan have described several alternative decision-making models. Mashaw's "Professional Treatment" model, for example, relies on the knowledge of trained experts to make decisions based on professional standards. In the Social Security Disability program, which Mashaw examined closely, such a process grants to physicians the power to decide whether someone is disabled (and thus eligible for benefits) or nondisabled.[58] Kagan's "Expert/Political Judgment" model combines professional knowledge about social problems with political judgment about what is considered acceptable to contending interests. Kagan gives as his example of this model the process by which government ministries in several European nations have developed occupational health and safety standards: through closed-door consensus-building discussions with business leaders, labor officials, and scientists.

Another model of decision making, which Kagan labels "Negotiation-Mediation," might instead simply be called "politics." As an example of this category Kagan mentions "bargaining among legislators representing contending interests."[59] This category fits precisely Aristotle's classical definition of politics as a process where equals who are both interdependent and in conflict deliberate together to choose outcomes through a combination of bargaining and persuasion.[60] Thus to bureaucratic rationality and adversarial legalism, we must add to the list of decision-making mechanisms such devices as professional treatment, expert judgment, and politics. As the drive for total justice marches on, government takes on a greater share of life's problems, and an increasing number of decisions must be made by institutions using one of these models.** Adversarial legalism competes with each of the other modes of social decision making for the expanded set of decisions. This competition underlies much of the litigation debate.

**This view, that government is destined to take on more and more social decisions as part of the drive for total justice, might well be rejected by proponents of markets. Markets are often held up as an alternative to government. But this is usually a false dichotomy. The structure of markets, and any market-based incentive, must, after all, be designed through some decision process, and this leads us back to the models Kagan and Mashaw have outlined. As Steven K. Vogel reminds us, competitive markets require rules (Vogel, *Freer Markets, More Rules* [Ithaca, N.Y.: Cornell University Press, 1996]). Similarly, private insurance, another market-based mechanism, also requires outside regulation. When, for example, there is a dispute between insurer and insured, some third party must arbitrate between them.

Markets can also be just another way of saying "lump it." Consider, for instance, how an advocate of markets might analyze the story of my grandmother. From a market perspective the story is a simple one: Grandmother made an unwise decision when she put all her money in a single (and probably badly managed) bank, and she paid for it. The market process simply tells my grandmother—and those who learn of her situation—to be more careful next time.

A related mechanism commonly employed is slyly referred to by some sociolegal scholars as "self-help." For example, large-scale creditors in debt collection disputes can threaten to harm the reputation ("credit rating") of debtors. Less powerful actors can use vigilantism, including physical force, to resolve their grievances. But self-help, like lumping it, involves a turning away from the use of government to solve social problems. If Lawrence Friedman is right, these approaches to dispute resolution will more and more fall out of favor as the desire for total justice grows. The social mechanisms that Kagan and Mashaw have described are bound to take over more and more of the space of social life.

On the surface, the debate over litigation in the United States seems to be about more versus less. The typical refrain of antilitigation reformers is that there are simply too many lawsuits, or alternatively, that we have to manage disputes in a more efficient manner. The typical reply of many sociolegal commentators is that, if anything, we have not enough litigation and that management of disputing poses its own dangers.

But a large part of the litigation debate is really about the division of responsibility in society for decision making. Do we need the tort system to police pharmaceutical companies, or can we trust a bureaucracy, the Food and Drug Administration? Should the handling of a toxic waste dump be decided through local politics, a federal bureaucracy, or litigation? Is disability a problem to be solved by rehabilitation professionals, welfare programs, or rights-based litigation? Are the decisions made by administrative agencies worthy of deference, or should courts step in and take a "hard look"? Should malpractice-damaged newborns be compensated through tort litigation or social insurance programs? Are the police public servants who should follow the dictates of their communities, professionals to whose judgment we should defer, bureaucrats who should follow the rules laid down by their superiors, or legal officers who need to be controlled through constitutional litigation? In each instance policy makers must decide which decision-making processes are most appropriate for the issue at hand.

This study has focused on controversies where the trade-offs between alternative decision-making processes were explicit. Replacement and resistance struggles are moments when American policy makers confront the negative effects of litigious policies and consciously contrast them with other approaches. But in this sense replacement and resistance battles are a misleading sample of the whole litigation debate, because policy makers rarely are confronted explicitly with the choice between litigation and its alternatives. As chapter 1 suggests, the vast majority of antilitigation efforts involve management and discouragement reforms, where alternative models are usually not part of the debate.

Management reforms retain the bilateral, party-centered form of litigation but seek to resolve legal conflicts more amicably and efficiently. Some management reforms seem primarily symbolic, with limited effects—for example, voluntary court-annexed arbitration. Others hold out the prospect of saving both defendant and plaintiff large amounts of time and money. Yet because management reforms are by their nature nested within a system of adversarial legalism, they mark only a modest movement away from litigation.

Discouragement reforms spark the most vigorous battles over litigation. This part of the litigation debate is much like the regulation debate, with Republicans simply wanting less and Democrats wanting either the status quo or more. While critics of litigation in such debates voice a range of complaints—the uncertainty created by jury verdicts, the high transaction costs, the long delays common in adjudication—the main purpose of discouragement reforms is simply to discourage plaintiffs. The rationale for many reforms is that many claims of plaintiffs are illegitimate. Yet most discouragement forms—caps on damages are a particularly vivid example—fail to separate legitimate and illegitimate claims. They just put a damper on all lawsuits.

Thus the alternative to litigation most congruent with many discouragement reforms is the one my grandmother chose: lumping it and depending on community or family. Indeed, antilitigation reformers sometimes use the language of community, as in George H. Bush's proclamation that Americans are "suing each other too much and caring for each other too little." But these stabs at communitarian rhetoric ring hollow in a society where the vast majority of citizens depend at some point in their lives on government support. In cases involving small grievances we might prefer more lumping, though lumping is pervasive already.[61] But few are willing to argue in cases of severe injury that we can rely solely on community and family resources. Fewer still would argue that families and communities by themselves can be expected to keep the environment clean, ensure the safety of products, and deter racial and sexual discrimination. To the extent that American policy makers choose "total justice," they will have to pick from the alternatives outlined—bureaucracy, politics, expert judgment, and adversarial legalism. The costs and benefits of these alternatives should be the main focus of the litigation debate.

A Revised Litigation Debate

How would the litigation debate be different if it took the turn I suggest? One answer comes from the continuing struggle over health care reform. During the early 1990s debate over the Clinton health care plan, many commentators, especially physician groups, argued that, because medical malpractice was a significant source of medical cost inflation, malpractice tort reform should be a part of any reform bill. Thus the issue of litigiousness was confined to a relatively narrow argument about tort reform measures, with the American Medical Association and the plaintiff lawyers flexing their legislative muscles.

But in focusing on the trees, many in the health care debate lost sight of the forest. They failed to note that national health care in itself is a tort reform because any system that provides greater access to health care will reduce incentives for tort litigation. Cross-national studies suggest that at least part of the disparity in tort litigation rates is due to differences in the provision of health care.[62] There is also research suggesting that within the United States those without health care are more likely to sue.[63] Yet this significant advantage of health care reform—much more far-reaching than many of the tort reforms considered—was entirely ignored. The more general point here is an important one: in arguing about social insurance and welfare policies, we should consider their effects on litigation as a part of the debate.

The current struggle over the patients' bill of rights provides another example of the failings of the litigation debate. Proponents of this legislation have raised the banner of total justice: something must be done, they say, to correct the injustices meted out by health maintenance organizations, which sometimes wrongly deny treatment to their patients. But what? While there have been proposals to create medical panels to resolve disputes, most of the attention has been focused on the adversarial legal solution: give patients the right to sue. Trenchant criticisms of this litigious policy have been voiced, but opponents have failed to demonstrate that they have a credible alternative. (No one, interestingly enough, has proposed the creation of a new federal bureaucracy to police HMOs, though in a different era this doubtless would have been one of the first options considered.) To the extent that everyone agrees that there is a problem with HMOs, participants in this debate should be considering the costs and benefits of alternative systems for resolving patients' claims—chief among them adversarial legalism, professional treatment, and bureaucratic rationality. But instead of focusing on these trade-offs among models, the debate mostly revolves around the virtue, or lack thereof, of HMOs and trial lawyers.

Another indication of a failed litigation debate is what has happened to the Equal Employment Opportunity Commission. When the EEOC was created, it was designed to resolve disputes bureaucratically, without recourse to litigation. But the EEOC has usually been too short staffed to do much about the vast majority of cases. Thus a common course of discrimination complaints is for determined plaintiffs, after filing with the agency, to ask for a right-to-sue letter and proceed to litigation. A better

staffed EEOC could mean that more disputes are resolved prior to litigation. Yet staffing has not kept up with the expanding scope of the
agency's responsibilities.[64]

The EEOC is just one of many regulatory bureaucracies that is, at
least by the standard of the law on the books, massively underfunded.
When regulatory agencies are given few resources and big tasks, one
agency response is to employ punitive sanctions and a legalistic mode of
enforcement. Regulated groups, in turn, respond to this approach by
challenging the sanctions in court, and what was a system of bureaucratic
regulation takes on the characteristics of adversarial legalism.[65] A flexi-
ble, creative, interactive style of regulation requires more resources but
also provides great benefits, as for example, advocates of "community
policing" argue. Community policing, in which the regulators—police
officers—spend time getting to know and understand the needs, norms,
and behavior patterns of the regulated, can create better relations
between the community and the police, and in the process lessen legal
conflict. As the example of community policing suggests, better staffing
of regulatory agencies is likely to reduce adversarial legalism.

Underfunding of regulatory agencies greatly increases the inclination
of activists to turn to the courts. Disability activists, dissatisfied with the
regulatory response to the first disability rights law, Section 504, turned
to litigation as a remedy. That experience may explain why they never
conceived of the ADA without a private right of action. Of course some
activists will always be unhappy with the level of regulatory enforcement
of the laws, but those who criticize citizen enforcement through litigation
as a poor mechanism are obliged to offer a more palatable alternative.
Building up regulatory agencies is one option.

On another track is the alternative of expert judgment. Experts are
much denigrated in the United States' populist culture. Even so, we might
consider giving them more latitude in certain areas. For example, experts
are part of the decision-making process of administrative agencies,
where the process often involves them in deliberation with the affected
interest groups. A line of writings on administrative law argues that
courts have gotten too involved in the substance of agency decision making, causing a host of ills including long delays and major disruptions in
agency missions.[66]

The literature on judicial review of administrative agencies illustrates
an important point. While political and popular debate on litigation is
typically framed in terms of "too much" versus "not enough," within

various policy communities there is a quieter, much less visible discussion of litigation and its alternatives. The 1991 American Law Institute study on the tort system, for example, is an extended exploration of the merits of various alternatives.[67] The Rand Institute for Civil Justice has for many years examined the costs and benefits of alternatives to litigation, including most recently no-fault systems.[68] Law professors such as Jeffrey O'Connell, Steve Sugarman, and Paul Weiler have analyzed the weaknesses of tort litigation and offered an array of replacement reforms.[69] They have helped to move the litigation debate in a more thoughtful and productive direction.

The Deep Roots of Litigious Policies

Policy entrepreneurs like O'Connell, Sugarman, and Weiler will ensure that replacement antilitigation reforms continue to be discussed and considered by policy makers. Yet the odds against enacting the more far-reaching replacement reforms are long. Many aspects of American politics seem stacked in favor of litigious policies. The Constitutional Theory suggests that the design of American government gives activists strong incentives to prefer litigious policies. Activists who seek to use government to achieve their ends find themselves drawn to litigious mechanisms as a way of triumphing over the diffuse, divided structure of American government. Moreover, the antistatism of the American constitutional tradition leads Americans to favor litigation as a way of taming the powerful and punishing bad behavior without creating more government. Further, there is the less fundamental but still significant influence of plaintiff lawyers, a group that has focused almost all its energy on defeating certain types of antilitigation reform. These cultural, structural, and political features are powerful constraints on attempts to curtail litigious policies. Sometimes, when political conditions are just right, they can be overcome. But major antilitigation reforms—those that eliminate whole classes of lawsuits—are likely to be few and far between.

I began this book by noting that many Americans think that litigation in the United States is out of control and that litigiousness is a sign that something is seriously wrong with their society. If the story of this book is right, the extension of litigation to more and more realms is a sign not of weakness but rather of a conjunction of traits many consider strengths.

On one hand there is the march toward total justice, the drive to treat people more fairly and equally and to help them recover from "the slings and arrows of outrageous fortune," as Shakespeare put it. On the other hand is the constitutional tradition of separated powers, federalism, and judicial independence, all reflected and reinforced by a strong distrust of government. When activist impulses collide with this constitutional tradition, litigious policies are often the result. In this sense litigation is the price Americans pay for aspects of their nation many hold dear.

NOTES

INTRODUCTION

1. My account of the Laskin Poplar Superfund dispute relies largely on the case study in Thomas W. Church and Robert T. Nakamura, *Cleaning Up the Mess: Implementation Strategies in Superfund* (Washington, D.C.: Brookings Institution, 1993), 47–58.

2. This estimate, which does not include EPA costs or money spent on lawyering, was provided by Jim Campbell, a trustee of the Laskin Poplar Superfund site (telephone conversation with author, November 15, 1995).

3. Church and Nakamura, *Cleaning Up the Mess*, 188 n. 16.

4. The lawsuit commenced in 1984; three consent decrees were lodged in 1993 ("Three Consent Decrees Lodged," *Ohio Industry Environmental Advisor* [October 8, 1993]).

5. Interview with Peter Poulos; Taft, Stettinius & Hollister; Cleveland, Ohio; April 16, 2001. Poulos estimates that less than 1 percent of the responsibility for the site is yet to be settled.

6. For a careful study of the building of the Stella Liebeck legend, see Judith Aks, William Haltom, and Michael McCann, "Symbolic Stella: On Media Coverage of Personal Injury Litigation and the Production of Legal Knowledge," *Law and Courts Newsletter* 7:3 (1997): 5–7.

7. For accounts of these and other lawsuits, see Meredith K. Wadman and Sam Delson, "A Nation of Lawyers: Avalanche of Civil Lawsuits Prompts Legislative Reform," *Oakland Tribune,* April 23, 1995, A1; Edward Felsenthal, "Avogadro's Number, You Say, Professor? I Don't Think So," *The Wall Street Journal,* May 9, 1995, A1; Zachary R. Dowdy, "Litigation Becoming a Pastime, Some Say," *Boston Globe,* March 8, 1996, 27; Neil MacFarquhar, "Extra and Errant Tee Shot May Hit Golfer's Wallet, Too," *New York Times,* January 28, 2000, A1; Richard B. Schmitt, "Uncharitable Acts: If Donors Fail to Give, More Nonprofit Groups Take Them to Court," *Wall Street Journal,* July 27, 1995, A1; "Try a Lighter Setting: Suit Claims Pastry Ignited," *ABA Journal* (May 1995), 38; Walter Berns, "Sue the Warden, Sue the Chef, Sue the Gardener . . . ," *Wall Street Journal,* April 24, 1995, A12; Di Mari Ricker, "Who Wants to Sue a

'Millionaire'?" *The Legal Intelligencer* (June 5, 2000), 4; and Robert J. Samuelson, "Whitewater: The Law as Pit Bull," *Washington Post,* March 16, 1994, A19.

8. Academics and journalists have attempted to track down the origins of these and other fabulous litigation stories. In the case of the ladder in the manure, popularized by the television show *60 Minutes,* reporters from *The American Lawyer* found that manure in fact had little to do with the case, which involved a ladder that broke apart due to defects in workmanship, severely injuring the plaintiff's leg (Stephen Brill and James Lyons, "The Not-So-Simple Crisis," *The American Lawyer* [May 1, 1986], 12). The $1 million award in the CAT scan case was based on adverse physical reactions to a dye that the patient had told the doctor she was allergic to—not the waning of her psychic powers. Further, the verdict was thrown out by the judge in the case (Robert M. Hayden, "The Cultural Logic of a Political Crisis," *Studies in Law, Politics and Society* 11 [1991]: 107). Some stories are pure inventions, as in the often repeated anecdote about a man who received $500,000 for injuries sustained when he attempted to use his lawnmower as a hedge trimmer (Stephen Daniels and Joanne Martin, "The Question of Jury Competence and the Politics of Civil Justice Reform: Symbols, Rhetoric and Agenda-Building," *Law and Contemporary Problems* 52:4 [1989]: 295 n. 105). As for the Kentucky Fried Rat story, it appears to be fictional, though widely believed. Another rodent litigation urban legend—concerning soda drinkers who find mice in their pop bottles—turns out to be based in reality. Gary Alan Fine has documented forty-five cases in which soda drinkers who found dead rodents in their bottles collected damages. See Gary Alan Fine, "The Kentucky Fried Rat: Legends and Modern Mass Society," *Journal of the Folklore Institute* 17 (1980) 222–243; Fine, "Cokelore and Coke Law: Urban Belief Tales and the Problem of Multiple Origins," *Journal of American Folklore* 92 [1979]: 477–482; and a collection of Fine's writings on contemporary folklore, *Manufacturing Tales: Sex and Money in Contemporary Legends* (Knoxville: University of Tennessee Press, 1992).

9. Philip K. Howard, *The Death of Common Sense: How Law Is Suffocating America* (New York: Random House, 1994).

10. See Marc Galanter, "Reading the Landscape of Disputes: What We Know and Don't Know (and Think We Know) about Our Allegedly Contentious and Litigious Society," *UCLA Law Review* 31 (1983): 4–71; Galanter, "The Day after the Litigation Explosion," *Maryland Law Review* 46:1 (1986): 3–39; and Michael J. Saks, "Do We Really Know Anything about the Behavior of the Tort Litigation System—and Why Not?" *University of Pennsylvania Law Review* 140:4 (1992): 1147–1292.

11. Lincoln Caplan, "Who Ya Gonna Call? 1-800-Sue Me," *Newsweek* (March 20, 1995), 36; Stephen Budiansky, "How Lawyers Abuse the Law," *U.S. News and World Report* (January 30, 1995), 50.

12. See, for example, *The Blame Game: Are We a Country of Victims?* (ABC News Special, August 17, 1995).

13. See the comprehensive study of accident compensation by the Rand Institute for Civil Justice, Deborah Hensler et al., *Compensation for Accidental Injuries in the United States* (Santa Monica, Calif.: Rand Institute for Civil Justice, 1991), 121.

14. The Civil Litigation Research Project, which studied patterns of litigation in American households, found that for every one thousand "grievances" perceived by respondents involving at least $1,000, only fifty cases were filed in court, a rate of 5 percent. See David M. Trubek et al., *Civil Litigation Research Project: Final Report—Summary of Principal Findings* (Madison: University of Wisconsin Law School, 1983), summary 19, figure 2; and Richard E. Miller and Austin Sarat, "Grievances, Claims, and Disputes: Assessing the Adversary Culture," *Law and Society Review* 15 (1980–81): 537–565.

15. See Paul C. Weiler et al., *A Measure of Malpractice: Medical Injury, Malpractice Litigation, and Patient Compensation* (Cambridge, Mass.: Harvard University Press, 1993). In this study medical experts combed through patient records to determine whether negligent medical practice had resulted in patient injury. That determination served as the baseline by which to determine the rate of claiming. In another study, a survey of 220 women who had suffered the death or permanent injury of a baby during delivery, none filed a medical malpractice claim (Frank A. Sloan and Chee Ruey Hsieh, "Injury, Liability, and the Decision to File a Medical Malpractice Claim," *Law and Society Review* 29:3 [1995]: 413–435).

16. Wayne McIntosh's study of litigation patterns in St. Louis over the past 150 years concludes that "there were far more complaints (per capita) registered with the court in the 1820s, '30s and '40s than in the 1960s and 1970s—far more" (Wayne V. McIntosh, *The Appeal of Civil Law: A Political-Economic Analysis of Litigation* [Urbana: University of Illinois Press, 1990], 191–192). A study of Accomack County, Virginia, in 1639 found a litigation rate of roughly 240 per thousand persons (George B. Curtis, "The Colonial County Court, Social Forum and Legislative Precedent, Accomack County, Virginia, 1633–1639," *Virginia Magazine of History and Biography* 85 [1977]: 287). That rate is more than four times that of any contemporary county for which data are available, according to Marc Galanter, "Reading the Landscape of Disputes," 41.

17. The Civil Litigation Research Project found that Americans took about 11 percent of their middle-range disputes to court, while a replication of the study in Australia found a 5.5 percent rate. It is difficult to say whether this counts as a large difference. Moreover, as Marc Galanter has pointed out, the gap in filings may simply reflect differences in practices, such as the absence in Australia of contingency fees (see Miller and Sarat, "Grievances, Claims, and Disputes: Assessing the Adversary Culture," 537, table 2; Galanter, "Reading the Landscape of Disputes," 60; Robert L. Nelson, "Ideology, Scholarship and Sociolegal Change: Lessons from Galanter and the 'Litigation Crisis,'" *Law and Society Review* 21:5 [1988]: 681; and Jeffrey M. FitzGerald, "Grievances, Disputes and Outcomes: A Comparison of Australia and the United States," *Law in Context* 1 [1983]: 15).

A study comparing Canadian and American accident victims found the Canadians less likely to claim compensation but more likely to seek legal assistance (Herbert M. Kritzer, W. A. Bogart, and Neil Vidmar, "The Aftermath of Injury: Cultural Factors in Compensation Seeking in Canada and the United States," *Law and Society Review* 25:3 [1991]: 499–544). Another study found the English less likely than Americans to blame someone else for an accident or claim compensation (Herbert M. Kritzer, "Propensity to Sue in England and the United States of America: Blaming and Claiming in Tort Cases," *Journal of Law and Society* 18 [1991]: 400–427).

All of these studies have difficulty disentangling the influence of cultural differences from the effects of differing structural incentives. For example, Gary Schwartz demonstrates that, despite relatively similar tort law doctrine, product liability and malpractice litigation rates are much higher in the United States than in Western Europe. Yet while Schwartz finds the notion of individual-level "litigiousness" intriguing, he suggests that the litigation gap is related to differences in procedure, especially the use of juries and contingency fees in the United States, and to the much greater provision of disability payments in Europe. P. S. Atiyah comes to similar conclusions in his comparison of tort litigation in the United States and Britain. See Schwartz, "Product Liability and Medical Malpractice in Comparative Context," in *The Liability Maze*, ed. Peter W. Huber and Robert E. Litan (Washington, D.C.: Brookings Institution, 1991); and P. S. Atiyah, "Tort Law and the Alternatives: Some Anglo-American Comparisons," *Duke Law Journal* (1987): 1002–1044.

The comparison with Japan is far more complicated than it at first appears. Several scholars of the Japanese legal system have argued that lower rates of litigation in Japan are not a result of a cultural aversion to conflict. Japanese sue less, these researchers say, because litigation simply doesn't pay as well in Japan as it does elsewhere. And that, the researchers argue, is no accident: Japanese elites have designed the disputing system to channel disputants away from litigation, either by making it hard to get a day in court or by making verdicts so predictable that it makes little sense to fully adjudicate claims. According to these studies, an American plucked from his or her litigation-encouraging environment in the United States and placed in the litigation-discouraging institutional structures of Japan would act just as the Japanese do. See John Haley, "The Myth of the Reluctant Litigant," *Journal of Japanese Studies* 4 (1978): 359; Takio Tanase, "The Management of Disputes: Automobile Accident Compensation in Japan," *Law and Society Review* 24 (1990): 651; Frank K. Upham, *Law and Social Change in Postwar Japan* (Cambridge, Mass.: Harvard University Press, 1987); and J. Mark Ramseyer and Minoru Nakazato, "The Rational Litigant: Settlement Amounts and Verdict Rates in Japan," *Journal of Legal Studies* 18:2 (1989): 263–290.

18. Dramatically large jury verdicts in tort lawsuits make wonderful fodder for the news media; verdicts for the defense and statistical data demonstrating the fate of the typical litigant are deemed boring and so tend to be ignored. The result is a highly skewed view of the tort system that nicely supports the tort reform movement's goals (Michael McCann and William Haltom, "Hegemonic Tales and Subversive Statistics: A 20-year Study of News Reporting about Civil Litigation" [paper presented at meeting of the Law and Society Association, Miami Beach, Fla., May 26, 2000]). See also Stephen Daniels and Joanne Martin, *Civil Juries and the Politics of Reform* (Evanston, Ill.: Northwestern University Press, 1995).

19. See Malcolm M. Feeley and Edward L. Rubin, *Judicial Policy Making and the Modern State: How the Courts Reformed America's Prisons* (Cambridge,

England: Cambridge University Press, 1998). Peanut butter may not be a matter fit for the attention of federal courts, but as Feeley and Rubin note, the Supreme Court has in recent years sustained the claim of a nonsmoking prisoner who wanted to be protected from secondhand smoke as well as the claim of a preoperative transsexual prisoner who wanted to be protected from his or her fellow prisoners (p. 15).

20. For a long list of these studies see Robert A. Kagan, *Adversarial Legalism: The American Way of Law* (Cambridge, Mass.: Harvard University Press, 2001), 8. See also Robert A. Kagan and Lee Axelrad, eds., *Regulatory Encounters: Multinational Corporations and American Adversarial Legalism* (Berkeley and Los Angeles: University of California Press, 2000); and Werner Pfennigstorf and Donald G. Gifford, eds., *A Comparative Study of Liability Law and Compensation Schemes in Ten Countries and the United States* (Oak Brook, Ill.: Insurance Research Council, 1991).

21. Some studies that take exception to the claim that American public policy is distinctively litigious are Eric Feldman, "Blood Justice: Courts, Conflict and Compensation in Japan, France and the United States," *Law and Society Review* 34 (2000): 561; Basil Markesinis, "Litigation-Mania in England, Germany, and the USA: Are We So Very Different?" *Cambridge Law Journal* 49 (1990): 233; and Jeffrey M. Sellers, "Litigation as a Local Political Resource: Courts in Controversies over Land Use in France, Germany and the United States," *Law and Society Review* 29 (1995): 475. The growth of judicial review, the ability of courts to strike down government actions as unconstitutional, and the development of transnational judicial institutions, especially in Europe, have been the main developments noted by scholars who see a growing role for courts across the globe. Whether this growth will filter down into nonconstitutional domains, such as injury compensation, remains an open question. See C. Neil Tate and Torban Vallinder, eds., *The Global Expansion of Judicial Power* (New York: New York University Press, 1995); and Alex Stone Sweet, *Governing with Judges: Constitutional Politics in Europe* (New York: Oxford University Press, 2000).

22. I thank Susan Silbey for this insight.

23. Erhard Blankenburg comes to a similar conclusion in comparing two neighboring countries, the former West Germany and the Netherlands, with widely disparate litigation rates. The cause of the difference, Blankenburg concludes, is the supply side rather than the demand side: German institutions encourage litigation, Dutch policies discourage it. See Blankenburg, "Civil Litigation Rates as Indicators for Legal Cultures," in *Comparing Legal Cultures*, ed. David Nelkin (Brookfield, Vt.: Dartmouth Press, 1997), 41–68.

24. Some litigious policies promote what Lawrence Friedman calls "judicialization"—the process of converting disputes or conflicts into court cases (Lawrence M. Friedman, "Limited Monarchy: The Rise and Fall of Student Rights," in *School Days, Rule Days: The Legalization and Regulation of Education*, ed. David L. Kirp and Donald N. Jensen [Philadelphia: Falmer Press, 1986], 239). The category of litigious policies includes laws that judicialize, but the category is broader: where courts *already* govern disputes, litigious policies serve to increase the volume of legal conflict by eliminating barriers to suing, creating new

types of satellite litigation, or increasing the rewards available to plaintiffs. Litigious policies thus expand the threat of litigation in both previously judicialized and nonjudicialized realms.

25. Church and Nakamura found that the Superfund program was administered differently from region to region, with some regional managers favoring a more prosecutorial, litigious approach. See generally Church and Nakamura, *Cleaning Up the Mess.*

26. A six-nation survey of toxic waste laws in the United States and Europe found only the Netherlands and the United States had retrospective liability; only the United States and Sweden had strict liability (Andrew Lohof, *The Cleanup of Inactive Hazardous Waste Sites in Selected Industrialized Countries,* discussion paper no. 069 [Washington D.C.: American Petroleum Institute, August 1991], vi, table 1).

27. This was the conclusion of a study comparing Superfund with hazardous waste efforts in Germany, the Netherlands, and Denmark (Thomas W. Church and Robert T. Nakamura, "Beyond Superfund: Hazardous Waste Cleanup in Europe and the United States," *Georgetown International Environmental Law Review* 7 [1994]: 15–57).

28. See Marc K. Landy, "Cleaning Up Superfund," *The Public Interest* (fall 1986), 58–71; Marc Landy and Mary Hague, "The Coalition for Waste: Private Interests and Superfund," in *Environmental Politics: Public Costs, Private Rewards,* ed. Michael S. Greve and Fred L. Smith, Jr. (New York: Praeger, 1992), 67–87; and Jerry Taylor, "Salting the Earth: The Case for Repealing Superfund," *Regulation* 18:2 (1995): 53–65. The Rand Institute for Civil Justice has published several studies on transaction costs incurred in the Superfund program. See, for example, Lloyd S. Dixon, Deborah S. Drezner, and James K. Hammitt, *Private-Sector Cleanup Expenditures and Transaction Costs at 18 Superfund Sites* (Santa Monica, Calif.: Rand Institute for Civil Justice, 1993).

29. Margaret Kriz, "Super Fight," *National Journal* (January 29, 1994), 226; and "How the Twain Met," *National Journal* (June 6, 1994), 1291–1295. Early in 2002 President Bush signed a modest Superfund reform shielding developers who buy abandoned industrial sites from being held responsible for toxic waste cleanups.

30. George Lardner, Jr., "'Tort Reform': Mixed Verdict; Bush's First Priority in Office Pleased Business, Spurred Donations and Cut Public Remedies," *Washington Post,* February 10, 2000, A6.

31. Walter K. Olson, *The Litigation Explosion: What Happened When America Unleashed the Lawsuit* (New York: Truman Talley Books-Dutton, 1991); Olson, *The Excuse Factory: How Employment Law Is Paralyzing the American Workplace* (New York: Free Press, 1997); Philip K. Howard, *Death of Common Sense;* Howard, *The Lost Art of Drawing the Line: How Fairness Went Too Far* (New York: Random House, 2001); and Max Boot, *Out of Order: Arrogance, Corruption and Incompetence on the Bench* (New York: Basic Books, 1998).

32. American Tort Reform Association, "An expectant mother has a right to expect more than this" (poster); Aetna Insurance Company, "Sue City, U.S.A." (advertisement), both reproduced in Daniels and Martin, "The Question of Jury Competence," 290.

33. Take, for example, an ABC television news documentary *The Trouble with Lawyers,* in which John Stossel portrays a society gone litigation mad (January 2, 1996). A typical newspaper version of this theme is Wadman and Delson, "A Nation of Lawyers: Avalanche of Civil Lawsuits Prompts Legislative Reform," A1.

34. See for example Gerald N. Rosenberg, *The Hollow Hope: Can Courts Bring about Social Change?* (Chicago: University of Chicago Press, 1991).

35. A series of studies by the Rand Institute for Civil Justice has documented the high transaction costs of litigation in such areas as auto accidents and asbestos injuries. See Rand Institute for Civil Justice, *Annual Report* (Santa Monica, Calif.: Rand Institute for Civil Justice, 1993–2001), for a summary of these findings.

36. Communitarian critics, such as Mary Ann Glendon, see American politics as overly influenced by rights talk and other forms of legalistic discourse that prevent political compromise. See, for example, Glendon's *Rights Talk: The Impoverishment of Political Discourse* (New York: Free Press, 1991).

37. Judith Resnik, "Failing Faith: Adjudicatory Procedure in Decline," *University of Chicago Law Review* 53 (1986): 494.

38. Robert A. Kagan, "Adversarial Legalism and American Government," *Journal of Public Policy and Management* 10:3 (1991): 369; *Adversarial Legalism,* 34–58; and "Trying to Have It Both Ways: Local Discretion, Central Control, and Adversarial Legalism in American Environmental Regulation," *Ecology Law Quarterly* 25:4 (1999): 718. Kagan's discussion of the effects of decentralization in American public policy draws on Mirjan Damaska's *The Faces of Justice and State Authority: A Comparative Approach to the Legal Process* (New Haven, Conn.: Yale University Press, 1986).

39. Alexis de Tocqueville, *Democracy In America,* trans. George Lawrence, ed. J. P. Mayer (New York: Harper and Row, 1969), 270.

40. The United States in the nineteenth century was, according to Stephen Skowronek, a state of "courts and parties." See his *Building a New American State: The Expansion of National Administrative Capacities, 1877–1920* (New York: Cambridge University Press, 1982).

41. For this account of changes in tort law, I rely on Donald G. Gifford, "The American Tort Liability System," in *A Comparative Study of Liability Law and Compensation Schemes,* 9–46; Edmund Ursin, "Judicial Creativity and Tort Law," *George Washington Law Review* 49:2 (1981): 229–308; Daniel Polisar and Aaron Wildavsky, "From Individual to System Blame: A Cultural Analysis of Historical Change in the Law of Torts," *Journal of Policy History* 1 (1989): 129–155; G. Edward White, *Tort Law in America: An Intellectual History* (New York: Oxford University Press, 1985); and Gary T. Schwartz, "The Beginning and the Possible End of the Rise of Modern American Tort Law," *Georgia Law Review* 26 (1992): 601–702.

42. See Deborah R. Hensler et al., *Class Action Dilemmas: Pursuing Public Goals for Private Gain* (Santa Monica, Calif.: Rand Institute for Civil Justice, 2000), 9–47; and Judith Resnik, "From 'Cases' to 'Litigation,'" *Law and Contemporary Problems* 54 (1991): 5–68. The plaintiffs in the Pentium chip litigation got a replacement chip and, in some cases, reimbursement for work ruined

by the chip's defects; their lawyers asked for $6 million in fees (Barry Meier, "Fistfuls of Coupons," *New York Times*, May 26, 1995, C1).

43. The expansion of personal liberties and focus on the rights of minorities did not start, of course, with the Warren Court. It can be traced at least as far back as Justice Stone's famous "Footnote Four" in his 1937 *Carolene Products* opinion, which presaged the Court's shift away from protecting economic rights toward guarding civil liberties (*U.S. v. Carolene Products Co.,* 304 U.S. 144 [1938]). It was under the Warren Court, however, that this new agenda reached its apex.

44. *Goldberg v. Kelly,* 397 U.S. 254 (1970).

45. Richard B. Stewart and Cass Sunstein, "Public Programs and Private Rights," *Harvard Law Review* 95 (1982): 1197. For a vivid description of the defects of this type of litigation, see Jeremy Rabkin, *Judicial Compulsions: How Public Law Distorts Public Policy* (New York: Basic Books, 1989).

46. Martin M. Shapiro, *Who Guards the Guardians: Judicial Control of Administration* (Athens: University of Georgia Press, 1988). The phrase comes from D.C. Circuit judge Harold Leventhal's opinion in *Greater Boston Television Corp. v. FCC,* 444 F. 2d 841 (1970).

47. The laws with citizen suit provisions include the Clean Air Act; Federal Water Pollution Control Act; Noise Control Act; Marine Protection, Research and Sanctuaries Act; Resource Conservation and Recovery Act; 1986 Superfund Amendment Act; Endangered Species Act; Consumer Product Safety Act; and Truth in Lending Act. For discussion about the politics of citizen suit provisions, see R. Shep Melnick, *Regulation and the Courts: The Case of the Clean Air Act* (Washington, D.C.: Brookings Institution, 1983); and Edward L. Rubin, "Legislative Methodology: Some Lessons from the Truth-in-Lending Act," *Georgetown Law Journal* 80 (1991): 233–309.

48. Brian K. Landsberg, *Enforcing Civil Rights: Race Discrimination and the Department of Justice* (Lawrence: University Press of Kansas, 1997), 43.

49. *Ruckelshaus v. Sierra Club,* 463 U.S. 680 (1983), cited in Susan Gluck Mezey and Susan M. Olson, "Fee Shifting and Public Policy: The Equal Access to Justice Act," *Judicature* 77 (1993): 13–20, at n. 5.

50. Karen O'Connor and Lee Epstein, "Bridging the Gap between Congress and the Supreme Court: Interest Groups and the Erosion of the American Rule Governing Award of Attorney's Fees," *Western Political Quarterly* 38 (1985): 238–249.

51. Barry Meier, "Bringing Lawsuits to Do What Congress Won't," *New York Times*, March 26, 2000, sec. 4, p. 3; Robert Reich, "Regulation Is Out, Litigation Is In," *USA Today*, February 11, 1999, 15A; Center for Legal Policy at the Manhattan Institute, *Regulation by Litigation: The New Wave of Government-Sponsored Litigation* (conference proceedings, June 22, 1999, Washington, D.C.).

52. E. J. Dionne, Jr., "Suddenly, Bush Likes the Lawyers," in *Bush v. Gore: The Court Cases and the Commentary*, ed. E. J. Dionne, Jr., and William Kristol (Washington, D.C.: Brookings Institution, 2001), 181–182.

53. William Kristol, "Crowning the Imperial Judiciary," and "A President by Judicial Fiat," in ibid., 209–10; and Robert N. Hochman, "Our Robed Masters," in ibid., 253–257.

54. See Kagan, "Adversarial Legalism and American Government," and "Trying to Have It Both Ways."

55. On the "constitutive turn" in sociolegal studies, see Patricia Ewick and Susan S. Silbey, *The Commonplace of Law: Stories from Everyday Life* (Chicago: University of Chicago Press, 1998); Sally Engle Merry, *Getting Justice and Getting Even: Legal Consciousness among Working-Class Americans* (Chicago: University of Chicago Press, 1990); Austin Sarat, " . . . 'The Law Is All Over': Power, Resistance, and the Legal Consciousness of the Welfare Poor," *Yale Journal of Law and Humanities* 2 (1990): 343–379; Carol J. Greenhouse, Barbara Yngvesson, and David M. Engel, *Law and Community in an American Town* (Ithaca, N.Y.: Cornell University Press, 1996); Austin Sarat and Thomas R. Kearns, eds., *Law in Everyday Life* (Ann Arbor: University of Michigan Press, 1993); Michael W. McCann, *Rights at Work: Pay Equity Reform and the Politics of Legal Mobilization* (Chicago: University of Chicago Press, 1994); and David M. Engel, "Law, Culture and Children with Disabilities: Educational Rights and the Construction of Difference," *Duke Law Journal* 1 (1991): 166–205.

56. Kagan discusses this point in *Adversarial Legalism,* 47–50.

57. See ibid., 44–46.

58. See generally Sven Steinmo, *Taxation and Democracy* (New Haven, Conn.: Yale University Press, 1993).

59. See Charles R. Shipan's much more fine-grained analysis of this point in *Designing Judicial Review: Interest Groups, Congress and Communications Policy* (Ann Arbor: University of Michigan Press, 1997). Shipan argues that, when interest groups are calculating whether or not to support judicial review of agency decision making, they consider such factors as previous experiences with the agency and with courts, the "legal regime" of the era, perceptions about each institution's capacities, and the costs and benefits to other groups (pp. 15–33). My analysis differs from Shipan's in two major respects. First, my level of analysis is broader since I am asking why activists might prefer court-based implementation of public policy generally, not simply in the context of judicial review of administrative agency decisions. Second, my analysis is grounded in comparative research: this book probes the mechanisms that make American public policy *generally* more court centered as compared to other advanced economies. Thus my emphasis is on broad comparative patterns rather than variation within the United States. I do, however, draw some tentative conclusions in the concluding chapter about the conditions under which litigious policies can be successfully attacked.

60. See Kagan, "Adversarial Legalism and American Government," and *Adversarial Legalism,* 9–13. The American judicial system is not, of course, the only structure that can be characterized as having an adversarial legal form of organization. Kagan shows that, for example, bureaucratic agencies can take on degrees of adversarial legalism to the extent that they structure issues as formal legal disputes between parties, decouple decision makers from higher authorities, and allow the rules to be argued over and modified. Conversely, judicial systems can vary in their degree of adversarial legalism to the extent that they vary in these attributes. For example, the Court of Federal Claims, which administers the Vaccine Injury Compensation Program described in chapter 4, scores much lower on adversarial legalism than the typical American court.

61. See, for example, Marc Galanter, "News from Nowhere: The Debased Debate on Civil Justice," *Denver University Law Review* 71 (1993): 77–113; David M. Engel, "The Oven Bird's Song: Insiders, Outsiders and Personal Injuries in an American Community," *Law and Society Review* 18 (1984): 1; Hayden, "The Cultural Logic of a Political Crisis"; and Daniels and Martin, *Civil Juries and the Politics of Reform.*

62. Two studies of legislative antilitigation efforts are Euel Elliot and Susette M. Talarico, "An Analysis of Statutory Development: The Correlates of State Activity in Product Liability Legislation," *Policy Studies Review* 10 (1991): 61–78; and Thomas J. Campbell, Daniel P. Kessler, and George B. Shepherd, *The Causes and Effects of Liability Reform: Some Empirical Evidence* (Cambridge, Mass.: National Bureau of Economic Research, 1994).

1. THE BATTLE OVER LITIGATION

1. For a history of attempts to keep disputes out of court in the United States, see Jerold Auerbach, *Justice without Law?* (New York: Oxford University Press, 1983). Auerbach demonstrates that conflicts over litigiousness are hardly unique to late-twentieth and early-twenty-first-century America.

2. Marc Galanter notes that Chief Justice Warren Burger, who would later become a leading spokesman for antilitigation efforts, omitted any mention of excessive litigiousness in his first "State of the Judiciary" address in 1970. Galanter, "Reading the Landscape of Disputes," 9.

3. Simon Rifkind, "Are We Asking Too Much of Our Courts?" in *The Pound Conference: Perspectives on Justice in the Future*, ed. A. Leo Levin and Russell R. Wheeler (St. Paul, Minn.: West, 1979), 51.

4. Walter V. Schaefer, "Is the Adversary System Working in Optimal Fashion?" in *Pound Conference*, 181.

5. Francis Kirkham, "Complex Civil Litigation—Have Good Intentions Gone Awry?" in *Pound Conference*, 212, 214.

6. Edward Levi, "The Business of Courts: A Summary and Sense of Perspective," in *Pound Conference*, 278.

7. Robert Bork, "Dealing with the Overload in Article III Courts," in *Pound Conference*, 151.

8. Kirkham, "Complex Civil Litigation," 213.

9. Geoffrey C. Hazard, "Social Justice through Civil Justice," *University of Chicago Law Review* 36 (1969): 699–712; Donald Horowitz, *The Courts and Social Policy* (Washington, D.C.: The Brookings Institution, 1977); Nathan Glazer, "Towards an Imperial Judiciary," *The Public Interest* 41:3 (1975) 104–23; Derek C. Bok, "A Flawed System," *Harvard Magazine*, May–June 1983, 38–45, 70; and Kristin Bumiller, *The Civil Rights Society: The Social Construction of Victims* (Baltimore: Johns Hopkins University Press, 1988). For criticism of the expansion of judicial review of administrative agencies, see Melnick, *Regulation and the Courts*; Shapiro, *Who Guards the Guardians*; and Rabkin, *Judicial Compulsions.*

10. Rosenberg, *The Hollow Hope: Can Courts Bring About Social Change?*

11. On the critical legal studies side see, for example, Peter Gabel and Duncan Kennedy, "Roll Over Beethoven," *Stanford Law Review* 36 (1984): 1; Mark Tushnet, "An Essay on Rights," *Texas Law Review* 62 (1984): 1363; and Alan D. Freeman, "Legitimizing Racial Discrimination through Anti-Discrimination Law: A Critical Review of Supreme Court Doctrine," *Minnesota Law Review* 62 (1978): 1049. The "father" of critical race theory is Derrick Bell; see his classic article "Serving Two Masters: Integration Ideals and Client Interests in School Desegregation Litigation," *Yale Law Journal* 85 (1976): 470; or his two best-known books, *Faces at the Bottom of the Well* (New York: Basic Books, 1992) and *And We Are Not Saved* (New York: Basic Books, 1987). For a defense of rights from a leading critical race theorist see Patricia Williams, "Alchemical Notes: Reconstructing Ideals from Deconstructed Rights," in *Harvard Civil Rights–Civil Liberties Review* 22 (1987): 401. Finally, for an overview of critical race theory there are two compendiums from which to choose: Kimberle Crenshaw, ed., *Critical Race Theory: The Key Writings That Formed the Movement* (New York: The New Press, 1995); and Richard Delgado, ed., *Critical Race Theory: The Cutting Edge* (Philadelphia: Temple University Press, 1995).

12. Glendon, *Abortion and Divorce in Western Law: American Failures, European Challenges* (Cambridge, Mass.: Harvard University Press, 1987), and *Rights Talk: The Impoverishment of Political Discourse*. Robert Bellah, another prominent academic associated with the communitarian movement, cites "the explosion of civil litigation" as evidence of a surfeit of blame and a deficit of responsibility in American society (Robert Bellah and Chris Adams, "Pessimism and Fantasy Reign in Presidential Race," *San Francisco Chronicle,* September 18, 1992).

13. Three studies, for example, argued that the American economy was suffering because of a surplus of lawyers: Stephen P. Magee, William A. Brock, and Leslie Young, *Black Hole Tariffs and Endogenous Policy Theory: Political Economy in General Equilibrium* (New York: Cambridge University Press, 1989); David N. Laband and John P. Sophocleus, "The Social Cost of Rent-Seeking: First Estimates," *Public Choice* 58 (1988): 269; and Kevin M. Murphy et al., *The Allocation of Talent: Implications for Growth* (National Bureau of Economic Research working paper, 1990).

14. See, for example, Craig Bradley, *The Failure of the Criminal Procedure Revolution* (Philadelphia: University of Pennsylvania Press, 1993); R. H. Helmholz et al., *The Privilege against Self-Incrimination: Its Origins and Development* (Chicago: University of Chicago Press, 1997); and Akhil Reed Amar, *The Constitution and Criminal Procedure: First Principles* (New Haven, Conn.: Yale University Press, 1997). Amar advocates eliminating the exclusionary rule and relying more on tort remedies to deter wrongful searches and seizures by police, so he is not exactly an antilitigationist. Amar does, however, mention the possibility of using an administrative process to determine damages rather than the traditional judicial process (see Amar, 159).

15. Gary Schwartz, writing in 1992, claimed that among tort scholars at the top twenty law schools in the nation, only one, Marshall Shapo at Northwestern, could be regarded as supportive of the existing state of tort law (Schwartz, "The

Beginning and the Possible End of the Rise of Modern American Tort Law,"
695). Many others are deeply critical of the whole tort system, from conservatives such as George Priest to liberals such as Steve Sugarman, Marc Franklin,
and John Fleming. While the conservatives would like to roll back liability, some
of the liberals want to abolish the tort system entirely and replace it with social
insurance and expanded regulation. This tendency is epitomized by Sugarman's
article "Doing Away with Tort Law," *California Law Review* 73 (1985): 555;
but see also John G. Fleming, "Is There a Future for Tort Law?" *Louisiana Law
Review* 44 (1984): 1193; George L. Priest, "The Current Insurance Crisis and
Modern Tort Law," *Yale Law Journal* 96 (1987): 1521; and Kenneth Abraham
and Lance Liebman, "Private Insurance, Social Insurance, and Tort Reform:
Toward a New Vision of Compensation for Illness and Injury," *Columbia Law
Review* 93 (1993): 75.

The American Law Institute, responsible for drafting the liberalizing *Second
Restatement of Torts,* published a highly critical report on the tort system, *Enterprise Responsibility for Personal Injury* (Philadelphia: American Law Institute,
1991). A team of researchers from Harvard, including legal scholars, found medical malpractice litigation inadequate both for deterrence and compensation
(Weiler et al., *A Measure of Malpractice: Medical Injury, Malpractice Litigation,
and Patient Compensation*).

In many respects these scholars are following in the footsteps of Jeffrey
O'Connell, a tort professor who since the mid-1960s has produced a relentless
stream of articles and books criticizing tort law and suggesting alternatives, par-
ticularly no-fault systems. See, for example, O'Connell and Robert E. Keeton,
*Basic Protection for the Traffic Victim: A Blueprint for Reforming Automobile
Insurance* (Boston: Little, Brown, 1965); O'Connell, *The Lawsuit Lottery: Only
the Lawyers Win* (New York: Free Press, 1979); O'Connell and C. Brian Kelly,
The Blame Game: Injuries, Insurance and Injustice (Lexington, Mass.: Lexington
Books, 1987); O'Connell, "A Draft Bill to Allow Choice between No-Fault and
Fault-Based Auto Insurance," *Harvard Journal on Legislation* 27:1 (1990):
143–171; and O'Connell, Lester Brickman, and Michael Horowitz, *Rethinking
Contingency Fees* (Washington, D.C.: Manhattan Institute, 1994).

16. The leading research organization on civil justice issues, the Rand Institute for Civil Justice (ICJ), was created in 1979, after an insurance executive,
inspired by the Pound Conference, suggested to colleagues that more systematic
research on the civil justice system was needed (Rand Institute for Civil Justice,
"How the ICJ Was Born," *1994–5 Annual Report* [Santa Monica, Calif.],
14–15). ICJ's research has, however, often disappointed ardent antilitigationists.
It contributed to debunking the myth of the litigation explosion, gave only mixed
reviews to alternative dispute resolution programs, and proved that accident victims are typically undercompensated yet rarely sue (Deborah Hensler, *Court-
Ordered Arbitration: An Alternative View* [Santa Monica, Calif.: Rand Institute
for Civil Justice, 1990]; Robert J. MacCoun, *Unintended Consequences of Court
Arbitration: A Cautionary Tale from New Jersey* [Santa Monica, Calif.: Rand
Institute for Civil Justice, 1992]; E. Allen Lind et al., *The Perception of Justice:
Tort Litigants' Views of Trial, Court-Annexed Arbitration and Judicial Settle-
ment Conferences* [Santa Monica, Calif.: Rand Institute for Civil Justice, 1989];

and Hensler et al., *Compensation for Accidental Injuries in the United States*). Still, the overall picture of civil litigation drawn by ICJ's researchers has not been pretty. For example, ICJ's research on tort litigation found high transaction costs and uneven awards (James S. Kakalik and Nicholas M. Pace, *Costs and Compensation Paid in Tort Litigation* [Santa Monica, Calif.: Rand Institute for Civil Justice, 1986]). Likewise, studies of the Superfund program found high transaction costs (Dixon, Drezner, and Hammitt, *Private-Sector Cleanup Expenditures and Transaction Costs at 18 Superfund Sites*; John P. Acton and Lloyd Dixon, *Superfund and Transaction Costs: The Experiences of Insurers and Very Large Industrial Firms* [Santa Monica, Calif.: Rand Institute for Civil Justice, 1992]). Further, a series of ICJ studies has provided strong support for antilitigation reforms in auto accident tort law (Stephen J. Carroll et al., *No-Fault Approaches to Compensating People Injured in Automobile Accidents* [Santa Monica, Calif.: Rand Institute for Civil Justice, 1991]; A. Abrahamse and Stephen J. Carroll, *The Effects of a Choice Auto Insurance Plan on Insurance Costs* [Santa Monica, Calif.: Rand Institute for Civil Justice, 1995]; and Jeffrey O'Connell et al., "The Comparative Costs of Consumer Choice for Auto Insurance in All Fifty States," *Maryland Law Review* 55 [1996]: 160).

The American Bar Foundation, the National Center for State Courts, and the Brookings Institution have also been active in the litigation debate. Some of the ABF studies are Stephen Daniels and Joanne Martin, "Empirical Patterns in Punitive Damage Cases," (Chicago: American Bar Foundation, 1987); "Jury Verdicts and the 'Crisis' in Civil Justice" (Chicago: American Bar Foundation, 1987); "The Man Who Mistook His Lawnmower for a Hedge Trimmer (and Collected $500,000): Examining Products Liability Verdicts," (Chicago: American Bar Foundation, 1992); and Daniels and Martin, *Civil Juries and the Politics of Reform*. Besides its own research, the National Center for State Courts regularly publishes *Examining the Work of State Courts,* which provides much of the raw data for the liability debate. Brookings has published four books on the litigation debate: Robert Litan and Clifford Winston, *Liability: Perspectives and Policy* (Washington, D.C.: The Brookings Institution, 1988); The Brookings Institution Task Force, *Justice for All: Reducing Costs and Delays in Civil Litigation* (Washington, D.C.: The Brookings Institution, 1989); Huber and Litan, eds., *The Liability Maze*; and Robert E. Litan, *Verdict: Assessing the Civil Jury System* (Washington, D.C.: Brookings Institution, 1993).

The most avowedly antilitigation research organization is the Center for Legal Policy at the Manhattan Institute Center for Policy Research. The institute is the home of the two most prominent antilitigation writers, Walter Olson and Peter Huber, whose books have fueled the tort reform movement and inspired antilitigation politicians, most famously Dan Quayle. Olson and Huber were dubbed "the intellectual gurus of the tort reform movement" by the *Washington Post* ("Walter Cronkite Video Helps Stir Debate over Tort Reform," *Washington Post,* September 14, 1992, C5). Olson's books are *The Litigation Explosion* and *The Excuse Factory*; Huber has written *Liability: The Legal Revolution and Its Causes* (New York: Basic Books, 1988) and *Galileo's Revenge: Junk Science in the Courtroom* (New York: Basic Books, 1991). Recent Manhattan Institute publications include *Regulation through Litigation: Assessing the Role of Bounty*

Hunters and Bureaucrats in the American Regulatory Regime, Manhattan Institute Conference Series no. 2 (New York: Center for Legal Policy, February 2000); Richard Painter, *The New American Rule: A First Amendment to the Client's Bill of Rights*, Civil Justice rpt. no. 1 (New York: Center for Legal Policy, March 2000); and John H. Beisner and Jessica Davidson Miller, "They're Making a Federal Case Out of It . . . in State Court," *Harvard Journal of Law and Public Policy* 25 (fall 2001): 143. Olson's latest venture is overlawyered.com, a website filled to overflowing with litigation "horror stories."

17. Dan Quayle, address to the annual meeting of the American Bar Association, Atlanta, Ga., August 13, 1991.

18. President's Council on Competitiveness, *Agenda for Civil Justice Reform in America* (Washington, D.C., August 1991).

19. John J. Curtin (president, American Bar Association), remarks in response to Vice President Dan Quayle's address (American Bar Association annual meeting, Atlanta, Ga., August 13, 1991).

20. Julie Johnson and Ratu Kamlani, "Do We Have Too Many Lawyers?" *Time Magazine*, August 26, 1991, 54; "Justice at What Price?" *Seattle Times*, August 14, 1991, A3; Michael Kinsley, "Quayle's Case," *New Republic*, September 9, 1991, 4; and Douglas Jehl, "Administration Calls for Wide Legal Reforms," *Los Angeles Times*, August 14, 1991, A1.

21. As Marc Galanter has demonstrated, Quayle's estimates of the proportion of lawyers practicing in the United States (70 percent) and the cost of tort litigation ($300 billion) were essentially made up and greatly exaggerate the true figures. See n. 92 (p. 225). The figure for the amount of civil cases filed—eighteen million—was correct but somewhat misleading since millions of them were routine uncontested probate, divorce, and debt collection matters and only a small percentage were tort claims, the type Quayle dwelt on in his speech. See Galanter, "News from Nowhere," 77–113.

22. Geoffrey C. Hazard, Jr., "Bush Report Not All That Controversial," *National Law Journal* (December 16, 1991), 13; Deborah Hensler, "Taking Aim at the American Legal System: The Council on Competitiveness's Agenda for Legal Reform," *Judicature* 75:5 (1992): 244–250.

23. For example, Quayle's proposed "loser pays" rule seemed on its face to be a revolutionary measure but actually amounted to much less. As its name suggests, the loser-pays rule requires the loser of a lawsuit to pay the legal costs incurred by the other side. This is the normal rule in most nations, but under the "American rule," losing parties are typically not required to pay the legal costs of their opponents. A move to make loser pays the normal rule in American civil law would have been a radical proposition. Quayle's initiative, however, was limited to diversity cases, those in which plaintiffs can choose either federal or state court, a limitation that would have greatly restricted the impact of the reform since plaintiffs could dodge it by lodging their cases in state courts.

24. Executive Order 12778, "Civil Justice Reform," *Public Papers of the Presidents* 27 (October 23, 1991): 1485. Some elements of the recommendations for discovery reform did end up in procedural rules changes adopted by the Judicial Conference the following year.

25. Joe Queenan, "Birth of a Notion: How the Think Tank Industry Came Up with an Issue That Dan Quayle Could Call His Own," *Washington Post,* September 20, 1992, C1.

26. Dole made the story of his fall from a campaign stage part of his standard campaign speech. At an event in San Diego he used it to illustrate the need for tort reform:

> Baseless litigation costs a lot of jobs and a lot of time and a lot of money. And obviously they enrich the trial lawyers. And I don't have any quarrel about people making money, but a lot of time these frivolous lawsuits put a lot of people out of business, take a lot of time, take a lot of your money. . . . I was out in Chico, California about five weeks ago. And to some of you who watch television, the railing wasn't very secure and I dove into the crowd. And on the way down, my cell phone rang. And this trial lawyer says, "Bob, I think we've got a case here." (laughter/applause)
>
> (Campaign speech by Bob Dole, San Diego, California,
> Federal News Service, October 15, 1996)

27. George Lardner, Jr., "'Tort Reform': Mixed Verdict," A6.

28. In the 2000 presidential election debate in St. Louis, George W. Bush proposed a "Teacher Protection Act" limiting lawsuits against teachers (*Transcript of the 2000 Presidential Election Debate, St. Louis, Missouri* [Federal News Service, October 17, 2000]). David A. Price, "Can Dole Reign In Trial Lawyers?" *Investor's Daily,* September 12, 1996, A1; Robert Dole, Republican Platform Committee address, CNN Transcript #869-2, August 6, 1996; Harriet Chiang, "Presidential Campaign Puts Lawyers on Trial," *San Francisco Chronicle*, September 24, 1992, A1.

29. Author's e-mail conversation with staff of the Court Statistics Project, National Center for State Courts, Williamsburg, Va., April 2, 2002. Although the ratio of tort to contract cases varies greatly over time, since 1984 there have always been at least 14 percent more contract than tort cases in the National Center for State Court's sample. Moreover, tort and contract cases together amount to only a small part of the work of state courts, which handle more than 97 percent of all cases filed in the United States. The NCSC staff estimates that only 2.9 million of the 31.7 million cases filed in general-jurisdiction state courts in 2000 involved tort and contract disputes; overall state case filings (including minor matters such as traffic tickets) numbered 92 million.

30. Ross E. Cheit, "Corporate Ambulance Chasers: The Charmed Life of Business Litigation," *Studies in Law, Politics and Society* 11 (1991): 119–40.

31. David Engel, "The Oven Bird's Song: Insiders, Outsiders, and Personal Injuries in an American Community."

32. William Glaberson, "When the Verdict Is Just a Fantasy," *New York Times,* June 6, 1999, sec. 4, p. 1; Aks, Haltom, and McCann, "Symbolic Stella," 5–7.

33. Interview with Diane Swenson, executive vice president, ATRA, Washington, D.C., May 19, 1994; "Special Report: Tort Reform Interests and Agendas," *Legal Times*, April 17, 1995, S30; interview with Michael Hotra, director of public education, ATRA, Washington, D.C., November 15, 2000.

34. Interview with William Fay, executive director, Product Liability Coordinating Committee, Arlington, Va., July 22, 1994.

35. Karen Alexander, "GC Group Knocks Out Tort Reform," *American Lawyer* (September 1992), 59.

36. The Alliance for Justice, a prolitigation public interest group, discusses these activities in a report on funding of the civil justice reform effort. According to the report, between 1989 and 1991 Aetna gave a total of $1.5 million for "reform of the civil justice system," including $250,000 to the American Law Institute, $600,000 to Rand's Institute for Civil Justice, and $180,000 to the Manhattan Institute (Alliance for Justice, *Justice for Sale: Shortchanging the Public Interest for Private Gain* [Washington, D.C., 1993], 59).

37. William Haltom, Michael W. McCann, and Jeffrey Dudas, "Smoke and Mirrors: Framing Fights over Tobacco" (paper presented at the annual meeting of the Western Political Science Association, Long Beach, California, March 24, 2002); Michael McCann, William Haltom, and Anne Bloom, "Java Jive: Genealogy of a Juridical Icon," *University of Miami Law Review,* forthcoming.

38. Department of Health, Education, and Welfare, *Medical Malpractice: Report of the Secretary's Commission on Medical Malpractice* (Washington, D.C., January 16, 1973).

39. In 1976 the Ford administration convened a White House conference on product liability, and in 1979, during the Carter administration, a special task force produced a model uniform product liability act for the states. The Reagan administration's Tort Policy Working Group released a report urging several tort reforms, including the elimination of joint and several liability, limits on contingency fees, and a $100,000 cap on all noneconomic damages (interview with Victor Schwartz, general counsel, American Tort Reform Association, Washington, D.C., November 14, 2000; U.S. Interagency Task Force on Product Liability, *Final Report: Executive Summary* [Washington, D.C., 1977]; U.S. Department of Commerce, *Uniform Product Liability Act: A Model for the States* [Washington D.C.: 1979]; Tort Policy Working Group, *Report on the Causes, Extent and Policy Implications of the Current Crisis in Insurance Availability and Affordability* [Washington, D.C.: February 1986]).

40. Jim VandeHei, "Bush's Cherished Tort Reform Plans Survive Enron—Barely," *Wall Street Journal,* March 14, 2002, A20.

41. Eleanor D. Kinney, "Malpractice Reform in the 1990s: Past Disappointments, Future Success?" *Journal of Health Politics, Policy and Law* 20 (1995): 112.

42. U.S. Chamber of Commerce Institute for Legal Reform, *A Primer on Civil Justice Reform at the Federal Level* (Washington, D.C., July 1999).

43. Schwartz, interview; Linda Lipsen, "The Evolution of Products Liability," in *Tort Law and the Public Interest,* ed. Peter H. Schuck (New York: Norton, 1991), 254.

44. Richard A. Epstein, "The Political Economy of Product Liability Reform," *American Economic Review* 78 (1988): 311–315.

45. Harry Nelson, "Medical Crisis: Doctors Finding Insurance Scarce," *Los Angeles Times,* January 7, 1975, 1.

46. Charles Oliver, "Have States Killed Tort Reform?" *Investor's Business Daily,* April 16, 1996, A1.

47. American Tort Reform Association, *State Tort Reform Enactments* (Washington, D.C.: 1995, 1996, and 1997).

48. For example, a study found that states that modified their joint and several liability rules found little or no effect (Han-Duck Lee, Mark J. Browne, and Joan T. Schmit, "How Does Joint and Several Tort Reform Affect the Rate of Tort Filings? Evidence from the State Courts," *The Journal of Risk and Insurance* 61:2 [1994]:295–316). See also Glenn Blackmon and Richard Zeckhauser, "State Tort Reform Legislation: Assessing Our Control of Risks," in *Tort Law and the Public Interest*; Patricia Danzon, *New Evidence on the Frequency and Severity of Medical Malpractice Claims* (Santa Monica, Calif.: Rand Institute for Civil Justice, 1986); Stephen J. Carroll and Nicholas Pace, *Assessing the Effects of Tort Reform* (Santa Monica, Calif.: Rand Institute for Civil Justice, 1987); and U.S. Office of Technology Assessment, *Impact of Legal Reforms on Medical Malpractice Costs* (Washington, D.C.: October 1993).

49. Valerie P. Hans, *Business on Trial: The Civil Jury and Corporate Responsibility* (New Haven, Conn.: Yale University Press, 2000) 22–78; Valerie P. Hans and William S. Lofquist, "Jurors' Judgments of Business Liability in Tort Cases: Implications for the Litigation Explosion Debate," *Law and Society Review* 26 (1992): 85–113. Whether this research demonstrates a change in attitude or simply a current of opinion that has always influenced jurors cannot be determined, because we do not have studies from earlier eras. Nor do we have evidence to indicate the extent to which antilitigation publicity campaigns by organizations such as Aetna have had an effect.

50. James Henderson and Theodore Eisenberg, "The Quiet Revolution in Products Liability: An Empirical Study of Legal Change," *UCLA Law Review* 37:3 (1990): 479–553; and "Inside the Quiet Revolution in Products Liability," *UCLA Law Review* 39:4 (1992): 731–810.

51. The beginning of this contraction came in *Stone v. Powell,* 428 U.S. 465 (1976); in *McClesky v. Zant,* 111 S. Ct. 1454 (1991), the Court expanded its "abuse of the writ" doctrine and promoted the state's interest in "finality."

52. Spencer Abraham, "Tough on Crime? Not the Clinton Justice Department," *Wall Street Journal,* September 25, 1996, A23.

53. Prisoner petitions constitute about one-quarter of the docket of U.S. district courts. Between 1992 and 1995, a period when overall federal district court filings grew by less than 10 percent, prisoner petitions rose by more than 25 percent, from forty-eight thousand to sixty-three thousand (Administrative Office of the United States Courts, *Judicial Business of the U.S. Courts: 1996 Report of the Director* [Washington, D.C.], 138, table C2A).

54. Margaret A. Jacobs, "Civil Rights Groups Fear Fast Senate Step," *Wall Street Journal,* April 21, 1995, B5.

55. Michael S. Greve, "Private Enforcement, Private Rewards: How Environmental Citizen Suits Became an Entitlement Program," in *Environmental Politics: Public Costs, Private Rewards,* ed. Michael S. Greve and Fred L. Smith, Jr. (New York: Praeger, 1992), 105–127.

56. Michael Grunwald, "Bush Seeks to Curb Endangered Species Suits," *Washington Post,* April 12, 2001, A2.

57. See Shapiro, *Who Guards the Guardians*; Melnick, *Regulation and the Courts*; and Rabkin, *Judicial Compulsions*. Cary Coglianese argues convincingly that the disruption created by lawsuits against one administrative agency, the Environmental Protection Agency, has been exaggerated (Coglianese, "Litigating within Relationships: Disputes and Disturbance in the Regulatory Process," *Law and Society Review* 30 (1996): 735–765).

58. On lower court deference to agencies, see Peter H. Schuck and E. D. Elliot, "To the Chevron Station: An Empirical Study of Federal Administrative Law," *Duke Law Journal* (1990): 984–1077. On the Supreme Court's post-*Chevron* jurisprudence, see Thomas W. Merrill, "Judicial Deference to Executive Precedent," *Yale Law Journal* 101 (1992): 969–1013; and Theodore W. Wern, "Judicial Deference to EEOC Interpretations of the Civil Rights Act, the ADA and the ADEA: Is the EEOC a Second Class Agency?" *Ohio State Law Journal* 60 (1999): 1533.

59. Hillary Stout, "Legal Services, the Agency That Wouldn't Die, Looks like It May Survive the Age of Gingrich," *Wall Street Journal*, July 21, 1995, 12; Richard B. Schmitt, "Legal Services for Poor Face Funding Woes in Congress," *Wall Street Journal*, July 25, 1994, B5. Congress has enacted a host of restrictions on the activities of lawyers receiving Legal Services Corporation (LSC) funding. For example, they generally cannot participate in class actions, win attorney's fees (even when permitted by statute), represent prisoners, or bring lawsuits regarding abortion. The Supreme Court, in *Legal Services Corporation v. Velazquez* (523 U.S. 903, 2001), overturned on First Amendment grounds a rule forbidding LSC-funded attorneys from challenging welfare laws in the course of representing their clients. *Velazquez* appears, however, to be a narrowly reasoned decision that does not portend judicial abolition of the many other restrictions Congress has imposed (Alan W. Houseman and Linda Perle, *What Can and Cannot Be Done: Representation of Clients by LSC-Funded Programs* [Center for Law and Social Policy, August 9, 2001], available at <http://www.clasp.org/pubs/legalservices/whatcancannot2001.pdf>, accessed March 26, 2002).

60. W. Kip Viscusi and colleagues found that significant reductions in general liability insurance costs resulted from caps on damages and elimination of the collateral source rule. They found that medical malpractice reforms, however, had little effect on malpractice insurance prices (W. Kip Viscusi et al., "The Effect of 1980s Tort Reform Legislation on General Liability and Medical Malpractice Insurance," *Journal of Risk and Uncertainty* 6 [1993]: 165–186). Others have found significant effects from the medical malpractice reforms. See, for example, Patricia Danzon, "The Frequency and Severity of Medical Malpractice Claims: New Evidence," *Law and Contemporary Problems* 49 (1986): 57–84; Drucilla Barker, "The Effects of Tort Reform on Medical Malpractice Insurance Markets: An Empirical Analysis," *Journal of Health Politics, Policy and Law* 17 (1992): 142–161; Daniel Kessler and Mark McClellan, "Do Doctors Practice Defensive Medicine?" *Quarterly Journal of Economics* 111 (1996): 353–390; and Albert Yoon, "Damage Caps and Civil Litigation: An Empirical Study of Medical Malpractice Litigation in the South," *American Law and Economics Review* 27 (2001): 199–227.

61. Auerbach, *Justice without Law?*

62. Ibid., 95–114.

63. For a fascinating review of the variety of motivations behind the ADR "movement," see Susan Silbey and Austin Sarat, "Dispute Processing in Law and Legal Scholarship: From Institutional Critique to the Reconstruction of the Juridical Subject," *University of Denver Law Review* 66 (1989): 437–498.

64. Frank Sander, for example, began his influential paper on alternative dispute resolution by citing the need to protect courts from an ever expanding docket (Sander, "Varieties of Dispute Processing," in *Pound Conference*, 65–67).

65. Christine Harrington, *Shadow Justice: The Ideology and Institutionalization of Alternatives to Court* (Westport, Conn.: Greenwood Press, 1985).

66. Burger, "Agenda 2000 A.D.: A Need for Systematic Anticipation," in *Pound Conference*, 31, 35.

67. Edgar S. and Jean C. Cahn, "What Price Justice: The Civilian Perspective Revisited," *Notre Dame Lawyer* 41 (1966): 921–60; Richard Danzig, "Toward the Creation of a Complementary, Decentralized System of Criminal Justice," *Stanford Law Review* 26 (1973): 1–54.

68. Lauren B. Edelman and Mark C. Suchman, "When the Haves Hold Court: Speculations on the Organizational Internationalization of Law," *Law and Society Review* 33 (1999): 941.

69. "Editorial: Overdue Limit on Arbitration," *San Francisco Chronicle*, January 17, 2002, A24. For a thoughtful discussion of the issues raised by contractual arbitration in employment, see Eileen Silverstein, "From Statute to Contract: The Law of the Employment Relationship Reconsidered," *Hofstra Labor and Employment Law Journal* 18 (2001): 472.

Data systematically comparing arbitration and litigation outcomes are scarce, so claims about the relative fairness of contractual arbitration systems are hard to assess. One study found mean and median jury verdicts in employment discrimination cases were at least three times higher than the comparable mean and median arbitration awards (William M. Howard, "Arbitrating Claims of Employment Discrimination: What Really Does Happen? What Really Should Happen?," *Journal of Dispute Resolution* 50 [1995]: 40, cited in Lisa B. Bingham, "On Repeat Players, Adhesive Contracts, and the Use of Statistics in Judicial Review of Employment Arbitration Awards," *McGeorge Law Review* 28 (1998): n. 31). A 1989 study by the Securities and Exchange Commission found that the median arbitration award in disputes between investors and brokerage firms was 42 percent lower than the median award in court (Margaret A. Jacobs and Michael Siconolfi, "Losing Battles: Investors Fare Poorly Fighting Wall Street—and May Do Worse," *Wall Street Journal*, February 8, 1995, A1). First USA, a credit card issuer, disclosed in a class action lawsuit in 2000 that it had prevailed in 99.6 percent of 19,618 disputes with consumers that reached an arbitrator, but this lopsided record may simply reflect the case mix, mostly claims by First USA against delinquent payees (Caroline E. Mayer, "Win Some, Lose Rarely? Arbitration Forum's Rulings Called One-Sided," *Washington Post*, March 1, 2000, E1).

Although arbitration provisions in employment contracts are increasingly common, there have been reversals. After years of controversy over an arbitration system heavily criticized as unfair by the press, some securities companies have backed away from contractually obligated arbitration of employment disputes (Diane E. Lewis, "Women Get Day in Court," *Boston Globe,* May 16, 1999, G4; Margaret A. Jacobs, "Men's Club: Riding Crop and Slurs: How Wall Street Dealt with a Sex-Bias Case," *Wall Street Journal,* June 9, 1994, A1).

70. Christopher R. Drahozal, in his defense of contractual arbitration, identifies nearly a dozen bills before Congress that would restrict the practice (Drahozal, "'Unfair' Arbitration Clauses," *University of Illinois Law Review* [2001]: 695). Contractual arbitration is also the subject of a steady stream of legal challenges, some of which have reached the Supreme Court. In its most recent decision on contractual arbitration, *EEOC v. Waffle House,* 122 S. Ct. 754 (2002), the Court ruled that the federal Equal Employment Opportunity Commission (EEOC) could litigate an Americans with Disabilities Act discrimination claim even though the complainant in the case had signed away his own right to sue in court. Generally, though, the Court has been supportive of contractual arbitration, as in the most often cited arbitration case, *Gilmer v. Interstate/Johnson Lane Company,* 500 U.S. 20 (1991).

71. Jeb Barnes, "Bankrupt Bargain? Bankruptcy Reform and the Politics of Adversarial Legalism," *Journal of Law and Politics* 13 (1997): 893.

72. John W. Kingdon, *Agendas, Alternatives, and Public Policies,* 2nd ed. (New York: HarperCollins, 1995), 122.

73. Price V. Fishback and Shawn Everett Kantor, *A Prelude to the Welfare State: The Origins of Workers' Compensation* (Chicago: University of Chicago Press, 2000).

74. Bob Van Voris, "New Terrorism Laws Raise Fears of Tort Reform," *Recorder* (November 29, 2001), 3; Juliet Eilperin, "Debating the Limits of Liability," *Washington Post,* November 17, 2001, A8.

75. [Note,] "Innovative No-Fault Tort Reform for an Endangered Specialty," *Virginia Law Review* 74 (1988): 1487.

76. For a description, see Richard L. Rabin, "Some Thoughts on the Efficacy of a Mass Toxics Administrative Compensation Scheme," *University of Maryland Law Review* 52 (1993): 956.

77. Paul Weiler reviews all the medical malpractice tort reforms that have been proposed and favors a no-fault system in *Medical Malpractice on Trial* (Cambridge, Mass.: Harvard University Press, 1991).

78. Rabin, "Some Thoughts on the Efficacy of a Mass Toxics Administrative Compensation Scheme."

79. George Miller, "Don't Let Industry Shirk Its Duty," and Gary Hart, "Let Government Bear Its Share," *New York Times,* September 5, 1982, F2.

80. Jeb Barnes, "Bankrupt Bargain?"

81. Kinney, "Malpractice Reform in the 1990s," 106; see also Patricia Danzon, "Tort Reform: The Case of Medical Malpractice," *Oxford Review of Economic Policy* 10:1 (1994): 84–98.

82. Under these laws, a custodial parent may apply to a state or local agency, which uses fixed rules to determine the appropriate level of support and enforces

its determination against the noncustodial parent. Thus what was a court-centered system has been largely replaced by a bureaucratic process (Jyl J. Josephson, *Gender, Families and State: Child Support Policy in the United States* [Lanham, Md.: Rowman and Littlefield, 1997], 29–55).

83. Phillipe Nonet, *Administrative Justice* (New York: Russell Sage, 1969).

84. Milo Geyelin and James S. Hirsch, "Bumped Fliers Can Sue Airlines for Damages," *Wall Street Journal*, June 7, 1993, B1.

85. Ellen Ruppell Shell, "An Element of Doubt," *Atlantic Monthly*, December 1995, 24–39.

86. Mark Hansen, "Just Say 'See You in Court,'" *ABA Journal*, December 1996, 30.

87. David E. Rosenbaum, "Going Easy on Parents Isn't So Easy," *New York Times*, May 6, 2000, sec. 4, p. 6.

88. Hillary Rodham proposed an array of rights for children, going so far as to suggest that age should be considered a "suspect classification" under the Constitution's Equal Protection Clause, since children are a "discrete and insular" minority. See Hillary Rodham, "Children under the Law," *Harvard Educational Review* 43 (1973): 512.

89. "No Lawyers for Kids," *Wall Street Journal*, November 8, 1994, B5; John Leo, "The Conflict over Children's Rights," *San Diego Union-Tribune*, August 27, 1992, B13.

90. But animal rights activists do seem to be making gains. A lawsuit filed under the Federal Animal Welfare Act gave a zoo visitor standing to sue the government to force it to create regulations concerning the living conditions of chimpanzees. See William Glaberson, "Legal Pioneers Seek to Raise Lowly Status of Animals," *New York Times*, August 18, 1999, A1.

91. Dietrich Rueschmeyer, "Comparing Legal Professions: A State-Centered Approach," in *Lawyers in Society: Comparative Theories,* ed. Richard L. Abel and Philip S. C. Lewis (Berkeley and Los Angeles: University of California Press, 1989), 3:306–308. On the political divisions within the American bar, see John P. Heinz and Edward O. Laumann, *Chicago Lawyers: The Social Structure of the Bar* (New York: Russell Sage Foundation, 1982).

92. Galanter shows that the correct figure for the U.S. share of lawyers is more like 25 to 33 percent, roughly the U.S. portion of world GNP (Galanter, "News From Nowhere," 78). The 70 percent figure was at one point quoted by antilitigation Supreme Court chief justice Warren Burger and has since echoed through the litigation debate. The $300 billion figure was made up from an executive's estimate of direct tort costs plus a very rough estimation of indirect costs. It almost certainly egregiously overestimates the true costs of the tort system (Galanter, "News from Nowhere," 83–90). Nor does each "excess" lawyer in the United States cost the nation $1 million, a figure estimated by antilitigation economist Stephen Magee (Galanter, "News from Nowhere," 81–83; see also Stephen P. Magee, "The Optimum Number of Lawyers: A Reply to Epp," *Law and Social Inquiry* 17 [1992]: 667–693; Charles R. Epp, "Do Lawyers Impair Economic Growth?" *Law and Social Inquiry* 17 [1992]: 585–623; and Frank B. Cross, "The First Thing We Do, Let's Kill All the Economists," *Texas Law Review* 70 [1992]: 645–683). Galanter's latest rebuttal to the claims of the tort

reform movement is "An Oil Strike in Hell: Contemporary Legends about the Civil Justice System," *Arizona Law Review* 40 (1998): 717–752.

93. True to the title, Dan Quayle repeats both figures in his recent book *Standing Firm* without even addressing Galanter's refutation (Quayle, "Too Many Lawyers," in *Standing Firm: A Vice Presidential Memoir* [New York: Harper Collins, 1994], 282–290.

94. I thank William Haltom and Michael McCann for helping me to see the significance of this pattern in the academic community; see McCann, Haltom, and Bloom, "Java Jive." On the Manhattan Institute see note 16. Some examples of research deflating the claims of tort reformers are Hensler et al., *Compensation for Accidental Injuries in the United States*; Daniels and Martin, *Civil Juries and the Politics of Reform*; Hans, *Business on Trial*; Henderson and Eisenberg, "The Quiet Revolution," and "Inside the Quiet Revolution"; Galanter, "Introduction: Shadow Play: The Fabled Menace of Punitive Damages" (introduction to special issue on punitive damages), *Wisconsin Law Review* (1998): 1; Galanter, "Reading the Landscape of Disputes"; Miller and Sarat, "Grievances, Claims and Disputes"; and Brian Ostrom, Neal Kauder, and Robert C. LaFountain, *Examining the Work of State Courts, 1999–2000* (Williamsburg, Va.: National Center for State Courts, 2000). Two recent protort books by academics are Carl T. Bogus, *Why Lawsuits Are Good for America* (New York: New York University Press, 2001), and Thomas H. Koenig and Michael L. Rustad, *In Defense of Tort Law* (New York: New York University Press, 2001). It is important to distinguish between tort reform and replacement schemes such as no-fault: there is much more support within academia for replacement efforts, and many academics—for example, Jeffrey O'Connell, Paul Weiler, and Steve Sugarman—have created replacement proposals (see n.15).

95. See, for example, Richard L. Abel, "The Contradictions of Informal Justice," in *The Politics of Informal Justice,* vol. 1: *The American Experience* (New York: Academic Press, 1982); Harrington, *Shadow Justice*; Sally Engle Merry, "The Social Organization of Mediation in Nonindustrial Societies: Implications for Informal Community Justice in America," in *The Politics of Informal Justice,* vol. 2: *Comparative Studies* (New York: Academic Press, 1982), 17–45; Richard Delgado, "ADR and the Dispossessed: Recent Books about the Deformalization Movement," *Law and Social Inquiry* 13 (1988): 145–154; and Laura Nader, "The ADR Explosion: The Implications of Rhetoric in Legal Reform," *Windsor Yearbook of Access to Justice* 8 (1988): 269–291.

96. Owen Fiss, "Against Settlement," *Yale Law Journal* 93 (1984): 1073; Judith Resnik, "Managerial Judges," *Harvard Law Review* 96 (1982): 374–448.

97. The concept of the "one-shotter" was developed by Marc Galanter in his classic article "Why the 'Haves' Come Out Ahead: Speculations on the Limits of Legal Change," *Law and Society Review* 9 (1974): 95–151.

98. Robert Evans, director, Governmental Affairs Office, American Bar Association, telephone conversation with author, February 8, 2002.

99. Information obtained from the website of the Center for Responsive Politics, <http://www.opensecrets.org/lobbyists/> and <http://www.opensecrets.org/pacs/>, accessed April 1, 2002.

100. The organization was first called the National Association of Claimants Compensation Attorneys (NACCA), later becoming ATLA. For a brief history of NACCA's origins, see Samuel B. Horovitz, "NACCA and Its Objectives," *NACCA Law Journal* (1952): 7–36.

101. The story of the rise of the plaintiff bar is told by one of its pioneers, Stuart M. Speiser, in *Lawyers and the American Dream* (New York: M. Evans, 1993). Speiser recounts Belli's crusade to educate the plaintiff bar and ATLA's development as an information-sharing forum for plaintiff lawyers at 222–236.

102. Interview with C. Thomas Bendorf, former lobbyist, Association of Trial Lawyers of America, Turton, S.D., August 6, 1994.

103. Interview with Alan A. Parker, senior director for public affairs, ATLA, 1984–94, Vienna, Va., July 12, 1994.

104. Speiser, *Lawyers and the American Dream*, 19.

105. Glenn R. Simpson, "Study of Trial Lawyers Finds Eight May Have Exceeded $25,000 Limit," *Roll Call* (May 1, 1995), 14; Jill Abramson and Amy Stevens, "Class-Action Clash: King of 'Strike Suits' Finds Style Cramped by Legal-Overhaul Bill," *Wall Street Journal,* March 30, 1995, A1.

106. The most prominent of the Pound-funded studies is Michael Rustad's work on punitive damages, which found them far less common than many suppose (Rustad, *Demystifying Punitive Damages in Products Liability Cases* [Washington, D.C.: Roscoe Pound Foundation, 1991]).

107. Rowland Evans and Robert Novak, "America's Most Powerful Lobby," *Reader's Digest,* April 1994, 131–35.

108. Interview with Pamela Gilbert, director, Public Citizen CongressWatch, Washington, D.C., June 10, 1994.

109. Interview with Ralph Nader, Washington, D.C., May 2, 1994.

110. Interview with Linda Lipsen, public affairs director, ATLA, Washington, D.C., July 7, 1994; Andrew Blum, "Trial Lawyers Set to Get Tough," *National Law Journal* (July 31, 1995), A6.

111. I derived this number using a list of such cases provided by the American Tort Reform Association that was updated through June 2001. Tort reformer Victor Schwartz, whose count (unlike mine) extends back to before 1990, identified a total of ninety-one state court decisions holding tort reform laws unconstitutional (Victor Schwartz and Leah Lorber, "Judicial Nullification of Tort Reforms: A Call to Arms to Stop It Now," *Metropolitan Corporate Counsel* [April 2000], 39). ATLA has provided much of the expertise in the tort reform lawsuits; in 2001, the association created the Center for Constitutional Litigation to support the work of challenging state tort laws (Fred Baron, "ATLA Helps Knock Down Florida 'Tort Reform' Law," *Trial* [April 2001], 9). For two competing perspectives on judicial review of tort reform legislation, see Robert S. Peck, "In Defense of Fundamental Principles: The Unconstitutionality of Tort Reform," *Seton Hall Law Review* 31 (2001): 672; and Victor Schwartz, "Judicial Nullification of Tort Reform: Ignoring History, Logic, and Fundamentals of Constitutional Law," *Seton Hall Law Review* 31 (2001): 688.

112. Deborah Goldberg, Craig Holman, and Samantha Sanchez, *The New Politics of Judicial Elections: How 2000 Was a Watershed Year for Big Money,*

Special Interest Pressure, and TV Advertising in State Supreme Court Campaigns
(New York: Brennan Center for Justice, 2002), 7, figure 1; 8, figure 2; 9, figure 3;
11, figure 5; 15, figure 8; and 16, figure 9.

113. Barry Bauman, Lawyers for Civil Justice, telephone conversation with
author, April 5, 2002.

114. Michael McCann, *Taking Reform Seriously: Perspectives on Public
Interest Liberalism* (Ithaca, N.Y.: Cornell University Press, 1986), 108.

115. An antilitigation workers' compensation reform plan proposed by California Governor Pete Wilson was an example, Nader said, of "Marie Antoinette
morality" and "a consistent display of cruelty" (Vlae Kershner, "Nader Blasts
Worker Comp Plan," *San Francisco Chronicle,* October 21, 1992). The antilitigation advertising campaign sponsored by Aetna, Nader said, would make "even
the most adept Kremlin propagandist . . . proud" (Nader, "Keynote Address,
Symposium on the Future of Tort Litigation in California," *Santa Clara Law
Review* 29 (1989): 511). For some other examples of Nader's prolitigation rhetoric, see Nader, "The Assault on Injured Victims Rights," *Denver University Law
Review* 64 (1988): 625–39; "The Corporate Drive to Restrict Their Victims'
Rights," *Gonzaga Law Review* 22 (1986): 15–29; and Nader and Joan Clay-
brook, "Preserving a Pillar of Our Democracy," *Trial* 27:12 (1991): 45.

116. Nader, "Keynote Address," 518.

117. Nader, "The Trial Bar and the Public Interest," *Trial Lawyers Quarterly*
19:3 (1988): 8, 16.

118. The story is told in David Sanford's relentlessly critical book, *Me &
Ralph: Is Nader Unsafe for America?* (Washington, D.C.: New Republic, 1976),
33–47.

119. Tatiana Boncompagni, "Nader Faces Trial Lawyer Backlash over Gore
Defeat," *Recorder* (February 13, 2001), 3. Nader identifies Baron as "a friend for
thirty years" who, inspired by a Nader speech while in law school, changed his
career aspirations from tax to tort law, becoming a "pioneering trial lawyer"
(Nader, *Crashing the Party: Taking on the Corporate Government in an Age of
Surrender* [New York: St. Martin's Press, 2002], 262).

120. Ibid., 262–66.

121. Charles McCarry, *Citizen Nader* (New York: Saturday Review Press,
1972), 197.

122. Nader, interview, May 2, 1994.

123. Ibid.; and Nader, "The Trial Bar and the Public Interest," 9–10.

124. "These executives like routine. They use the word 'predictability.' They
don't like to have their golf game disturbed on weekends. Litigation upsets them
in that way and the economic cost is trivial." Nader, "Keynote Address," 513.

125. Nader, "Trial Lawyers and the Public Interest," 9.

126. Nader, interview.

127. See *Lujan v. Defenders of Wildlife,* 504 U.S. 555 (1992), in which the
Court ruled that the plaintiffs lacked standing under the Endangered Species Act
because they failed to allege concrete injuries. In *Bennett v. Spear,* 117 S. Ct. 1154
(1997), however, the Court found that property owners, along with environmentalists, can have standing under the act.

128. *Rust v. Sullivan,* 500 U.S. 173 (1991).

129. *Amchem Products v. Windsor,* 521 U.S. 591 (1997).

130. *Daubert v. Merrell Dow Pharmaceuticals,* 509 U.S. 579 (1993); *Kumho Tire v. Carmichael,* 526 U.S. 137 (1999).

131. *Felker v. Turpin,* 519 U.S. 989 (1996).

132. *Seminole Tribes v. Florida,* 517 U.S. 44 (1996); *City of Boerne v. Flores,* 521 U.S. 507 (1997); *Alden v. Maine,* 527 U.S. 706 (1999); *College Savings Bank v. Florida Prepaid Postsecondary Education Expense Board,* 527 U.S. 666 (1999); *Kimel v. Florida Board of Regents,* 528 U.S. 62 (2000); and *University of Alabama v. Garrett,* 531 U.S. 356 (2001).

133. *United States v. Morrison,* 529 U.S. 598 (2000), struck down the Violence against Women Act; *Bourne v. Flores* overturned the Religious Freedom Restoration Act as applied to states; *Kimel v. Florida* and *Alabama v. Garrett* ruled that state sovereignty as recognized in the Eleventh Amendment precluded citizen lawsuits for money damages against the states under the Age Discrimination in Employment Act and the Americans with Disabilities Act, respectively.

134. *BMW of North America v. Gore,* 517 U.S. 559 (1996). In the case, the jury's punitive damage award was more than five hundred times actual damages.

135. *Honda Motor Co. v. Oberg,* 517 U.S. 1219 (1994).

136. Stuart Taylor, Jr., "Not So Conservative: The Supreme Court and the Disability Decisions," *National Journal,* July 3, 1999, 1933.

137. Lori Johnson, "Congress versus the Judicial Branch in the Battle over the Scope of Federal Court Jurisdiction" (paper presented at the annual meeting of the Western Political Science Association, Long Beach, Calif., March 24, 2002). See also Ann Althouse, "Inside the Federalism Cases: Concern about Federal Courts," *Annals of the American Academy of Political and Social Science* 574 (2001): 132.

138. Some works that have influenced my approach to case study research are Gary King, Robert O. Keohane, and Sidney Verba, *Designing Social Inquiry: Scientific Inference in Qualitative Research* (Princeton, N.J.: Princeton University Press, 1994); Alexander George, "Case Studies and Theory Development: The Method of Structured, Focused Comparison, in *Diplomacy: New Approaches in History, Theory and Policy,* ed. Paul Gordon (New York: Free Press, 1979), 43–68; Harry Eckstein, "Case Studies and Theory Development," in *Handbook of Political Science,* vol. 7: *Strategies of Inquiry,* ed. Fred Greenstein and Nelson W. Polsby (Reading, Mass.: Addison-Wesley, 1975); David Collier, "The Comparative Method: Two Decades of Change," in *Comparative Political Dynamics: Global Research Perspectives,* ed. Dankwart A. Rustow and Kenneth Paul Erickson (New York: Harper Collins, 1991), 7–31; Charles Ragin, *The Comparative Method: Moving beyond Qualitative and Quantitative Strategies* (Berkeley and Los Angeles: University of California Press, 1987); and Robert Yin, *Case Study Research: Design and Methods* (Beverly Hills, Calif.: Sage, 1984).

139. In small-*n* studies the purpose of case selection is to maximize the range of values for the most significant variables, those that theory suggests are crucial. The researcher should try to get as much variety as possible so that all the mechanisms that shape relationships between variables can be assessed. Guided by this

criterion, I picked three cases that varied on many counts including partisanship (high/low), public visibility (high/low), level of government (state/federal), lawyer interest group involvement (high/low), rights discourse (high/low), area of law (tort/nontort), and effort to reform old law/resistance to new law. Most important, I picked one case in which the antilitigation effort was successful and two in which it was not.

Although the small-n design limits the scope of this study's conclusions, in a few instances more rigorous tests of theories are conducted. For example, within two of the cases, I employ a roll-call vote study to test a theory about the behavior of lawyer legislators. In addition, at several points, particularly the conclusion, I expand my number of cases (n) by considering comparable cases in the United States or comparisons with patterns of policy in other industrialized nations.

The case studies are detailed descriptions that include measurements of all the variables suggested by the explanations considered. The narratives of each case were generated from a variety of sources, including court cases, reports, hearings, and floor debates. For the case studies, I interviewed sixty participants, some in person, others by telephone. The interviews ranged in length from five minutes to two hours. The interviews are footnoted wherever data from them is introduced, with only a few exceptions—for five of the interviews I agreed not to cite the participant by name. There was no attempt to standardize interviews since participants were involved in many different aspects of the cases. Interviewees were selected from references in primary and secondary documents and by referral—a "snowball sampling" technique appropriate for narrative case studies. Where possible and helpful for measuring variables I gathered quantitative data, including the roll-call votes.

140. I define a "serious attempt" to include any bill or amendment on which a hearing or a floor debate has been held. This simply eliminates bills that are introduced but gather dust and cases in which new litigation rights are enacted but are not opposed. The fact that in some cases new litigation rights are created without any opposition is, as I have suggested, theoretically interesting and worthy of study in itself. This study is, however, limited in scope to antilitigation *efforts*.

2. THE CREATION OF A LITIGIOUS POLICY:
THE AMERICANS WITH DISABILITIES ACT

1. These statistics come from the *1998 National Organization on Disability/Harris Survey of Americans with Disabilities* (New York: Lou Harris and Associates, 1998), 15, exhibit 1.

2. The 43 million figure appears in the preamble of the Americans with Disabilities Act (ADA) (*U.S. Code,* vol. 42, sec. 12101(a)1 [1990]). A more appropriate measure of disability, according to some researchers, is the number of people who are limited in their abilities to perform everyday activities. This approach generates an estimate of 36 million, including 2 million people in institutionalized

settings. See Mitchell P. LaPlante, "The Demographics of Disability," *Milbank Quarterly* 69, supplement 1/2 (1991): 65.

The ADA itself defines disability as "a physical or mental impairment that substantially limits one or more . . . major life activities," though the law also applies to those who have "a record of such an impairment" or are "regarded as having such an impairment" (*U.S. Code*, vol. 42, sec. 12102[2]). Courts have narrowly interpreted these provisions, so that the number of people actually covered by the ADA may be much lower than the 43 million cited in the statute's preamble.

3. Deborah Stone traces the evolution of the concept of disability in *The Disabled State* (London: Macmillan, 1984).

4. *U.S. Code*, vol. 42, sec. 12112.

5. Ibid., secs. 12131, 12148, 12181, 12182, 12183.

6. Ibid., secs. 12131, 12181, 12182, 12183, 12188.

7. "The Lawyer's Employment Act" [editorial], *Wall Street Journal*, September 11, 1989, A18.

8. Paul K. Longmore and David Golberger document a fascinating spurt of 1930s disability activism, the formation and dissolution of the League of the Physically Handicapped. League members, like disability activists much later in the twentieth century, protested against government programs that treated them as helpless children; they demanded that the Works Projects Administration (WPA) provide jobs equally to the disabled and nondisabled (Longmore and Goldberger, "The League of the Physically Handicapped and the Great Depression: A Case Study in the New Disability History," *The Journal of American History* 87 (2000): 888–922). The National Association of the Deaf fought employment discrimination beginning in the early twentieth century and protested laws prohibiting deaf people from obtaining driver's licenses in the 1940s. Organizations for blind people pushed for laws, first enacted in the 1930s, protecting guide dogs and white canes. Congress banned discrimination against people with disabilities in the civil service in 1948. Five states adopted similar bans; a few even had nondiscrimination laws in certain job categories, particularly teaching. See Jacobus ten Broek, "The Right to Live in the World: The Disabled and the Law of Torts," *California Law Review* 54 (1966): 846.

Rita Varela notes that the issue of access for mobility-impaired people was raised in the 1950s by paralyzed veterans, who fought for accessible facilities at Veterans Administration hospitals. In 1959 several disability groups met with the American Standards Association to agree on a set of standards for architectural accessibility. These standards were adopted by many states in the mid-1960s as part of building accessibility laws and eventually by the federal government for its buildings. See Varela, "Changing Social Attitudes and Legislation Regarding Disability," in *Independent Living for Physically Disabled People*, ed. Nancy M. Crewe and Irvina Kenneth Zola (San Francisco: Jossey-Bass, 1983), 28–48. These early laws were generally enforced by administrative mechanisms. An exception was Wisconsin's accessibility law, which created a private right of action (ten Broek, "The Right to Live in the World," 863).

9. Susan M. Olson, *Clients and Lawyers: Securing the Rights of Disabled Persons* (Westport, Conn.: Greenwood Press, 1984), 42.

10. Richard K. Scotch, *From Good Will to Civil Rights* (Philadelphia: Temple University Press, 1984), 36.

11. Edward D. Berkowitz, "The American Disability System in Historical Perspective," in *Disability Policies and Government Programs,* ed. Edward Berkowitz (New York: Praeger, 1979), 44–45.

12. Gerben DeJong, *The Movement for Independent Living: Origins, Ideology and Implications for Disability Research* (Boston: Medical Rehabilitation Institute, Tufts-New England Medical Center, March 1979), 34–36.

13. Ibid., 60.

14. Edward D. Berkowitz, *Disabled Policy: America's Programs for the Handicapped* (New York: Cambridge University Press, 1987), 203.

15. Institute for Educational Leadership, *Challenges of Emerging Leadership: Community-Based Independent Living Programs and the Disability Rights Movement* (Washington, D.C., 1982), 21–22.

16. Olson, *Clients and Lawyers,* 46.

17. Jacobus ten Broek, "The Disabled and the Law of Welfare," *California Law Review* 54 (1966): 809; and "The Right to Live in the World," 841.

18. In *Pennsylvania Association for Retarded Children v. Commonwealth of Pennsylvania,* 343 F. Supp. 279 (1972), a federal court concluded that the plaintiffs had a "colorable claim" under both the Equal Protection Clause and the Due Process Clause in approving a settlement reached between the parties, but the court did not reach the issue of suspect or semisuspect status. In *Mills v. Board of Education of the District of Columbia,* 348 F. Supp. 866 (1972), the court found a violation of the Due Process Clause because the district was excluding mentally retarded children from schooling, but the decision also rested on local statutes. These cases paved the way for the 1975 passage of the Education for All Handicapped Children Act, which guaranteed all children with disabilities a "free, appropriate education." (On the enactment of the Education for all Handicapped Children Act, see R. Shep Melnick, *Between the Lines: Interpreting Welfare Rights* [Washington, D.C.: Brookings Institution, 1994], 135–159.) The clearest discussion of the place of the disabled in constitutional law came much later, in *Cleburne v. Cleburne Living Centers,* 473 U.S. 432 (1985). Here the Supreme Court ruled that the mentally retarded were not a suspect class deserving of special protection under the Fourteenth Amendment.

19. Interviews with Evan Kemp and Bob Funk, Washington, D.C., December 16, 1993, and with Lex Frieden, Washington D.C., April 21, 1994. Funk contends that the civil rights model might not have come to prominence if not for 504, because the proponents of independent living were interested mainly in creating a more effective model of service delivery. Frieden notes that in Berkeley one could quite easily see the distinction between the two parts of the disability movement: "CIL [The Center for Independent Living] was on one side of Telegraph Avenue and DREDF [the Disability Rights and Education Defense Fund] was on the other side of the street. And a lot of times that street was pretty wide. There were differences of opinion even on Telegraph Avenue on where the movement should go, and there still are." In contrast, Arlene Mayerson, a top DREDF attorney, sees little distinction between the independent living movement and the civil rights movement (interview with Mayerson, Berkeley, Calif., June 2, 1994).

20. Robert A. Katzmann, *Institutional Disability: The Saga of Transportation Policy for the Disabled* (Washington, D.C.: Brookings Institution, 1986), 46.

21. Scotch, *From Good Will to Civil Rights*, 44–45.

22. Ibid., 51–52.

23. Katzmann, *Institutional Disability*, 47.

24. *Rehabilitation Act of 1973, U.S. Code*, vol. 28, sec. 794(a) (1998).

25. Katzmann, *Institutional Disability*, 53.

26. Scotch, *From Good Will to Civil Rights*, 63.

27. Ibid., 75.

28. Scotch, *From Good Will to Civil Rights*, 46.

29. Interview with Robert Funk, former executive director, DREDF, Washington D.C., December 16, 1993.

30. Edward V. Roberts, "Into the Mainstream: The Civil Rights of People with Disabilities," *Civil Rights Digest* (winter 1979), 23–24.

31. Susan Olson notes that the bylaws of the National Federation of the Blind went so far as to prohibit coalitions with other disability groups (Olson, *Clients and Lawyers*, 48).

32. Robert Funk, "Disability Rights: From Caste to Class in the Context of Civil Rights," in *Images of the Disabled, Disabling Images*, ed. Alan Gartner and Tom Joe (New York: Praeger, 1986), 7.

33. Frank Bowe, *Handicapping America: Barriers to Disabled People* (New York: Harper and Row, 1978), 224. See also Harlan Hahn, "Disability Policy and the Problem of Discrimination," *American Behavioral Scientist* 28:3 (1985): 293–318.

34. Evan Kemp, Jr., "Aiding the Disabled: No Pity, Please," *New York Times*, September 3, 1981, A19.

35. Bowe, *Handicapping America*, 171.

36. Kemp, "Aiding the Disabled."

37. Joseph P. Shapiro, *No Pity: People with Disabilities Forging a New Civil Rights Movement* (New York: Times Books, 1993), 22.

38. See Harlan Hahn, "Civil Rights for Disabled Americans: The Foundation of a Political Agenda," in *Images of the Disabled, Disabling Images*, 188.

39. John Gliedman and William Roth, *The Unexpected Minority: Handicapped Children in America* (New York: Carnegie Corporation, 1980), 34. Renee Anspach sees in disability activism a kind of identity politics (Anspach, "From Stigma to Identity Politics: Political Activism among the Physically Disabled and Former Mental Patients," *Social Science and Medicine* 13 [1979]: 765–773).

40. *APTA v. Lewis*, 655 F. 2d 1272 (D.C. Cir., 1981).

41. For examples of backlash reportage, see Henry Fairlie, "We're Overdoing Help for the Handicapped," *Washington Post*, June 1, 1980, D1; and "Must Every Bus Kneel to the Disabled?" *New York Times*, November 18, 1979, 18E.

42. Charles R. Babcock, "Handicapped Policy Undergoing a Rewrite," *Washington Post*, March 2, 1982, A27; Felicity Barringer, "How Handicapped Won Access Rule Fight," *Washington Post*, April 12, 1983, A10.

43. Funk, interview; Barringer, "How Handicapped Won Access Rule Fight."

44. Interview with C. Boyden Gray, White House counsel in the George H.

Bush administration, Washington, D.C., December 13, 1993; Shapiro, *No Pity*, 120.

45. Interview with Evan Kemp, Jr., Washington, D.C., December 16, 1993.

46. Interviews with Gray, Kemp, and Funk.

47. Katzmann, *Institutional Disability*, 125. David Pfeiffer, a disability activist and historian of the disability movement, argues that the Reagan administration's turn on Section 504 arose from its interest in the two "Baby Doe" cases, which involved controversy over whether to provide lifesaving medical treatments to disabled babies. The administration found Section 504 useful in arguing that treatment should be provided (telephone conversation with author, May 6, 1996).

48. Interview with Pat Wright, executive director, DREDF, Washington, D.C., February 3, 1994.

49. Gray, interview.

50. National Council on the Handicapped, *Toward Independence: An Assessment of Federal Laws and Programs Affecting Persons with Disabilities—with Legislative Recommendations* (Washington, D.C.: Government Printing Office, 1986), iv.

51. Interview with Justin Dart, Jr., Washington, D.C., June 18, 1994.

52. Justin W. Dart, Jr., "The ADA: A Promise to Be Kept," in *The Americans with Disabilities Act: From Policy to Practice,* ed. Jane West (New York: Milbank Memorial Fund, 1991), xxi.

53. Dart, interview.

54. Ibid.

55. Dart, "The ADA: A Promise to Be Kept," xxii.

56. National Council on the Handicapped, U.S. Department of Education, *National Policy for Persons with Disabilities* (Washington, D.C., 1983), 7.

57. U.S. Commission on Civil Rights, *Accommodating the Spectrum of Individual Abilities* (Washington, D.C., September 1983).

58. Robert Burgdorf and Christopher Bell, "Eliminating Discrimination against Physically and Mentally Handicapped Persons: A Statutory Blueprint," *Mental and Physical Disability Law Reporter* 8 (1984): 64.

59. Interview with Robert Burgdorf, Jr., Washington, D.C., February 23, 1994.

60. Interviews with Dart, Frieden, and Burgdorf.

61. National Council on the Handicapped, *Toward Independence*, 1.

62. Ibid., 12.

63. Ibid., 1.

64. Ibid., 2. In her transmittal letter to President Reagan, Chairperson Parrino argued that if the recommendations of the council were implemented, "current Federal expenditures for disability can be significantly redirected from dependency-related approaches to programs that enhance independence and productivity of people with disabilities, thereby engendering future efficiencies in Federal spending" (ii).

65. Ibid., 8.

66. Ibid.

67. Ibid.

68. Ibid., 20.

69. See generally Katzmann, *Institutional Disability*.

70. Justin Dart, Jr., interview.

71. Reagan responded in a written statement: "I agree with the goals implicit in *Toward Independence*—equal opportunity and full social participation for all Americans, and I am pleased to see that your report sets forth a comprehensive agenda for progress toward these goals. . . . [However] the road toward full independence will not be easy" (Ronald Reagan, January 1986, quoted in National Council on the Handicapped, *On the Threshold of Independence: A Report to the President and to the Congress of the United States* [Washington, D.C., January 1988], xvii).

72. Louis Harris and Associates, *The ICD Survey of Disabled Americans: Bringing Disabled Americans into the Mainstream* (New York, March 1986).

73. National Council on the Handicapped, *On the Threshold of Independence*, 25–39.

74. S.R. 2345, 100th Cong., 2d sess., *Congressional Record* (hereafter cited as *Cong. Rec.*), daily ed. (April 28, 1988): S5089; H.R. 4498, 100th Cong., 2d sess., *Cong. Rec.*, daily ed. (April 19, 1988), H2757.

75. Julie Kosterlitz, "Joining Forces," *National Journal* (January 28, 1989), 194; United States Presidential Commission on the Human Immunodeficiency Virus Epidemic (1988), 123, reproduced in U.S House of Representatives, Committee on Education and Labor, *Legislative History of the Americans with Disabilities Act* (Washington, D.C.: Government Printing Office, 1990), 981.

76. Shapiro, *No Pity*, 96.

77. Phil McCombs, "The Distant Drum of C. Boyden Gray," *Washington Post*, March 31, 1989, D1–D8; Gray, interview.

78. Interview with Bill Roper, former deputy assistant to the president for domestic policy, Atlanta, Ga., June 6, 1994. Roger Clegg, a deputy assistant attorney general in the civil rights division, remembers that he expressed "fundamental misgivings" but recalls only limited public discussion in the White House over the merits of the ADA (interview with Roger Clegg, Washington D.C., May 17, 1994).

79. Interview with Robert Silverstein, chief counsel, Senate Subcommittee on Disability, Washington, D.C., December 16, 1993.

80. Paula Yost, "Tedious Meetings, Testy Exchanges Produced Disability-Rights Bill," *Washington Post*, August 7, 1989, A4.

81. Interview with Chai Feldblum, former legislative counsel, AIDS Project, American Civil Liberties Union, Washington, D.C., March 21, 1994; interview with Pat Wright, executive director, DREDF, Washington, D.C., February 3, 1994.

82. Interview with Arlene Mayerson, DREDF, Berkeley, Calif., June 2, 1994.

83. Interview with Ralph Neas, Washington, D.C., July 19, 1994.

84. Ibid.

85. Ibid.

86. 465 U.S. 555 (1984).

87. *Consolidated Rail Corporation v. LeStrange Darrone*, 465 U.S. 102 (1984).

88. Jane West, "Moving toward the Mainstream: Disability Rights Policy and Politics in the 100th Congress" (Jane West and Associates, Chevy Chase, Md., 1992, photocopy), 56–57.

89. Wright, interview.

90. NFIB representative Sally Douglas argued in congressional testimony that the ADA was in fundamental respects different from other civil rights laws because it (1) covered a broader scope of private businesses, (2) required affirmative and possibly costly actions by a business, (3) had stiffer remedies, and (4) was more adversarial and legalistic in tone. Thus far more compromise was necessary, Douglas argued, to make the bill workable and fair. See "Statement of Sally Douglas, National Federation of Independent Business," in House Committee on Labor and Human Resources and Senate Subcommittee on the Handicapped, *Americans with Disabilities Act of 1989: Hearings on S. 933,* 101st Cong., 1st sess., May 10, 1989, 499–511.

91. Interview with John Motley, director of federal governmental relations, National Federation of Independent Businesses, Washington, D.C., June 9, 1994.

92. Sara Watson makes this point in her article "A Study in Legislative Strategy: The Passage of the ADA," in *From Policy to Practice,* 25–34.

93. Interviews with John Tysse, lobbyist, Labor Policy Association, Washington, D.C., May 27, 1994; Wendy Lechner, legislative representative, National Federation of Independent Businesses, Washington, D.C., July 29, 1994; Lawrence Lorber, lobbyist, National Association of Manufacturers, Washington, D.C., May 19 and 26, 1994; and Bill Roper.

94. Quoted by Senator Tom Harkin, House Committee on Labor and Human Resources and Senate Subcommittee on the Handicapped, *Americans with Disabilities Act of 1989,* May 9, 1989, 23.

95. Testimony of Richard L. Thornburgh, Attorney General of the United States, Senate Committee on Labor and Human Resources and Subcommittee on the Handicapped, *Americans with Disabilities Act of 1989,* June 22, 1989.

96. *Americans with Disabilities Act,* sec. 12188.

97. Letter from Attorney General Richard Thornburgh, March 12, 1990, quoted in *Cong. Rec.,* daily ed. (May 29, 1990), 101st Cong., 2d sess., H2613.

98. *Cong. Rec.,* daily ed. (September 7, 1989), 101st Cong., 1st sess., S10714.

99. At a hearing in which one NFIB member attacked several provisions in the bill, Bartlett criticized the member for not providing concrete advice: "I am not suggesting you didn't give us good testimony, you did, but your testimony doesn't lead us anywhere" (House Committee on Education and Labor, *Legislative History of Public Law 101-336: The Americans with Disabilities Act of 1989,* 101st Cong., 2d sess., 1990, Committee Print, 2:1651).

100. See *Cong. Rec.,* daily ed. (May 17, 1990), 101st Cong., 2d sess., H2472. A ceiling on reasonable accommodations amounting to 10 percent of an employee's annual wages was defeated on the House floor, 187 to 213 (see ibid., H2475).

101. "Bush Vetoes Job Bias Bill; Override Fails," *1990 Congressional Quarterly Almanac,* 462–73.

102. Letter from Attorney General Richard Thornburgh.

103. Interviews with Silverstein, Wright, and Feldblum.

104. *Cong. Rec.,* daily ed. (May 22, 1990), 101st Cong., 1st sess., H2612.

105. Ibid., H2615.

106. Ibid.

107. Ibid., H2616.

108. Testimony of Sandra Parrino, chairperson, National Council on the Handicapped, in House Committee on Education and Labor, *Legislative History of Public Law 101-336*, 2:955.

109. Testimony of Lisa Carl, May 10, 1989, in House Committee on Labor and Human Resources and Senate Subcommittee on the Handicapped, *Americans with Disabilities Act of 1989*, 64–65.

110. Testimony of Betty Correy and Emory Correy, May 10, 1989, in ibid.,102.

111. Testimony of Tony Coelho, September 27, 1988, House Committee on Education and Labor, *Legislative History of Public Law 101-336*, 2:939–40.

112. Some of these divergences are discussed in U.S. Commission on Civil Rights, *Accommodating the Spectrum of Individual Abilities*, 142–158; and Jane West, "The Evolution of Disability Rights," in *From Policy to Practice*, 4–9.

113. U.S. Commission on Civil Rights, *Accommodating the Spectrum of Individual Abilities*, 144.

114. In the Harris survey commissioned by the National Council on the Handicapped, disabled people were asked which was more of an obstacle to a better job, employer reactions to their disability or the disability itself. Seventy-one percent said that the disability was more of a barrier; only 18 percent thought employer reactions were more important. Thus the respondents disagreed with a central tenet of the rights model, that socially imposed barriers limit disabled people more than their physical impairments (Louis Harris and Associates, *The ICD Survey of Disabled Americans*, 79).

115. In addition, only 45 percent of the survey respondents agreed that disabled people "are a minority group in the same sense as are blacks and Hispanics." Among those who considered themselves disabled, 46 percent said they had a "very strong" or "somewhat strong" sense of common identity with other disabled people, while 35 percent said they had "some sense" and 8 percent said they had no sense of common identity at all (Ibid., 15, 114, 111).

116. According to the Harris survey, 13 percent of all disabled people acquired their condition at birth or in adolescence (Ibid., 27, table 9).

117. The National Federation of Independent Businesses (NFIB) was the most critical of the business groups and thus at times pointed to some of the divergences between disability rights law and traditional civil rights law (see note 90).

In floor debate and hearings on the ADA I could locate only one instance in which a member of Congress directly challenged the civil rights model. Bud Shuster, a representative from Pennsylvania, argued that the ADA was not a civil rights bill, because it was riddled with exceptions and compromises: "Mr. Chairman, by calling this a civil rights bill, that does not make it a civil rights bill except that I suppose we can do anything we want to do in this Congress in terms of passing laws, using whatever words we choose to use. However, if my colleagues look at the logic of this bill, there are numerous exceptions to it" (*Congr. Rec.*, daily ed. [May 17, 1990], 101st Cong., 2d sess., H2437). Shuster favored reducing mandates on local transit systems and argued that mandates in the ADA should be evaluated strictly on a cost-benefit basis, not as a matter of civil rights. One subtle way in which members of Congress undermined the rights model was by describing the ADA as a bill to help out disabled people; but this was never part of a critique of the rights model.

In floor debate and in the hearings I could locate only one suggestion of a non-litigious alternative to the ADA. During final consideration of the ADA on the Senate floor, Senator Armstrong suggested that Congress should have created a tax credit. He called the ADA "a legislative Rorschach test, an inkblot whose meaning and significance will be determined through years of costly litigation." Armstrong did, however, vote for passage (*Cong. Rec.*, daily ed. [July 13, 1990], 101st Cong., 2d sess., S9694).

118. Gary Orfield tells this story in his book *The Reconstruction of Southern Education: The Schools and the 1964 Civil Rights Act* (New York: John Wiley, 1969).

119. Gerald Rosenberg argues that the role of litigation in the achievement of civil rights has been greatly exaggerated. See Rosenberg, *The Hollow Hope: Can Courts Bring About Social Change?*

120. See Mark C. Miller, *The High Priests of American Politics: The Role of Lawyers in American Political Institutions* (Knoxville, Tenn.: University of Tennessee Press, 1995), 57–75.

121. Bonnie Tucker, "Section 504 of the Rehabilitation Act after Ten Years of Enforcement: The Past and the Future," *University of Illinois Law Review* (1989): 877.

122. Although this case is about judicial enforcement as an alternative to agency enforcement rather than judicial review of agency decisions, it does seem to provide some support to Charles Shipan's approach to modeling interest group and legislator choices about judicial review provisions. Shipan argues that experiences with agencies and courts, institutional theories about the capabilities of the two, an understanding of the dominant legal philosophies of the day, and recognition of the capacities of other interest groups all shape preferences over judicial review (Shipan, *Designing Judicial Review*, 15–36). The case of the ADA demonstrates how experiences and institutional theories can shape preferences. But notice that all actors in this case *assumed* courts would be involved. This makes it hard to know exactly what was behind their preferences and whether their preferences were as goal directed as both Shipan's account and mine suggests.

123. See Katzmann, *Institutional Disability,* for a full account.

124. See Stephen L. Percy, "ADA, Disability Rights, and Evolving Regulatory Federalism," *Publius* 23:4 (1993): 87–105. By the late 1980s forty-six states had laws regarding discrimination against disabled people in employment. The ADA leaves these laws in place but adds ADA regulations on top of them.

125. Civil rights activists attempted to empower the EEOC to enforce its own rulings, through "cease and desist" orders, but this was resisted on several grounds. Opponents argued, for example, that it "would be inconsistent with our system of division of government powers to subject state and local authorities to the cease-and-desist power of a federal commission" (House Committee on Education and Labor, *Equal Employment Opportunities Enforcement Act of 1971,* 64, quoted in Landsberg, *Enforcing Civil Rights,* 68).

126. Stanley Herr, "Reforming Disability Nondiscrimination Laws: A Comparative Perspective," *University of Michigan Law Review,* forthcoming. In

Britain, Herr notes, the newly formed Disability Rights Commission has been granted power to compel compliance with nondiscrimination rulings. Canadian discrimination complaints are brought to the Canadian Human Rights Commission, which investigates, mediates, and if necessary, brings cases to the Human Rights Tribunal (Marcia H. Rioux and Catherine L. Frazee, "The Canadian Framework for Disability Equality Rights," in *Disability, Diversability and Legal Change*, ed. Melinda Jones and Lee Ann Basser Marks [Boston: M. Nijhoff, 1999], 173). In Australia the Human Rights and Equal Opportunity Commission takes complaints, attempts conciliation, and when no agreement can be reached, holds hearings. Originally the commission was empowered to enforce its decisions, but the Australian High Court ruled this unconstitutional. As a result, complainants who face unyielding defendants must, as in the United States, gain their victories in court (Jones and Basser, "Disability, Rights and Law in Australia," in *Disability, Diversability and Legal Change*, 199–200). Herr counts forty-one nations with disability rights laws, but this figure lumps together purely symbolic laws—constitutional proclamations and never-used criminal statutes—with a much smaller number of policies that individuals can mobilize through complaints (Herr, "Reforming Disability Nondiscrimination Laws").

127. Kathryn Moss et al., "Unfunded Mandate: An Empirical Study of the Implementation of the Americans with Disabilities Act by the Equal Employment Opportunity Commission," *Kansas Law Review* 50 (2001): 1.

128. *Sutton v. United Air Lines*, 527 U.S. 471 (1999).

129. Chai R. Feldblum, "Definition of Disability under Federal Anti-Discrimination Law: What Happened? Why? and What Can We Do about It?" *Berkeley Journal of Employment and Labor Law* 21 (2000): 91; Bonnie Poitras Tucker, "The Supreme Court's Definition of Disability under the ADA: A Return to the Dark Ages," *Alabama Law Review* 52 (2000): 321; and Matthew Diller, "Judicial Backlash, the ADA, and the Civil Rights Model," *Berkeley Journal of Employment and Labor Law* 21 (2000): 19. A study by Ruth Colker found that defendants prevailed in around 93 percent of ADA employment discrimination trials from 1992 to 1998 (Colker, "The Americans with Disabilities Act: A Windfall for Defendants," *Harvard Civil Rights–Civil Liberties Law Review* 34 [1999]: 99). As an indicator of the effectiveness of the ADA, this figure should be interpreted with some caution, since defendants may be settling strong claims before trial and fighting only weak claims in court. See Scott Burris et al., "Disputing under the Americans with Disabilities Act: Empirical Answers, and Some Questions," *Temple Political and Civil Rights Law Review* 9 (2000): 237.

130. Herr, "Reforming Disability Nondiscrimination Laws."

131. Interviews with Torbjorn Andersson, legal adviser, Labor Law, and with Lars Loow, head of the Office of the Disability Ombudsman, both Stockholm, Sweden, March 8, 2002.

132. European Union, European Council Directive 2000/78/EC, *Official Journal of the European Communities*, November 27, 2000.

133. Brian Doyle, *Disability, Discrimination and Equal Opportunities: A Comparative Study of the Employment Rights of Disabled Persons* (London: Mansell, 1995), 260.

134. Lisa Waddington, *Disability, Employment and the European Community* (Antwerp, Belgium: Metro Press, 1995), 230–32.

135. Heyer, "From Special Needs to Equal Rights: Japanese Disability Law," *University of Hawaii Asian-Pacific Law and Policy Journal* 1 (2000): 6.

136. For an overview of disability policy among the affluent democracies, see Neil Lunt and Patricia Thornton, *Employment Policies for Disabled People in Eighteen Countries: A Review* (York, England: Social Policy Research Unit, 1997).

3. A FAILED ANTILITIGATION EFFORT: THE STRUGGLE OVER NO-FAULT AUTO INSURANCE IN CALIFORNIA

1. Deborah Hensler et al., *Compensation for Accidental Injuries in the United States*, 121. The accident rate for motor vehicles is calculated based on information in table 5.2. The Rand study's estimates are based on a massive household survey administered in 1988–89 covering injuries that were suffered in the previous year.

2. Ibid., 101. These figures are rough estimates derived from calculations from table 4.20 in the Rand study. It should be noted that these statistics include any kind of claim, not just a lawsuit filing. Auto accident claims, like most kinds of claims, typically do not result in litigation; most claims are settled after negotiation with an insurer.

Some corroborating evidence on the dominance of automobile accidents in tort litigation comes from the National Center for State Courts. An NCSC study of tort caseloads in ten state courts of general jurisdiction between 1984 and 1993 found that 60 percent of all cases arose from auto accidents. In another study, of eleven courts of general jurisdiction in 1993, auto cases were a somewhat smaller proportion of tort cases going to trial, 42 percent, but they were still the predominant type of tort (Brian J. Ostrom and Neal B. Kauder, *Examining the Work of State Courts, 1993: A National Perspective from the Court Statistics Project* [Williamsburg, Va.: National Center for State Courts, 1994], 23–24).

3. Perhaps not coincidentally, more than 90 percent of drivers in two-car accidents blamed someone else for the crash, according to the Rand study cited above. Thirty-seven percent of drivers managed to find someone else to blame in *one-car* accidents. And perhaps most incredibly, the few drivers who admitted driving illegally before the crash overwhelmingly blamed another party for their accidents. See Hensler et al., *Compensation for Accidental Injuries in the United States*, 159, table 6.7. Herbert Kritzer finds that Americans are more likely to blame someone else for an auto accident and more likely to claim compensation than English drivers. He suggests that this gap is due partly to economic incentives and partly to cultural differences between the two nations. See Kritzer, "Propensity to Sue," 400–427.

4. Of course, even in the traditional liability system, drivers can choose to insure themselves against accidents they cause or accidents in which the party at fault cannot fully compensate them for injuries suffered. Uninsured motorist coverage is an example of this kind of insurance.

It is also important to remember that the liability system is only one source of compensation for car accidents and not by any means the dominant one. The Rand Institute for Civil Justice study cited earlier estimated that, of $25.7 billion in compensation doled out to car accident victims, $9.8 billion came through the tort system. First-party accident insurance, employer benefits, health insurance, and various public programs accounted for the rest. See Hensler, 101, table 4.20, and 108, table 4.22.

5. In addition to using governmental social insurance, some of the advanced economies have also adopted no-fault accident systems, public and private, to handle tort liability claims. See generally Robert H. Joost, *Automobile Insurance and No-Fault Law,* 2d ed. (Deerfield, Ill.: Clark Boardman Callaghan, 1992 [updated through October 2001]), sec. 7:1–43; Pfennigstorf and Gifford, eds., *A Comparative Study of Liability Law and Compensation Schemes.*

6. The cost-shifting incentive is beside the point because privately run no-fault systems don't require government expenditures. The insulation incentive is similarly irrelevant, because there is no need to wrest control of implementation away from wavering government bureaucrats. Lastly, the control incentive is irrelevant because this case takes place at the state level—the control incentive is applicable only when national-level actors wish to gain power over the actions of state and local agencies, as in the ADA case.

7. *Appears* is the correct word here since even in a no-fault system insurers can raise rates after accidents. Moreover, it should be remembered that, even in a traditional liability system, claims are typically paid by insurers, not individuals. Tom Baker finds in his study of Connecticut trial lawyers that among plaintiff attorneys there is a general norm against seeking "blood money"—the assets of individual defendants. Instead, plaintiffs usually content themselves with whatever they can obtain from the defendant's insurer (Baker, "Blood Money, New Money, and the Moral Economy of Tort Law in Action," *Law and Society Review* 35 [2001]: 275–319).

8. Jonathan Simon, "Driving Governmentality: Automobile Accidents, Insurance and the Challenge to Social Order in the Inter-War Years, 1919–1941," *Connecticut Insurance Law Journal* 4 (1997–98): 521.

9. Keeton and O'Connell, *Basic Protection for the Traffic Victim.*

10. Interview with Michael Dukakis, former governor of the Commonwealth of Massachusetts, Boston, August 9, 2000.

11. Joost, *Automobile Insurance and No-Fault Law,* sec. 57–22.

12. U.S. Department of Transportation, *Compensating Auto Accident Victims: A Follow-Up Report on No-Fault Auto Insurance Experiences* (Washington, D.C., 1985).

13. On the merits of auto no-fault, see the stunningly thorough review of the evidence in Don Dewees, David Duff, and Michael Trebilcock, *Exploring the Domain of Accident Law: Taking the Facts Seriously* (New York: Oxford University Press, 1996), 15–94. See also U.S. Department of Transportation, *Compensating Auto Accident Victims;* Carroll et al., *No-Fault Approaches to Compensating People Injured in Auto Accidents*; and Kenneth J. Meier and Robert M. LaFollette, "The Policy Impact of No-Fault Automobile Insurance," *Policy Studies Review* 6:3 (February 1987): 496–504.

14. Joost, *Automobile Insurance and No-Fault Law,* sec. 6:44–45.

15. States with a higher percentage of Republican politicians were more likely to adopt no-fault plans. See Meier and LaFollette, "The Policy Impact of No-Fault Auto Insurance," 503 n. 5.

16. A follow-up study of the Massachusetts no-fault system, the first in the nation, concluded that it had "a marked economic impact on the trial bar and on at least a portion of the lawyers in general practice." See Alan Widiss, "Massachusetts No-Fault Automobile Insurance: Its Impact on the Legal Profession," in *No-Fault Automobile Insurance in Action: The Experiences in Massachusetts, Florida, Delaware and Michigan,* ed. Alan Widiss et al. (Dobbs Ferry, N.Y.: Oceana Publications, 1977), 87–126.

17. Philip B. Heyman and Lance Liebman, "No Fault, No Fee: The Legal Profession and Federal No-Fault Automobile Insurance Legislation," in *The Social Responsibilities of Lawyers: Case Studies,* ed. Lance Liebman and Philip B. Heyman (New York: Foundation Press, 1988), 309–330.

18. Jeffrey O'Connell and Peter Spiro, "Whatever Happened to No-Fault?" *Washington Monthly* (April 1986), 35.

19. By one count twenty-eight no-fault bills had been introduced up to 1988; only six had been reported out of the chamber of origin and none had reached the governor. See William C. George, "No-Fault in California," *San Diego Law Review* 26 (1989): 1067.

20. Benjamin Zycher, "Automobile Insurance Regulation, Direct Democracy, and the Interests of Consumers," *Regulation* (summer 1990), 68.

21. James D. Richardson, "Willie Brown: The Play for Power," *APF Reporter* 16:1 (1996): 23–35.

22. Steven A. Clucas carefully analyzes the means by which Brown maintained his position in the assembly in *The Speaker's Electoral Connection: Willie Brown and the California Assembly* (Berkeley, Calif.: Institute of Governmental Studies Press, 1995).

23. California Fair Political Practices Commission, *1986 Primary Election Campaign Receipts and Expenditures* (Sacramento, Calif.: October 1986), 2:F34.

24. Interview with Will Glennon, legislative analyst, California Trial Lawyers Association, Berkeley, Calif., August 6, 1993.

25. Interview with Bill Lockyer, state senator, Hayward, Calif., March 12, 1994.

26. Interview with Judith Bell, director, West Coast office of Consumers Union, San Francisco, Calif., August 10, 1993; interview with Ralph Nader, Washington, D.C., May 2, 1994.

27. Zycher, "Automobile Insurance Regulation," 68.

28. Testimony of John Garamendi, state of California insurance commissioner, California Senate-Assembly Conference Committee on SB 10, 1991 Fall Interim Hearings, in *Automobile Insurance: Identification of Issues and Possible Solutions,* summary of October 3, 1991, meeting (Sacramento, 1991), 1.

29. Testimony of Tom Wiebel, State of California Department of Motor Vehicles, in ibid., 3.

30. Interview with Dick Woodward, Woodward & McDowell, Burlingame, Calif., August 13, 1993.

31. Ibid.

32. Mervin Field, "Large Majority of Voters Believe Car Insurance Rates Much Too High," *The California Poll*, June 10, 1988.

33. Ibid.

34. Arthur Lupia, "Short Cuts versus Encyclopedias: Information and Voting Behavior in California Insurance Reform Elections," *American Political Science Review* 88 (1994): 63–76. Lupia's analysis is based on exit polls of Los Angeles–area voters. The one exception to the "the more you know them the less you favor them" rule was opinion on Prop. 106, where those who knew the lawyer position were, inexplicably, more likely to vote for it, though this relationship did not reach statistical significance.

35. The previous record was held by Proposition 51, the 1986 "deep pockets" initiative whose victory led CTLA to the bargaining that resulted in the Napkin Deal. The two sides of the Prop. 51 battle together spent nearly $11 million (California Fair Political Practices Commission, *Historical Overview of Receipts and Expenditures By Ballot Measure Committees* [Sacramento, Calif., April 1988]).

36. California Fair Political Practices Commission, *1988 Ballot Issues* (Sacramento, Calif.), A8–A11.

37. Interview with Dan Dunmoyer, Personal Insurance Federation, Sacramento, Calif., September 24, 1993.

38. "The most obnoxious aspect of the insurance industry's no-fault initiative is that it's a Trojan horse to cloak what the initiative also calls for, the total prohibition of any regulation or public accountability of their operations" (Steven Miller, drafter of Proposition 100, quoted in Kenneth Reich, "Insurance Industry's No-Fault Auto Initiative Certified for Fall Election," *Los Angeles Times*, June 25, 1988, I-26). In the ballot pamphlet distributed to each voter, the anti-104 statement (written by Rosenfield and Ralph Nader) began with this argument, devoting relatively little space to no-fault itself (California Secretary of State, *California Ballot Pamphlet: General Election, November 8, 1988* (Sacramento, Calif., August 18, 1988), 104–5.

39. Edward L. Lascher, Jr., "Commentary: Source Cues and Voting on California Insurance Reform Measures" (manuscript in author's possession); Ross E. Cheit and Jonathan D. Youngwood, "How Not to Reform Auto Insurance," *The Public Interest* 104 (1991): 71.

40. This result would not necessarily surprise those political scientists who study the financing of ballot initiatives. Their research indicates that there is little correlation between the level of spending *in favor* of an initiative and its success. John R. Owens and Larry L. Wade go so far as to claim that both spending for and spending against an initiative has at best only a modest impact. See Owens and Wade, "Campaign Spending on California Ballot Propositions, 1924–1984: Trends and Voting Effects," *Western Political Quarterly* 39 (1986): 675.

41. Interview with Patrick Johnston, California state senator, Sacramento, Calif., March 8, 1994.

42. Ibid.

43. Judith Bell, "Despite 103, Insurance Needs a Legislative Cure," *Los Angeles Times*, November 11, 1988, II-5.

44. Interview with Jeff Shelton, principal consultant to the California assembly Finance and Insurance Committee, Sacramento, Calif., August 2, 1993.

45. Jan Hoffman, "Life on Wheels: New No-Fault Insurance Effort Emerges in Capitol," *Los Angeles Times* (Orange County edition), February 9, 1989, IX-3.

46. U.S. Department of Labor, Bureau of Labor Statistics, *1995 Consumer Expenditure Survey* (Washington, D.C.: Government Printing Office), cited in Joost, *Automobile Insurance and No-Fault Law,* sec. 8:18.

47. See testimony of Tom Wiebel, Department of Motor Vehicles, in *Automobile Insurance: Identification of Issues and Possible Solutions,* 3. Wiebel estimated that of 18 million registered drivers, between 25 and 29 percent were uninsured.

48. Interview with John Gamboa, executive director, Latino Issues Forum, San Francisco, Calif., July 30, 1993.

49. Interview with Robert Gnaizda, Public Advocates, San Francisco, Calif., March 14, 1994.

50. Gamboa, interview.

51. Ibid.

52. Gnaizda, interview.

53. Kenneth Reich, "Group Proposes No-Frills Auto Policy for $160," *Los Angeles Times,* March 23, 1989, 1-3.

54. Johnston, interview.

55. Kenneth Reich, "Push Starts for No-Frills, No-Fault Car Insurance, *Los Angeles Times,* May 24, 1989, 1-3.

56. Douglas Shuit, "Panel Approves Insurer-Backed No-Fault Bill," *Los Angeles Times,* April 19, 1989, 1-3.

57. Rick Kushman, "Brown Unveils Auto Insurance Plan," *Sacramento Bee,* May 23, 1989, A1.

58. Ibid.

59. Kenneth Reich, "Nader Draws Criticism by Consumers for No-Fault View," *Los Angeles Times,* May 28, 1989, 1–3.

60. Interviews with Gnaizda and Gamboa.

61. Kenneth Reich, "Nader Draws Criticism."

62. Nader, interview.

63. Daniel Weintraub, "Two Conflicting Car Insurance Bills Advance in Assembly," *Los Angeles Times,* June 22, 1989, 1-3.

64. "The Anything-But-No-Fault Bill," *Sacramento Bee,* September 6, 1989, B5.

65. "Take Another Stab at No-Fault," *Los Angeles Times,* September 24, 1989, V-4.

66. Interview with Billy Rutland, former chief consultant to assembly speaker Willie Brown, and Alan Zarenberg, former legislative secretary to Governor George Deukmajian, Sacramento, Calif., August 5, 1993. At the end of the 1990 session, Rutland and Zarenberg had worked out a compromise auto insurance bill that involved limiting lawyer fees in minor accidents. Both believe that they were close to getting their respective bosses to sign on to the bill, but the legislative session ran out before a deal could be made.

67. Daniel Weintraub, "Car Insurance Bill's Death Is Laid to Brown," *Los Angeles Times,* January 18, 1990, A3.

68. Dan Walters, "Insurance Bill 'Speakerized,'" *Sacramento Bee,* January 18, 1990, A3.

69. Bill Ainsworth, "Lockyer's Legendary Temper: Political Tactic, or Curse? Insiders Say Senate Judiciary Chairman's Personality Undermines His Potential," *Recorder* (September 5, 1991), 1.

70. Lockyer, interview.

71. Ibid.

72. Vlae Kershner, "Wilson, Brown Square Off on Auto Insurance Bill," *San Francisco Chronicle,* March 28, 1991, A1.

73. Kenneth Reich, "Wilson Intensifies Push for No-Fault Insurance," *Los Angeles Times,* May 30, 1991, A1.

74. Consumers Union, letter to Senator Bill Lockyer, May 22, 1991 (copy in author's possession).

75. Bell, interview.

76. Dunmoyer, interview.

77. Ibid.

78. Interview with Tim Hart, legislative advocate, Association of California Insurance Companies, Sacramento, Calif., October 11, 1993. In one newspaper account the insurers were said to have spent $1.2 million (Kenneth Reich, "Brown Attacks Funding of No-Fault Ads," *Los Angeles Times,* May 11, 1991, A21).

79. Petris, like Lockyer, was a lawyer with some experience in plaintiff tort litigation, though tort was only a small part of his practice (interview with Nicholas Petris, Oakland, Calif., January 26, 1996).

80. Johnston believed that the crucial vote was Art Torres's and that he would be unable to get either Marks, Watson, or Roberti to vote for no-fault (Johnston, interview).

81. Interview with Sal Russo, Russo Marsh & Associates, Sacramento, Calif., August 13, 1993.

82. Gamboa, interview.

83. Kenneth Reich, "Insurance Industry Targets Legislators," *Los Angeles Times,* May 10, 1991, A39.

84. Ibid.

85. Kenneth Reich, "Brown Attacks Funding of No-Fault Ads," A21.

86. Kenneth Reich, "Nader Alters Criticism of No-Fault," *Los Angeles Times,* May 21, 1991, B8.

87. Kenneth Reich, "Brown Attacks Funding of No-Fault Ads."

88. Daniel Weintraub, "No-Fault Bill Is Rejected by Senate Panel," *Los Angeles Times,* May 29, 1991, A3.

89. Bill Ainsworth, "When CTLA Talks, Legislators Listen," *Recorder* (June 7, 1991), 1.

90. Tom Dressler, "Former Allies Now Enemies in Tort Battle," *Los Angeles Daily Journal,* March 15, 1996.

91. Dan Morain, "Ex Allies Now Split over Anti-Lawyer Measure," *Los Angeles Times,* March 4, 1996, A3.

92. G. Pascal Zachary, "California's Defeat of Legal, Insurance Overhaul Raises Questions about Tort Reform Nationwide," *Wall Street Journal,* March 28, 1996, A16.

93. Dan Bernstein, "Voters Decisively Reject No-Fault Auto Insurance," *Sacramento Bee,* March 27, 1996, A4.

94. This was the conclusion of A. G. Block, the editor of the *California Journal,* and University of California–San Diego political scientist Gary Jacobson. See Zachary, "California's Defeat of Legal, Insurance Overhaul Raises Questions."

95. This characterization was made by Max Boot, a crusading antilitigation *Wall Street Journal* columnist who sympathized with the goals of the initiative campaign (Max Boot, "Will Tort Reformers Miss a Golden (State) Opportunity?" *Wall Street Journal,* February 21, 1996, A13).

96. Kingdon, *Agendas, Alternatives, and Public Policies.*

97. Reynolds Holding, "No-Fault Insurance Rejected by Voters," *San Francisco Chronicle,* March 27, 1996, A3.

98. Edward Lascher concludes in his study that the outcome of no-fault struggles depends on how policy makers allocate responsibility for rising costs of automobile insurance. No-fault proponents must convince policy makers that the problem is with consumers and trial lawyers who abuse the tort system; no-fault opponents can effectively counter this by arguing that the problem is caused by "profiteering" insurers. Lascher's case study of no-fault in Rhode Island looks much like my study of California: plaintiff lawyers and Nader-backed consumer activists successfully stalled no-fault legislation, in part by persuading legislators of the insurer "profiteer" story and advocating regulation of insurers as an alternative. In Lascher's account of the battle in Pennsylvania, by contrast, no-fault opponents failed to advance the profiteer story, in part because the anti-no-fault coalition was unusual: it failed to include Naderite consumer groups but did include insurers! (Edward L. Lascher, Jr., *The Politics of Automobile Insurance Reform: Ideas, Institutions and Public Policy in North America* [Washington, D.C.: Georgetown University Press, 1999]).

99. Daniel Weintraub, "Road to No-Fault Plan Stops at Brown's Office," *Los Angeles Times,* May 30, 1991, A1.

100. This figure was computed by combining CTLA's contributions for the 1988 primary and general elections, the 1989 off-year election, and the 1990 primary election.

101. California Fair Political Practices Commission, *1988 Primary Contributions* (Sacramento, Calif., 1988), B3.

102. Bill Ainsworth, "A Little Help for Its Friends; Trial Lawyers Group Gives Most to No-Fault Opponents," *Recorder,* August 19, 1991, 1.

103. The assembly member, Gerald Eaves, was part of the "Gang of Five," a group of Democrats who rebelled against Brown's leadership. CTLA contributed $109,982 to Eaves's 1988 primary opponent, Joe Baca, who nonetheless lost. The Gang of Five rebellion was quashed by Brown, who stripped all five of their committee assignments. After two years, the five made peace with Brown. One of the five was Steve Peace, the coauthor of the Johnston bill who abstained on the January 1990 Ways and Means vote, dooming the bill in the assembly.

104. Bill Ainsworth, "Lockyer's Legendary Temper," 1.

105. Lockyer, interview.

106. Weintraub, "Road to No-Fault Plan Stops at Brown's Office," A1.

107. Glennon, interview.

108. Hensler et al., *Compensation for Accidental Injuries in the United States,* 101. The estimate is derived from table 4.20.

109. See Widiss, "Massachusetts No-Fault Automobile Insurance," 87–126.

110. Stephen Green, ed., *California Political Almanac, 1991–1992,* 2d ed. (Sacramento, Calif.: California Journal Press, 1991). Four seats were listed as vacant and thus were excluded. I counted as lawyers all those who were listed as having received a J.D. Edward Lascher's study of no-fault politics in Pennsylvania and Rhode Island comes to similarly ambiguous conclusions about the influence of lawyer legislators. See Lascher, *The Politics of Automobile Insurance Reform,* 83–85.

111. Joost, *Automobile Insurance and No-Fault Law,* sec. 7:5. Of course, if there are disputes between claimant and insurer the matter will end up being resolved by a public agency, either a court (auto insurance) or an administrative tribunal (workers' compensation). In addition, twenty states have a public workers' compensation fund. In the United States 20 percent of firms in workers' compensation are insured through a state-run fund (American Law Institute, *Enterprise Responsibility for Personal Injury,* 1:121).

112. Takao Tanase, "The Management of Disputes: Automobile Accident Compensation in Japan," *Law and Society Review* 24 (1990): 641.

113. Hensler et al., *Compensation for Accidental Injuries in the United States,* 101, table 4.20; 108, table 4.22.

114. Pfennigstorf and Gifford, eds., *A Comparative Study of Liability Law and Compensation Schemes,* 158–159.

4. A SHOT OF ANTILITIGATION REFORM: THE VACCINE INJURY COMPENSATION PROGRAM

1. Quoted in testimony of Jeffrey Schwartz, U.S. House Subcommittee on Health and the Environment, *Vaccine Injury Compensation: Hearings on H.R. 5810,* 98th Cong., 2d sess., September 10, 1984, 81.

2. Estimates of the number of children seriously injured by reactions to vaccines are a matter of dispute. A study commissioned by the Department of Health and Human Services estimated that between 143 and 325 children each year suffered injuries ranging from acute brain swelling to death (U.S. Office of Technology Assessment, *Compensation for Vaccine-Related Injuries: A Technical Memorandum* [Washington, D.C.: Government Printing Office, 1980], 60). A report by the American Medical Association, drawing on several published studies, estimated that on average sixty-three children suffer permanent brain damage or death each year from vaccines (American Medical Association Board of Trustees, "Report of Ad Hoc Commission on Vaccine Injury Compensation," *Connecticut Medicine* [March 1985], 172.) However, Barbara Loe Fisher, a parent of a DPT-injured child, estimated, based on her own analysis of published research, that eleven thousand infants each year had lasting neurological symptoms and nearly one thousand died from reactions to DPT alone (Barbara Loe Fisher and Harris L. Coulter, *DPT: A Shot in the Dark* [San Diego: Harcourt Brace Jovanovich, 1985]).

3. Interview with Andrew Dodd (plaintiff lawyer in vaccine litigation), Torrance, Calif., July 7, 1994.

4. Comment k of section 402A of the second *Restatement of Torts* says that the seller of unavoidably dangerous products such as drugs and vaccines "is not to be held to strict liability for unfortunate consequences attending their use merely because he has undertaken to supply the public with an apparently useful and desirable product, attended with a known but apparently reasonable risk" (American Law Institute, *Restatement of the Law, Second, Torts* [St. Paul, Minn.: ALI, 1965], sec. 402A).

5. A study by the Institute of Medicine of the National Academy of Sciences found only eight reported cases in which manufacturers were found liable for defective vaccines given to humans (Institute of Medicine, Division of Health Promotion and Disease Prevention, *Vaccine Supply and Innovation* [Washington, D.C.: National Academy Press, 1985], 86).

6. In *Reyes v. Wyeth Laboratories* (498 F. 2d 1264 [5th Cir. 1974]) the court upheld a verdict in the case of a young Texas girl vaccinated with the Sabin polio vaccine. The court accepted the argument that Wyeth had failed to warn, even though the vaccines had been delivered to a Texas state clinic with a package insert warning of risks. Commentators have criticized the decision for not explaining how Wyeth was supposed to warn all recipients of its vaccines without relying on intermediaries such as clinics. Further, critics of the *Reyes* decision point out that, if the plaintiff had been warned of the dangers of the Sabin polio vaccine, he would have no alternative but to take it since the Salk polio vaccine was unavailable (Marc A. Franklin and Joseph Mais, Jr., "Tort Law and Mass Immunization Programs: Lessons from the Polio and Flu Epidemics," *California Law Review* 65 [1977]: 754).

The logic of the *Reyes* decision can probably best be explained by the court's discussion of the larger issues in vaccine compensation:

> "Until Americans have a comprehensive scheme of social insurance, courts must resolve by a balancing process the head-on collision between the need for adequate recovery and viable enterprise." . . . Statistically predictable as are these rare cases of vaccine-induced polio, a strong argument can be advanced that the loss ought not lie where it falls (on the victim), but should be borne by the manufacturer as a foreseeable cost of doing business, and passed on to the public in the form of price increases to his customers.
>
> (*Reyes v. Wyeth,* 1294, quoting *Helene Curtis Industries v. Pruitt,* 385 F. 2d 862 [1968]).

7. An exception to this pattern of minimal compensation is the swine flu vaccine program. The U.S. government accepted liability for all those who developed a severe illness called Guillain-Barre syndrome from the vaccine, so that a large number were compensated. Several cases were contested on the issue of causation, however. See U.S. Office of Technology Assessment, *Compensation for Vaccine-Related Injuries,* 93-104.

8. Edward W. Kitch, "Vaccines and Product Liability: A Case of Contagious Litigation," *Regulation* (May/June 1985), 13.

9. *Toner v. Lederle,* 828 F. 2d 510 (1987). The jury concluded that another version of DPT, which had been tested but never licensed, would have been safer.

10. The verdict was later reversed by the Kansas Supreme Court in *Johnson v. American Cyanamid Co.*, 718 P. 2d 1318 (1986).

11. See generally Peter William Huber, *Liability: The Legal Revolution and Its Consequences* (New York: Basic Books, 1988); and Edward W. Kitch, "Vaccines and Product Liability."

12. Michael J. Conlon, United Press International, *Washington News*, April 19, 1982.

13. Some observers attributed the report and a *Nightline* program the same year to the rise in filings of personal injury lawsuits in the early 1980s (Francesca Lunzero, "Scared Shotless," *Forbes* [November 18, 1985], 256).

14. In DPT's statement of purpose the first six goals listed involve either further study of the DPT vaccine or promotion of debate about the dangers of the pertussis vaccine in particular. The final two goals advocate the adoption of a compensation program and the development of treatment centers for vaccine-injured children (Testimony of Jeffrey Schwartz, Senate Labor and Human Resources Committee, *Task Force Report on Pertussis: Hearing before the Committee on Labor and Human Resources*, 98th Cong., 1st sess., July 22, 1983, 44, 52).

15. Testimony of Martin H. Smith, American Academy of Pediatrics, ibid., 60.

16. The nations were Britain, France, West Germany, Switzerland, Denmark, and Japan. The California program provided up to $25,000 in medical benefits. See Wendy K. Mariner, "Compensation Programs for Vaccine-Related Injury Abroad: A Comparative Analysis," *Saint Louis University Law Journal* 31 (1987): 599–654.

17. Nonet, *Administrative Justice*.

18. New Zealand allows lawsuits for "exemplary damages" beyond the economic compensation victims get from the state fund and for mental injuries that are unconnected to a physical injury. In 1998 the government partially privatized workplace accident compensation, but this change was reversed in 2000 (Stephen Todd, "Privatization of Accident Compensation: Policy and Politics in New Zealand," *Washburn Law Journal* 39 [2000]: 404).

19. Interview with Stephen Lawton, representative, American Academy of Pediatrics, Washington D.C., May 25, 1994. Testimony of Martin H. Smith, American Academy of Pediatrics, Senate Labor and Human Resources Committee, *Task Force Report on Pertussis*, 63.

20. Interview with Jeffrey Schwartz, Washington D.C., June 17, 1994; Lawton, interview.

21. Fisher and Coulter, *A Shot in the Dark*, 371–377.

22. Barbara Loe Fisher, editorial, *Dissatisfied Parents Together News* 1:1 (1983): 17.

23. Testimony of Jeffrey Schwartz, Senate Labor and Human Resources Committee, *Task Force Report on Pertussis*, 57.

24. Testimony of Robert Kaufman, Advocates for Safe Vaccines, ibid., 94.

25. Testimony of Jeffrey Schwartz, ibid., 50–51, 56–57; Schwartz, interview.

26. Lawton, interview.

27. *National Childhood Vaccine-Injury Compensation Act*, 98th Cong., 1st sess., S. 2117, *Cong. Rec.*, 129, pt. 24 (1983): 33796–33804.

28. The state health departments of Michigan and Massachusetts also manu-factured DPT, primarily for use within their states.

29. Testimony of James Mason, director, Division of Immunization of the Center for Prevention Services, Centers for Disease Control, Public Health Service, House Subcommittee on Health and the Environment, *Vaccine Injury Compensation,* December 19, 1984, 268.

30. Statement of Robert B. Johnson, president, Lederle Laboratories Division, American Cyanamid, ibid., September 10, 1984, 235.

31. Lunzer, "Scared Shotless," 256.

32. Waxman concluded the hearing by noting that what had appeared to be a shortage one day had turned out not to be a shortage the next. Waxman pledged not to get into a game of "chicken" with manufacturers and get stampeded into legislation that was overly generous to them (House Subcommittee on Health and the Environment, *Vaccine Injury Compensation,* December 19, 1984, 349).

33. Testimony of Jeffrey Schwartz, ibid., 347.

34. "Dwindling Supply of Vaccines Threat to Public Health," *Chicago Tribune,* August 4, 1985, 15.

35. Sally Squires, "Pediatricians Warn of Vaccine 'Crisis,'" *Washington Post,* April 23, 1986, 7.

36. Testimony of Robert B. Johnson, House Subcommittee on Health and the Environment, *Vaccine Injury Compensation: Hearings before the Subcommittee on Health and the Environment,* 99th Cong., 2d sess., July 25, 1986, 233.

37. *National Childhood Vaccine Injury Act,* 99th Cong., 1st sess., S. 827, *Cong. Rec.,* 131, pt. 6 (1985): 7031–7032.

38. Senate Labor and Human Resources Committee, *National Childhood Vaccine Injury Compensation Act: Hearing on S. 2117,* 98th Cong., 2d sess., May 3, 1984; and Senate Labor and Human Resources Committee, *National Childhood Vaccine Injury Compensation Act of 1985: Hearing on S. 827,* 99th Cong., 1st sess., July 18, 1985.

39. Testimony of Robert L. Willmore, deputy assistant attorney general, Civil Division (answers to written questions), ibid., 228.

40. Statement of Edward N. Brandt, Jr., assistant secretary for health, Senate Labor and Human Resources Committee, *Hearing on S. 2117,* May 3, 1984, 16–18.

41. Robert A. McConnell, assistant attorney general, Office of Legislative and Intergovernmental Affairs, to Orrin G. Hatch, June 12, 1984, reproduced in Senate Labor and Human Resources Committee, *Hearing on S. 2117,* 292–293.

42. Council on Human Resources, *Working Group on Vaccine Supply and Liability,* (Washington, D.C., 1985).

43. *Report of Ad Hoc Commission on Vaccine Injury Compensation,* reprinted in *Connecticut Medicine* (March 1985), 172–176.

44. The quote comes from Madigan's aide on the subcommittee, Eddie Allen (interview with Eddie Allen, Washington, D.C., May 18, 1995).

45. Marjorie Sun, "Three Plans Proposed to Avert Vaccine Shortage," *Science* (April 19, 1985), 308.

46. "President Reagan Signs Vaccine Injury Compensation and Safety Bill into Law," *DPT News* 3 (spring 1987): 13.

47. Testimony of John E. Lyons, president, Merck Sharp & Dohme, Senate Labor and Human Resources Committee, *Hearing on S. 2117,* May 3, 1984, 276–278.

48. Testimony of John E. Lyons, executive vice president, Merck & Co., Inc., House Subcommittee on Health and the Environment, *Vaccine Injury Compensation,* July 25, 1986, 222–230.

49. Testimony of Jeffrey Schwartz, president, Dissatisfied Parents Together, ibid., 186–195.

50. Julie Rovner, "House Passes Vaccine Injury Compensation Bill," *Congressional Quarterly Weekly Report,* October 18, 1986, 2626.

51. Interview with Nancy Taylor, aide to Senator Orrin Hatch, Washington, D.C., May 18, 1995; Allen, interview.

52. Taylor, interview.

53. Barbara J. Culliton, "Omnibus Health Bill," *Science* (December 12, 1986), 1313.

54. J. Edward Fox, assistant secretary, State Department, to James C. Miller, III, director, Office of Management and Budget, October 24, 1986; Robert M. Kimmitt, general counsel, Treasury Department, to Miller, October 30, 1986; Douglas Riggs, general counsel, Commerce Department, to Miller, November 6, 1986; and Peter Meyers, deputy secretary, Agriculture Department, to Miller, October 27, 1986, Clayton Yeutter, U.S. trade representative, to Miller, October 31, 1986, all in HE A11 subject file, Ronald Reagan National Library, Simi Valley, Calif.

55. Riggs to Miller; Kimmitt to Miller; Mari Maseng, director, Public Liaison, to Donald T. Regan, chief of staff, November 12, 1986. A memo from Alfred Kingon, cabinet secretary and assistant to the president, to Donald Regan, the president's chief of staff, summarized the conclusion of a meeting of White House and departmental officials: the Health and Human Services representative recommended signing the law, the Justice Department and OMB representatives recommended a veto, and the labor secretary, William Brock, advised that the president should either "sign before election day or, after that, 'flip a coin'" (Alfred H. Kingon to Donald T. Regan, October 24, 1986, HE A11 subject file, Ronald Reagan National Library).

56. David L. Chew, assistant to the president, to Ronald Reagan, November 14, 1986, HE A11 subject file, Ronald Reagan National Library.

57. John R. Bolton, assistant attorney general, to James C. Miller, III, director, OMB, October 31, 1986, HE A11 subject file, Ronald Reagan National Library.

58. Peter J. Wallison to Donald T. Regan, November 3, 1986, HE A11 subject file, Ronald Reagan National Library.

59. Kingon to Regan, October 24, 1986.

60. Memo from Owen to Miller, October 28, 1986, HE A11 subject file, Ronald Reagan National Library.

61. Joseph Wright to Ronald Reagan, memo on Enrolled Bill S. 1744, November 13, 1986, HE A11 subject file, Ronald Reagan National Library.

62. In the first version of his memo Wright noted that in addition to the vaccine program, several other provisions of the bill, including the medical

malpractice measure, were "very troublesome" and concluded that, despite the importance of the export measure, "S. 1744 is so objectionable . . . that I believe its disapproval is warranted." In the final draft, Wright noted that, until funding was provided, the vaccine program could not become operational and "we have received assurances from industry that will support efforts to perfect the defects" in the program's design (Wright to Reagan, draft memorandum on Enrolled Bill S. 1744, November 10, 1986; Wright to Reagan, memorandum on Enrolled Bill S.1744, November 13, 1986, both in HE A11 subject file, Ronald Reagan National Library).

63. "Statement on Signing S. 1744 into Law, November 14, 1986," *Public Papers of the Presidents of the United States: Ronald Reagan, 1981–1989* (Washington, D.C.: Government Printing Office, 1988), 1565–1366.

64. Ibid., 1565.

65. Testimony of Robert B. Johnson, president, Lederle Laboratories Division, American Cyanamid Company, House Subcommittee on Select Revenue Measures, *Funding of the Childhood Vaccine Program: Hearing before the Subcommittee on Select Revenue Measures*, 100th Cong., 1st sess., March 5, 1987, 82.

66. Testimony of Dennis E. Ross, tax legislative counsel, Department of the Treasury, ibid., 19–20, 31.

67. Julie Rovner, "Vaccine Compensation Plan Cut Back by Two House Panels," *Congressional Quarterly Weekly Report*, October 17, 1987, 2510.

68. Ibid. Lederle had already dropped its price for DPT from the 1986 high of $11.40 to $8.92 in May of 1987. Connaught, the other maker of DPT, had followed suit. "DPT Prices Drop," *DPT News*, Summer/Fall 1987, 4.

69. "Vaccine Compensation," *Congressional Quarterly Almanac* (Washington, D.C.: Congressional Quarterly Press, 1987), 537.

70. Ibid.

71. The total awarded, $1.323 billion, includes lawyer's fees paid to 1,698 unsuccessful claimants (U.S. Department of Health and Human Services, Health Resources and Services Administration, Vaccine Injury Compensation Program, *Monthly Statistics Report* (February 28, 2002), available at <http://www.hrsa.gov/osp/vicp/montly.htm>, accessed April 5, 2002).

72. Interviews with Thomas Balbier, administrator, Vaccine Injury Compensation Program, Washington, D.C., May 13, 1994; and Gary Golkiewicz, Office of Special Masters, U.S. Claims Court, Arlington, Virg., May 26, 1994.

73. The appeal number is taken from Molly Treadway Johnson, Carol E. Drew, and Dean P. Miletich, *Use of Expert Testimony, Specialized Decision Makers, and Case-Management Innovations in the National Vaccine Injury Compensation Program* (Washington, D.C.: Federal Judicial Center, 1998), 23. This number was compared to the overall adjudications in the program's *Monthly Statistics Report*.

74. U.S. Department of Health and Human Services, Office of Special Programs, Vaccine Injury Compensation Program, "Commonly Asked Questions about the National Vaccine Injury Compensation Program—Revised 01/2002," available at <http://www.hrsa.gov/osp/vicp/quanda.htm>, accessed April 5, 2002.

75. Success rate calculated from Table II, Vaccine Injury Compensation Pro-

gram, *Monthly Statistics Report* (February 28, 2002), available at <http://www.
hrsa.gov/osp/vicp/monthly.htm>, accessed April 5, 2002.

76. Vaccine Injury Compensation Program, "Commonly Asked Questions."

77. Denis J. Hauptly and Mary Mason, "The National Childhood Vaccine
Injury Act," *Federal Bar News and Journal* 37:8 (1990): 455.

78. United States General Accounting Office, *Vaccine Injury Compensation:
Program Challenged to Settle Claims Quickly and Easily* (Washington D.C.:
December 1999), 8, fig. 1.

79. House Subcommittee on Criminal Justice, Drug Policy, and Human
Resources, *Compensating Vaccine Injuries: Are Reforms Needed?* 106th Cong.,
1st sess., September 28, 1999, Committee Print; Arthur Allen, "Shots in the
Dark," *Washington Post Magazine* (August 30, 1998), W10; and Elizabeth C.
Scott, "The National Childhood Vaccine Injury Act Turns Fifteen," *Food and
Drug Law Journal* 56 (2001): 351.

80. Derry Ridgway, "No-Fault Vaccine Insurance: Lessons from the National
Vaccine Injury Compensation Program," *Journal of Health Politics, Policy and
Law* 24 (1999): 70.

81. *Terran v. HHS,* 195 F. 3d 1302 (1999), and *O'Connell v. HHS,* 217 F. 3d
857 (1999).

82. U.S. General Accounting Office, *Vaccine Injury Compensation,* 12, table 4.

83. Ibid., 14, table 6.

84. Oddly enough, program statistics do not show the success rate of complainants dropping after 1995, the year in which residual seizure disorder was
removed from the table. From 1988 to 1995 postprogram claimants prevailed in
41 percent of cases; from 1996 to 2001 they won 44 percent of the time. The
record of preprogram claimants actually improved markedly, from 21 percent to
40 percent (calculated from table II in Vaccine Injury Compensation Program,
Monthly Statistics Report [February 28, 2002]).

85. House Committee on Government Reform, *The Vaccine Injury Compensation Program: Addressing Needs and Improving Practices,* 106th Cong., 2d
sess., 2000, H. Rept. 977, 2.

86. Ibid., 12.

87. Testimony of Cliff Shoemaker, attorney, Shoemaker and Horn, House
Subcommittee on Criminal Justice, Drug Policy, and Human Resources, *Compensating Vaccine Injuries,* 89–90, 95–96.

88. House Committee on Government Reform, *The Vaccine Injury Compensation Program,* 11–14.

89. U.S. Department of Health and Human Services, Office of Special Programs, "Background Information on VICP," available at <http://www.hrsa.gov/
osp/vicp/abdvic.htm>, accessed April 5, 2002.

90. Alice Dembner, "Two Mass[achusetts] Families Sue Vaccine Makers,"
Boston Globe, September 1, 2001, A1.

91. Elyse Tanouye, "The Vaccine Business Gets a Shot in the Arm," *Wall
Street Journal,* February 25, 1998, B1.

92. Interview with Alan A. Parker, senior director, Public Affairs, Association
of Trial Lawyers of America, Vienna, Virg., July 12, 1994.

93. Interview with Robert D. Evans, director; Lillian Gaskin, senior legislative counsel; Irene Emselmen, senior legislative counsel; Kevin Driscoll, senior legislative counsel; and Gary Sellers, legislative counsel, ABA Governmental Affairs Office, Washington D.C., April 28, 1994.

94. Interview with Andrew Dodd, Advocates for a Safer Vaccine, Torrance, Calif., July 7, 1994.

95. Testimony of Robert B. Johnson, House Subcommittee on Health and the Environment, *Vaccine Injury Compensation,* September 10, 1984, 237.

96. Geoffrey Evans finds vaccine compensation programs operating in Germany, France, Italy, Japan, Switzerland, Norway, Denmark, Sweden, New Zealand, the United Kingdom, Quebec, and Taiwan. In these nations claims for compensation are decided by a health or social welfare agency or by an expert panel of doctors, with the exception of France, where an administrative tribunal may be used, and Sweden, where the program is administered by private insurers. The compensation programs are funded through general tax revenues, except in Sweden and Taiwan, which finance their programs through fees paid by manufacturers. See Geoffrey Evans, "Vaccine Injury Compensation Programs Worldwide," *Vaccine* 17 (1999): S26, table 1.

5. UNDERSTANDING THE LITIGATION DEBATE

1. October 11, 1992, presidential debate, Transcript no. 2-6 (Cable News Network, 1992), available from Lexis-Nexis Academic Universe at <http://www.lexis-nexis.com>, accessed April 9, 2002.

2. These sorry tales of litigiousness are told, respectively, in Zachary R. Dowdy, "Litigation Becoming a Pastime, Some Say," *Boston Globe,* March 8, 1996, 27; Edward Felsenthal, "Weekend Warriors Find a New Arena: Court," *Wall Street Journal,* June 23, 1995, B1; and Lisa Miller, "Clergy Shy Away from Counseling; Surge in Lawsuits Is Scaring Them Off," *Houston Chronicle,* February 14, 1998, Religion Section, 1.

3. Terry M. Moe, "Political Institutions: The Neglected Side of the Story," *Journal of Law, Economics, and Organization* 6 (1990): 213–253; "The Politics of Bureaucratic Structure," in *Can the Government Govern?* ed. John E. Chubb and Paul E. Peterson (Washington, D.C.: Brookings Institution, 1989), 267–329; and "The Politics of Structural Choice: Toward a Theory of Public Bureaucracy," in *Organization Theory: From Chester Barnard to the Present and Beyond,* ed. Oliver E. Williamson (New York: Oxford University Press, 1995).

4. The analysis here differs in crucial respects from that of Morris Fiorina in his writing on the court-versus-agency delegation decision (Fiorina, "Legislative Choice of Regulatory Forms: Legal Process or Administrative Process?" *Public Choice* 39 [1982]: 33–66; and "Group Concentration and the Delegation of Legislative Authority," in *Regulatory Policy and the Social Sciences,* ed. Roger G. Noll [Berkeley and Los Angeles: University of California Press, 1985], 175–199).

First, Fiorina assumes that courts will more predictably interpret statutes than agencies. I know of no evidence for this assumption and it does not enter into my analysis. Second, Fiorina assumes that delegation to agencies shifts blame away from legislators more than delegation to courts. Again, in the policy arenas I have studied I see no evidence to support this assumption, and so it does not play a part in my analysis. (To be fair to Fiorina, he is really analyzing the choice between broad delegation to agencies versus narrow delegation to courts. My analysis differs in that I treat "scope of delegation" as exogenous to the choice of where to delegate.)

Finally, and most importantly, Fiorina is considering the decision to delegate solely from the perspective of the legislator. I consider the decision from the position of all "activists"—all those who seek public action on a social problem, in particular interest groups, policy entrepreneurs in various positions, and policy makers in the legislative and executive branches. Lumping the incentives of all these actors together, of course, greatly oversimplifies the complexity of delegation politics. For one analysis of how incentives differ between presidents and legislators, see David E. Lewis, "The Presidential Advantage in the Design of Bureaucratic Agencies" (paper presented at the American Political Science Association Annual Meeting, Boston, Mass., September 1998).

5. Terry M. Moe, "Political Institutions," 239–242.

6. Mirjan R. Damaska, *The Faces of Justice and State Authority* (New Haven, Conn.: Yale University Press, 1986), 16–46.

7. Herbert Jacob et al., *Courts, Law, and Politics in Comparative Perspective* (New Haven, Conn.: Yale University Press, 1996), 19.

8. This point was suggested to me by R. Shep Melnick, who makes a similar argument in his book *Between the Lines* (Washington, D.C.: Brookings Institution, 1994), 177–178.

9. For an account of the various techniques Congress has at its disposal for disciplining bureaucracies, see William T. Gormley, Jr., *Taming the Bureaucracy: Muscles, Prayers and Other Strategies* (Princeton, N.J.: Princeton University Press, 1989).

10. *Martin v. PGA,* 121 S. Ct. 1879 (2001).

11. William N. Eskridge, Jr.'s study of congressional attempts to override statutory judicial decisions found that only 7 percent of Supreme Court statutory decisions were overridden, though more than a third were at least scrutinized by a congressional committee (Eskridge, "Overriding Supreme Court Statutory Interpretation Decisions," *Yale Law Journal* 101:2 [1991]: 350, table VIII). This finding, combined with Eskridge's modeling of court-Congress-president interactions, demonstrated, he concludes, "the significant power of the Court to read its own raw preferences into statutes without congressional override." Moreover, Eskridge finds "an unimpressive knowledge of and response to the far more numerous lower federal court statutory decisions" (416). Congress, of course, can't overrule decisions it never learns about.

12. Douglas Arnold, *The Logic of Congressional Action* (New Haven, Conn.: Yale University Press, 1990), 47.

13. This point was suggested to me by Martin Shapiro.

14. Melnick, *Between the Lines*, 221–229.

15. Steven M. Teles tells this story and many others in his penetrating political history of Aid to Families with Dependent Children, *Whose Welfare? AFDC and Elite Politics* (Lawrence: University Press of Kansas, 1996).

16. My analysis concerns the decision to lodge implementation power in the courts as an adjunct to, or as a substitute for, agency implementation. The choice

of how to structure judicial review of agency decisions involves another set of considerations that are beyond the scope of this book. For a careful study of this choice, see Charles R. Shipan, *Designing Judicial Review*.

17. See Frank R. Baumgartner and Bryan D. Jones, *Agendas and Instability in American Politics* (Chicago: University of Chicago Press, 1993), 6–9.

18. Ibid., 68.

19. Melnick notes that the traditional veterans' affairs policy monopoly was challenged by the Vietnam Veterans of America, who sought judicial review because they believed courts would prove more sympathetic to their claims about Agent Orange than the Veterans Administration (Melnick, *Between the Lines*, 268).

20. Epstein and O'Halloran's *Delegating Powers* provides some support for the existence of the insulation incentive, though this support is mostly indirect since the authors focus on delegation to bureaucratic agencies rather than courts. The study finds that in periods of divided government, Congress is more apt to delegate to state agencies, local authorities, and courts rather than to the executive branch. (Unfortunately, the authors do not provide separate analysis of delegation to courts but instead lump them together with states and localities. See 156–157.) The authors also find that Congress generally delegates less and grants less discretion to implementing authorities during periods of divided government (David Epstein and Sharyn O'Halloran, *Delegating Powers: A Transaction Cost Politics Approach to Policy Making under Separate Powers* [New York: Cambridge University Press, 1999]).

21. Sven Steinmo, *Taxation and Democracy*, 196.

22. A 1974 survey, for example, found Americans less likely than citizens of Britain, the Netherlands, or West Germany to hold government responsible for education, health care, housing, old age security, and unemployment (Arnold Heidenheimer, Hugh Heclo, and Carolyn Teich Adams, *Comparative Public Policy: The Politics of Social Choice in America*, 3rd ed. [New York: St. Martin's Press, 1990], 354). See also Herbert McClosky and John Zaller, *The American Ethos: Public Attitudes toward Capitalism and Democracy* (New York: Twentieth Century Fund, 1984); and Seymour Martin Lipset, *American Exceptionalism: A Double-Edged Sword* (New York: Norton, 1996).

23. An unfunded-mandates point of order can be defeated by a majority of the membership. Moreover, the unfunded-mandates law excludes many actions by the federal government, including those enforcing constitutional rights and preventing discrimination, two main uses of litigious policies aimed at states and localities (Paul I. Posner, *The Politics of Unfunded Mandates* [Washington, D.C.: Georgetown University Press, 1998], 175).

24. *City of Boerne v. Flores*, 521 U.S. 507 (1997).

25. See, respectively, *Seminole Tribe of Florida v. Florida*, 517 U.S. 44 (1996); *Alden v. Maine*, 527 U.S. 706 (1999); and *Kimel v. Florida Board of Regents*, 528 U.S. 62 (2000).

26. *University of Alabama v. Garrett*, 121 S. Ct. 955 (2001).

27. C. Neal Tate and Torbjorn Vallinder, eds., *The Global Expansion of Judicial Power*.

28. McCann, *Rights at Work: Pay Equity Reform and the Politics of Legal Mobilization*.

29. Gerald N. Rosenberg, *The Hollow Hope: Can Courts Bring About Social Change?*

30. Glendon, *Rights Talk: The Impoverishment of Political Discourse.* See also Glendon, *Abortion and Divorce in Western Law.*

31. Ibid., 22–25.

32. On the failings of the welfare rights movement, see Teles, *Whose Welfare?* 85–118.

33. Mary Ann Glendon, "Rights in Twentieth Century Constitutions," in *Rights and the Common Good: The Communitarian Perspective,* ed. Amitai Etzioni (New York: St. Martin's Press, 1995), 27–36.

34. Kelman quotes Edmund Burke's famous remark about this dark side of liberal philosophers: "In the groves of their academy . . . at the end of every vista you see nothing but the gallows" (Kelman, *Regulating America, Regulating Sweden: A Comparative Study of Occupational Safety and Health Policy* [Cambridge, Mass.: MIT Press, 1981], 198).

35. James Lynch, "Crime in International Perspective," in James Q. Wilson and Joan Petersilia, *Crime* (San Francisco: Institute for Contemporary Studies Press, 1995), 11–38. The Bureau of Justice Statistics reports that on June 30, 2001, there were 472 prison inmates per 100,000 U.S. residents, up from 292 at the end of 1990 (Bureau of Justice Statistics, *Prison Statistics,* available at <http://www.ojp.usdoj.gov/bjs/prisons.htm>, accessed April 9, 2002).

36. For a classic argument against the belief that courts even the odds between the powerful and the lowly, see Marc Galanter, "Why the Haves Come Out Ahead: Speculations on the Limits of Legal Change," *Law and Society Review* 9 (1974): 95. See also Gillian K. Hadfield, "The Price of Law: How the Market for Lawyers Distorts the Justice System," *Michigan Law Review* 98 (2000): 953.

37. A study of Texas lawyer interest groups found a pattern very similar to the one found in the California no-fault case, with the plaintiff lawyer organization far more mobilized than either the bar association or the civil defense lawyer group. See William De Soto, "Texas Lawyers and the Mobilization of Interests" (paper presented at the American Political Science Association Annual Meeting, Washington, D.C., September 2–5, 1993).

38. The few studies that move beyond the focus on intra–bar association politics are De Soto, "Texas Lawyers and the Mobilization of Interests," which includes a survey of political activity of plaintiff and defense lawyers; Richard A. Watson and Rondal G. Downing, *The Politics of the Bench and the Bar* (New York: John Wiley, 1969), which describes conflicts between proplaintiff and prodefendant lawyer groups over judicial selection in Missouri; Theodore Schneyer, "Professionalism as Politics: The Making of a Modern Legal Ethics Code," in *Lawyer's Ideals, Lawyer's Practices,* ed. Robert L. Nelson, David M. Trubek, and Rayman L. Solomon (Ithaca, N.Y.: Cornell University Press, 1992), 95–143, which details the conflicts between the ABA and ATLA over a code of professionalism; and Philip Heymann and Lance Liebman, *The Social Responsibilities of Lawyers* (Ithaca, N.Y.: Foundation Press, 1988), 309–335, which discusses how both ABA and ATLA mobilized to beat a national no-fault auto insurance bill.

39. On the formation of a coalition in favor of workers' compensation, see Fishback and Kantor, *A Prelude to the Welfare State: The Origins of Workers' Compensation*, 88–93, 120–147.

40. Ed Gillespie and Bob Schellhas, eds., *Contract With America* (New York: Times Books, 1994), 37–64, 143–155.

41. To determine whether the main matter in dispute involved a litigious policy, I used the roll-call vote descriptions provided by the *Congressional Quarterly Almanac* for 1995 and 1996 (Washington, D.C.: Congressional Quarterly Press).

42. The measure employed is the first-dimension Poole-Rosenthal W-nominate scores for the 104th Congress. Poole-Rosenthal scores are widely used in congressional research, and I, like many others, owe a debt of thanks to Professors Poole and Rosenthal for developing them.

43.

OLS Regression Analysis of Support for Litigious Policies	
Degree (J.D. = 1)	4.46 (1.08)*
Poole-Rosenthal Voting Record	−46.12 (2.76)*
(1 = most conservative to −1 = most liberal)	
Republican (= 1)	−0.38 (3.26)
Southern Democrat (= 1)	−4.76 (1.86)*
Percentage Black in District	0.06 (0.04)
Constant	45.92 (2.12)*

n = 434
adjusted r-squared = 0.86
*Significant at 0.01

The dependent variable is the percentage of votes on which a member took a prolitigation position, so the range is 0 to 100 (mean = 40.2, standard deviation = 29.05).

A significant minority of members with law degrees have little or no experience as lawyers. In view of this fact, I developed a separate variable, "lawyer," which was coded as a "1" only if the member had practiced law in at least three separate years. When I plugged "lawyer" into the regression equation instead of "degree," however, the results were similar.

I also ran separate regressions with only Democrats and only Republicans and got similar results for both "degree" and "lawyer" in these equations.

Several additional variables involving characteristics of the representative's district (median household income, percentage rural households, and presidential vote in the 1996 election) were dropped from the final equation. They did not significantly affect the variables of interest, "degree" and "lawyer." Finally, I ran the regression with the Huber-White estimator for standard errors, which doesn't require the assumption of a normally distributed dependent variable. This too had no effect on the findings I report.

44. Richard L. Hall and Frank W. Wayman, "Buying Time: Moneyed Interests and the Mobilization of Bias in Congressional Committees," *American Political Science Review* 84 (1990): 797–820.

45. See Heinz Eulau and John D. Sprague, *Lawyers in Politics: A Study in Professional Convergence* (Indianapolis: Bobbs-Merrill, 1964); David R. Derge, "The Lawyer as Decision-Maker in the American State Legislature," *Journal of Politics* 21 (1959): 408–433; Derge, "The Lawyer in the Indiana General Assembly," *Midwest Journal of Political Science* 6 (1962): 19–53; and Justin J. Green et

al., "Lawyers in Congress: A New Look at Some Old Assumptions," *Western Political Quarterly* 26 (1973): 440–452; but see Richard L. Engstrom and Patrick F. O'Connor, "Lawyer-Legislators and Support for State Legislative Reform," *Journal of Politics* 42 (1980): 267–76; and more generally, Mark Miller, *The High Priests of American Politics;* and Robert A. Kagan, "Do Lawyers Cause Adversarial Legalism?" *Law and Social Inquiry* 19 (1994): 1.

46. Barry Meier, "Cigarette Makers in a $368 Billion Accord to Curb Lawsuits and Curtail Marketing," *New York Times,* June 21, 1997, A1.

47. Michael K. Frisby, "Tobacco Officials Balk at Changes Proposed to Beef Up Settlement," *Wall Street Journal,* August 15, 1997, B6. For an account of both this and the later, successful state attorneys general–led tobacco settlement, see Martha A. Derthick, *Up in Smoke: From Legislation to Litigation in Tobacco Politics* (Washington, D.C.: Congressional Quarterly Press, 2002).

48. Stephen Labaton, "Asbestos Cases in for Overhaul by Lawmakers," *New York Times,* June 28, 1999, A1.

49. Diana B. Henriques and David Barstow, "A Nation Challenged: Victims' Compensation: Fund for Victims' Families Already Proves Sore Point," *New York Times,* October 1, 2001, A1.

50. Pace and Kakalik, *Costs and Compensation Paid in Tort Litigation.*

51. Galanter, "News From Nowhere"; Daniels and Martin, "The Question of Jury Competence," 309.

52. See, for example, Saks, "Do We Really Know Anything about the Behavior of the Tort Litigation System—and Why Not?" Although Saks spends more than one hundred pages reviewing a huge number of studies, his main point is that we lack good data about tort litigation, so that any reform will be the product of "guesswork" (1288).

53. For a classic study of how an individualism of "self-sufficiency and personal responsibility" in traditional rural communities led residents to "lump it" when they were injured, see David M. Engel's "The Oven Bird's Song," 551.

54. Robert A. Kagan, "The Routinization of Debt Collection: An Essay on Social Change and Conflict in the Courts," *Law and Society Review* 18 (1984): 323–83.

55. Lawrence M. Friedman, *Total Justice* (Boston: Beacon Press, 1987).

56. Kagan, "Adversarial Legalism and American Government," 394.

57. Ibid., 374. Jerry L. Mashaw makes a similar distinction between "bureaucratic rationality" and "moral judgment" in *Bureaucratic Justice* (New Haven, Conn.: Yale University Press, 1983), 25–34.

58. Ibid., 26–29.

59. Kagan, "Adversarial Legalism and American Government," 373.

60. Aristotle labeled as "political rule" decision making through deliberation by "persons who are similar in birth to the ruler, and are similarly free" (Aristotle, *The Politics,* trans. Ernest Barker [New York: Oxford University Press, 1979], 105).

61. Lumping is one of the dominant responses to injury, far more common than litigation. For example, much of the costs of accidents is borne by the injured themselves. See Hensler et al., *Compensation for Accidental Injuries in the United States.* A household study conducted as part of the Civil Litigation

Research Project found that, for every ten instances in which people perceive that they have been illegally discriminated against, only three result in some claim for redress, and most of those who claim get nothing in response (Miller and Sarat, "Grievances, Claims and Disputes: Assessing the Adversary Culture," 527–565).

62. Pfennigstorf and Gifford, *A Comparative Study of Liability Law and Compensation Schemes in Ten Countries and the United States,* 145.

63. Cross and Hsieh, "Injury, Liability, and the Decision to File a Medical Malpractice Claim," 413–436. The study found that in cases of severe neonatal injuries, families without health insurance were more likely to sue for malpractice. One reason for this, however, may have been that Florida, the state in which the study was conducted, has repealed the collateral source rule. This means that those families who had their medical costs paid by insurers could not collect these as damages in a malpractice suit.

64. See Kathryn Moss et al., "Unfunded Mandate." In recent years EEOC officials have instituted a claim prioritization system and a mediation program in order to resolve a larger number of claims more efficiently. Despite improvements in management, however, observers suggest the agency is still overwhelmed by its tasks (Reed Abelson, "Anti-Bias Agency Is Short of Will and Cash," *New York Times,* July 1, 2001, sec. 3, 1).

65. Robert A. Kagan and Eugene Bardach, *Going by the Book: The Problem of Regulatory Unreasonableness* (Philadelphia: Temple University Press, 1982); and Kagan, "Managing Regulatory Enforcement in the United States," in *Handbook of Regulation and Administrative Law,* ed. David Rosenbloom and Richard Schwartz (New York: M. Dekker, 1994).

66. See, for example, Shapiro, *Who Guards the Guardians;* Mashaw, *Bureaucratic Justice;* Melnick, *Regulation and the Courts;* and Rabkin, *Judicial Compulsions;* but see Coglianese, "Litigating within Relationships."

67. American Law Institute, *Reporters' Study: Enterprise Responsibility for Personal Injury* (Philadelphia: ALI, 1991).

68. Carroll et al., *No-Fault Approaches to Compensating People Injured in Automobile Accidents.*

69. See, for example, Steven Sugarman, "Doing Away with Tort Law," 555; Paul C. Weiler, *Medical Malpractice on Trial;* and Jeffrey O'Connell, "A Draft Bill to Allow Choice between No-Fault and Fault-Based Auto Insurance."

INDEX

Designer: Victoria Kuskowski
Compositor: Michael Bass & Associates
Text: 10/13 Sabon
Display: Frutiger
Printer and Binder: Maple-Vail Book Manufacturing Group